The Land Question in China

This book interrogates the inevitability and practicability of full-scale, land-intensive capitalist agriculture in China, while analyzing the labor-intensive industrious revolution as an alternative rural development path. It presents a critical account of the recent rise of agrarian capitalism as a force that would undermine hundreds of millions of people's livelihoods in the populous country.

The Land Question in China traces the roots of the industrious revolution in China back to the eighteenth century, drawing comparisons between contemporary rural development and economic prosperity in the mid-Qing dynasty. In the context of neoliberal restructuring, it argues that vigorous rural development with broad access to land offers a solution to mitigate precarious urban employment and population pressure, while the transfer of land from villagers to large producers and urban investors will exacerbate these problems. Comparisons with South Africa and the East Asian economies of Japan, South Korea, and Taiwan further illustrate this and help to develop a new interpretation of the industrious revolution and its contemporary relevance.

Providing a critical examination of the "new land reform" in China from a world historical perspective, this book will be useful to students and scholars of sociology, economics, and development, as well as Chinese Studies.

Shaohua Zhan is Assistant Professor of Sociology at Nanyang Technological University, Singapore. His research interests include Chinese political economy, land politics, food security, and migration.

Routledge Contemporary China Series

China's Climate-Energy Policy
Domestic and International Impacts
Edited by Akihisa Mori

Western Bankers in China
Institutional Change and Corporate Governance
Jane Nolan

Xinjiang in the Twenty-First Century
Islam, Ethnicity and Resistance
Michael Dillon

China Studies in the Philippines
Intellectual Paths and the Formation of a Field
Edited by Tina S. Clemente and Chih-yu Shih

Innovative and Creative Industries in Hong Kong
A Global City in China and Asia
Grace L. K. Leung

Illicit Industries and China's Shadow Economy
Challenges and Prospects for Global Governance and Human Security
Edited by Victor Teo and Sungwon Yoon

Re-Engineering Affordable Care Policy in China
Is Marketization a Solution?
Peter Nan-shong Lee

The Land Question in China
Agrarian Capitalism, Industrious Revolution, and East Asian Development
Shaohua Zhan

The Land Question in China

Agrarian Capitalism, Industrious Revolution, and East Asian Development

Shaohua Zhan

Routledge
Taylor & Francis Group
LONDON AND NEW YORK

First published 2019 by Routledge
2 Park Square, Milton Park, Abingdon, Oxon OX14 4RN
52 Vanderbilt Avenue, New York, NY 10017

First issued in paperback 2020

Routledge is an imprint of the Taylor & Francis Group, an informa business

British Library Cataloguing-in-Publication Data
A catalogue record for this book is available from the British Library

Library of Congress Cataloging-in-Publication Data
A catalog record has been requested for this book

ISBN 13: 978-0-367-66265-3 (pbk)
ISBN 13: 978-0-415-78910-3 (hbk)

Typeset in Times New Roman
by Wearset Ltd, Boldon, Tyne, and Wear

To my mentors
Giovanni Arrighi, Beverly Silver, Joel Andreas, and Huang Ping

Contents

List of illustrations

Figures

Tables

Preface

This book is a product of my two-decade search for alternative solutions to rural development problems in China. At the end of the 1990s, when I started graduate studies at the Chinese Academy of Social Sciences (CASS), the fervent push for agricultural modernization, large-scale land expropriations, and massive rural-urban migration had already begun in China. Proponents of such changes often use rural underdevelopment as justification, no matter how often these changes have led to injustices against peasants and migrant workers. I have been unable to clear the image from my head since one colleague described the booming business of replanting migrant workers' machine-severed fingers in the streets of Wenzhou, one of the migrant-receiving locations. I also felt an acute pain in my chest when one of my friends, whom I grew up with, showed me his broken finger. I was disturbed by the tremendous human costs of China's development, with work injuries being just one example of the many gruesome consequences.

Huang Ping, my supervisor at the CASS, brought to my attention a range of alternative development theories. He also motivated me to pursue my PhD study at Johns Hopkins University in Baltimore, Maryland, in the United States. Giovanni Arrighi, who was my advisor before he passed away in 2009, inspired me to study China's rural development from a macro-historical perspective. His last magnum opus, *Adam Smith in Beijing*, became the most important source of intellectual inspiration of my dissertation research. I am very grateful that he attended my proposal defense at a time he was already very ill. Beverly Silver and Joel Andreas supervised me after Giovanni's passing. Beverly's harshness on my intellectual work and kindness in daily life are the assets of a lifetime that have had and will continue to have profound influence on me both as a scholar and as a human being. Joel advised me throughout my study. With his rich knowledge on China, he has offered me numerous insightful suggestions and pulled me back whenever I shifted away from the reality.

I also owe an enormous debt to William Rowe. His classes on Qing history took me into a field to which I was a complete stranger. He read my research proposal and made revisions sentence by sentence. Without him, Chapter 1 would not be the way it is now. Kellee Tsai offered me a great deal of advice on literature and the overall structure of the book. Her support on my historical analysis of state-society relations in China was very important in the development of my thesis. Ho-fung Hung advised me even before he came to Johns Hopkins. As an expert on both the Qing dynasty and contemporary China, he was particularly helpful in guiding me to make the connection between the two periods and trace the roots of contemporary development to the eighteenth century.

This book could not have been written without financial support from a number of institutions. A National Science Foundation Dissertation Improvement Grant funded my one-year fieldwork in China. After that, the Center for a Livable Future at the Bloomberg School of Public Health at Johns Hopkins offered me a one-year fellowship to write up the dissertation. A postdoctoral fellowship in China Studies from the Henry Luce Foundation and the American Council of Learned Society supported me to turn the dissertation into a book. A start-up research grant from the Nanyang Technological University supported my fieldwork in recent years and the final stage of writing. I have also received smaller research grants from the Johns Hopkins University and the Chinese Academy of Social Sciences.

On the way toward the completion of the book, a number of people read the whole, part, or summary of the book, and offered valuable advice and comments. They are Ching Kwan Lee, Roberto Patricio Korzeniewicz, William Martin, Jason Moore, Heather Zhang, Evelyn Hu-Dehart, Jack Goldstone, Lingxin Hao, Sara Berry, Siba Grovogui, Mel Kohn, Stefanie Deluca, Perry Anderson, Chaohua Wang, Jeffrey Wasserstrom, and Rhacel Salazar Parrenas. I also benefited greatly from discussions with fellow students at Johns Hopkins, particularly Astra Bonini, Rachel Core, Yige Dong, Burak Gurel, Kevin Harris, Sahan Savas Karatasli, Sefika Kumral, Ricado Jacobs, Yao Li, Daniel Pasciuti, Irene Peng, Ke Ren, Peter Rosenblatt, Ben Scully, Erdem Yoruk, Yin Yue, Juan Wang, and Lu Zhang. Ben Scully and Ricado Jacobs offered valuable suggestions on Chapter 5.

My colleagues at the Nanyang Technological University have also been a great support. Kwok Kian Woon, Min Zhou, Baogang He, and Francis Lim have offered valuable suggestions on the early drafts of the book. I also benefited from intellectual exchange with other colleagues, particularly Xiao Hong, Teo You Yenn, Shirley Sun, Premchand Dommaraju, Md Saidul Islam, and Sam Han. Tan Yu Xun and Yaw Chue Yan Grace have proofread and commented on a few chapters. Chen Xingyan helped with preparing the appendix. I also thank Stephanie Rogers and Georgina Bishop at Routledge for their generous support and for being so patient with my preparation of the manuscript over an extended period of time.

I thank my colleagues and friends in China who provided institutional and personal support for my data collection and fieldwork, including Li Peilin, Wang Xiaoxi, Wang Xiaoyi, Zhao Kebin, Wang Hongyan, and Zhang Yunpeng at the Chinese Academy of Social Sciences; Liu Wenpeng, Gao Wanglin, and Wang Weidong at the Renmin University; Jin Yihong at the Nanjing Normal University; He Huili at the China Agricultural University. I also express my wholehearted gratitude to my informants and interviewees (officials, entrepreneurs, peasants, and migrants) in the field sites. Without their participation in my research this book would be impossible.

Finally I owe special thanks to my wife, Lingli Huang, and my daughter, Elizabeth. I am so lucky to have Lingli as my life and intellectual partner. She has always been the first critic of my work and urged me to take my analysis to a higher level. Elizabeth has brought us the greatest joy, and added much needed elements to my intellectual life.

Introduction

On November 12, 2013, the Third Plenary Session of the 18th Central Committee of the Chinese Communist Party, a meeting that would set the government's agenda for at least the next ten years, declared to reform the rural land system. The decision, which the party claims would turn peasants' land rights into marketable assets, was dubbed "the new land reform."[1] This reform, as well as the follow-up policy specifications, signaled a decisive move to recentralize and transfer land rights from peasants to large producers, including large farms, agribusiness companies, and urban investors. The new land reform came as no surprise to the students of Chinese agrarian change, as the efforts to scale up agriculture had been going on for more than a decade (Andreas and Zhan 2016; Wilmsen 2016; Ye 2015). Nevertheless, it intensified the long debate over the land question in China, which is the key to understanding agrarian transitions, the future of the countryside, and most importantly, the choice of different development paths.

The land question in China, simply put, is whether rural smallholders – including peasants, migrant workers, and rural entrepreneurs – should maintain land rights in a rapidly industrializing and urbanizing economy. The land question is certainly not new or exceptional to China. The issue who owns, uses, controls, and receives benefits from the land has been a central issue in Chinese revolutions, socialist experiments, and the market reform; it has also been a crucial issue in agrarian change worldwide (Bernstein 2010). This book situates the land question in contemporary China in a historical-comparative context and highlights the critical importance of land against the background of population pressure and the precarization[2] of urban employment in our times.

China carried out a sweeping nationwide land reform between 1946 and 1952, one that redistributed land from landlords to poor peasants. The country then organized peasants into collective units, including communes, brigades, and production teams. The market reform in the early 1980s dismantled the collective system and shifted agriculture from collective farming to household farming, giving rise to a household land tenure system. Under this system, land rights comprise two components: land ownership, which is held collectively by the village community, and land use rights, which are contracted to individual households (Dong 1996; Ho 2001; Unger 2002). While keeping collective ownership unchanged, the recent reform further divided land use rights into contract rights (*chengbao quan*) and use rights.[3] Peasants hold contract rights, but they can (and are often forced to) transfer out use rights to other parties. This is to accelerate long-term land transfer to large producers, and after the transfer, peasants would only hold nominal contract rights (Box I.1; Figure I.1).

Box I.1 China's land system and the new land reform

Land in China can be basically classified into rural and urban lands (Figure I.1). Urban land is state-owned, while villages or production teams collectively own rural land. The conversion of rural land into urban land must be carried out through land expropriations by the state. Local governments have a keen interest in expropriating rural lands, as their value will be greatly appreciated after the conversion. However, the central government set up a quota system restricting how much land can be converted for the sake of food security and for ecological reasons.

Rural land includes farmland, residential land (for rural houses), and construction land (for rural factories and public facilities). There are other lands such as woodlands, riverbeds, and wastelands, but these are beyond the scope of the research in this book. The conversion of farmland into construction and residential lands must be approved by the state. Rural households hold use rights of farmland, residential land, and some of construction land. The new land reform is aimed to transfer the use rights of farmland to large producers such as large farms, agribusinesses, and rural cooperatives. The reform also permits the transfer of the use rights of rural construction and residential lands to buyers in the market, mostly urban investors or urban residents.

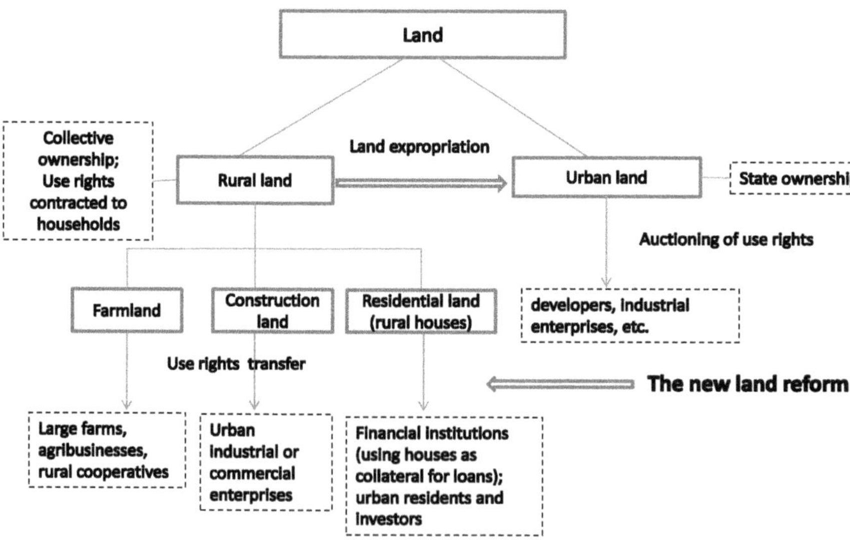

Figure I.1 China's land system.

The push for agrarian capitalism, however, has not proceeded without resistance. Besides resistance from peasants themselves, many scholars and agricultural practitioners in China have engaged in fierce debates over the importance of small-scale farming and the protection of peasants' land rights. For example, Tiejun Wen and Changping Li, who brought the plight of Chinese peasants to the spotlight around the year 2000, argued against the expansion of large capital and large farms, while advocating the protection of peasants' land rights and greater support for the household economy (Li 2003; Wen 2009). Recently, university professors Jingzhong Ye and Xuefeng He, among many others, have called attention to the advantages of household farming in the economy and the benefits of small peasants to the society. Citing Jan Douwe Van der Ploeg's *The New Peasantries*, Jingzhong Ye (2013) argues that peasant production contributes to the autonomy of labor, the morality of economy, the security of food, and the sustainability of the environment. Xuefeng He (2013) argues that the combination of peasant production in the countryside and wage employment in the city is the strength of the Chinese economy, rather than a disadvantage. It reduces the cost of reproduction, provides a safety net for migrant workers, and contributes to social stability. From a historical and practical perspective, Philip Huang (2014) proposes that small, capital-intensive family farms should be promoted as the main units of production in the Chinese countryside.

The contradiction between large farms and peasant production is certainly not new; it was a recurring phenomenon in Chinese dynastic transitions, during which the concentration of land often led to peasant rebellions, precipitating the fall of old regimes. This contradiction was particularly sharpened during the eighteenth century, when China witnessed a steady population growth roughly from 150 million in 1700 to 360 million in 1810 (Ho 1959; Shi 2017, 148–58). This means that the land, which already faced population pressures before the turn of the century, had to sustain more than twice the population. Nevertheless, the eighteenth century was known as the most prosperous period in imperial China. According to Kenneth Pomeranz (2000), some key indicators of the standard of living in China, such as levels of sugar and cloth consumption, were comparable to those in England, and the Great Divergence between these two countries did not take place until the early nineteenth century.

How was China able to sustain such a large population with a limited amount of land? This question carries world-historical significance. Over the past three centuries, the rise and expansion of capitalism has contributed to high productivity and exceptional economic growth, but it has also created (and seems unable to solve) mass underemployment and poverty. More than half of the world population is currently living in urban areas, but a great number of urban dwellers are unemployed or underemployed with a precarious livelihood, particularly in the global South (Davis 2006; Kalleberg 2009; Standing 2011). As Arrighi and Silver noted,

> … the underlying contradiction of a world capitalist system that promotes the formation of a world proletariat but cannot accommodate a generalized

> living wage (that is, the most basic of reproduction costs), far from being solved, has become more acute than ever.
>
> (2001, 276–7)

This diagnosis of capitalism is highly relevant to the reality in China. The transition of the country to capitalism since the 1980s has led to rapid economic growth. Millions of rural laborers have migrated to urban areas and become wage laborers. Yet, the majority of them is earning a precarious livelihood and is unable to bring their families to the city; in other words, they cannot fulfill social reproduction in the city as members of the proletariat (Gallagher, Lee, and Kuruvilla 2011; Huang 2009; Lee 2007, 2016; Zhou 2013). Among 168 million migrant workers in 2014, only 16.4 percent were covered by urban pension insurance, 18.2 percent by urban health care insurance, and 29.7 percent by work injury insurance (NBS 2015). Meanwhile, there were 58 million migrant children and 45 million elderly left behind in the countryside (Ye *et al.* 2013). In this situation, the issue of land is of critical importance because land and land-based economic activities are important sources of livelihood for rural laborers whom the capitalist sector is unable to employ or provide a living wage for. As Henry Bernstein noted, "… land redistribution acquires a new significance in agrarian questions of labour, given the inability of contemporary capitalism to provide adequate and secure employment to the great majority of the working poor in the South" (2007, 28–9). Bernstein was addressing the question of whether land reform (land redistribution) is necessary in Southern countries such as South Africa, where land is concentrated. In China, however, debates revolve around whether the previous land reform should be reversed to provide conditions for large farms and agribusinesses.

Industrious revolution, agrarian capitalism, and argument of the book

This book interrogates the inevitability and practicability of a full-scale, land-intensive capitalist agriculture in China and draws attention to a labor-intensive path of development – industrious revolution, which historically grew out of East Asia, but can also be found in many other parts of the world. The concept of industrious revolution was coined by Japanese scholars, first by Akira Hayami in a Japanese work in 1967. He argued that Japan, during the Tokugawa period (1603–1868), embarked on a development path that he called an "industrious revolution," in contrast to the Industrial Revolution taking place in Britain. This was because Japan was a resource-scarce and labor-abundant society, whereas Britain faced much less pressure from a labor surplus. In Japan, the revolution nurtured an industrious work ethic that motivated people to dedicate more time and effort to work (Hayami 1992). Kaoru Sugihara extended Hayami's analysis to other countries in East Asia, including China. He showed how the industrious revolution path gave rise to labor-absorbing technologies and institutions in the region. According to him, households and village communities in East Asia tended to increase labor inputs in farming (e.g., irrigated rice production) and handicraft production, combine multiple economic activities, and encourage the same worker to perform multiple tasks (Sugihara 2003, 2007).

Historically, a complete division between the Industrial Revolution and industrious revolutions is debatable, because long working hours and labor intensification also existed in factories in the West before and after the Industrial Revolution. For example, Jan de Vries argued that an industrious revolution also took place in England and much of Northwestern Europe and America from the seventeenth century through the early nineteenth century (1994, 2008). The industrious revolution that de Vries articulates refers to a change in household behavior, a change in which households allocate more resources; particularly labor, to market-oriented activities in response to rising demand for goods in the market.

The literature on industrious revolutions makes at least two contributions to the contemporary debate. First, since capitalism is unable to absorb the "surplus" population, particularly in the global South, the labor-intensive industrious revolution model would provide a viable alternative to balance and even replace capitalism in certain sectors or regions. This is one of the central themes in Giovanni Arrighi's *Adam Smith in Beijing: Lineages of the Twenty-First Century*. As he noted,

> Western success along the extroverted, Industrial Revolution path was based upon the exclusion of the vast majority of the world's population from access to the natural and human resources.... As such, it never was an option for that majority.
>
> (2007, 386)

The path of industrious revolution has the potential to be "an option for the majority." Next, the concept suggests that economic progress is possible in non-capitalist modes of economy, which are commonly perceived as backward and inefficient from the angle of modernization. Households, small enterprises, labor-intensive production, and multitasking arrangements, which are emphasized in literature on industrious revolution, can contribute to economic development and provide a livelihood for a great number of people.

Although the model of industrious revolution was formulated to be the opposite of the Industrial Revolution, the contrast has been most salient in the rural economy, particularly with regards to land. Sugihara (2004) compared land use in England and Japan from the sixteenth century to the nineteenth century and showed that land in Japan had absorbed much more labor than that in England. In addition, land policy in Japan restricted land concentration and land purchase, especially by political and economic elites from outside the village community, whereas England saw the enlargement of farm size and the displacement of peasants from the common land (see Brenner 1982; Brenner and Isett 2002).

I apply the concept of industrious revolution to the study of agrarian change. An industrious revolution refers to an economic change when great economic progress is made by and shared among a large population in rural areas. It usually takes place when peasants and rural entrepreneurs have access to and use land resources for farm and nonfarm purposes. This definition is highly relevant to contemporary rural China.

On the one hand, China still has a large rural population and a large rural migrant population, 576.6 million and 172 million in 2017 respectively (NBS 2018), who have to rely on the rural economy for a significant proportion of their livelihood and social reproduction. On the other hand, the rise of China started with the rural economy's takeoff in the 1980s, which can be characterized as another industrious revolution, given its labor-intensive nature and small-scale, community-based production. It can be argued that this recent industrious revolution laid the foundation for sustained growth of the Chinese economy over the past four decades. Thus this book attempts to shed light on the two episodes of industrious revolution in the recent Chinese history. The first is during the eighteenth century, when China in the Qing dynasty reached a new height of prosperity against the background of considerable population growth. The second is in the 1980s and early 1990s, when the market-oriented reform unleashed rapid economic growth in rural areas, lifting 400 million out of poverty and absorbing 160 million rural laborers into nonfarm sectors including rural industry. Figure I.2 shows that the two episodes coincided with the increase in China's standing in the world economy, attesting to the importance of labor-intensive industrious revolution in the populous country.

Based on historical comparisons and empirical investigations, this book puts forward three broad arguments.

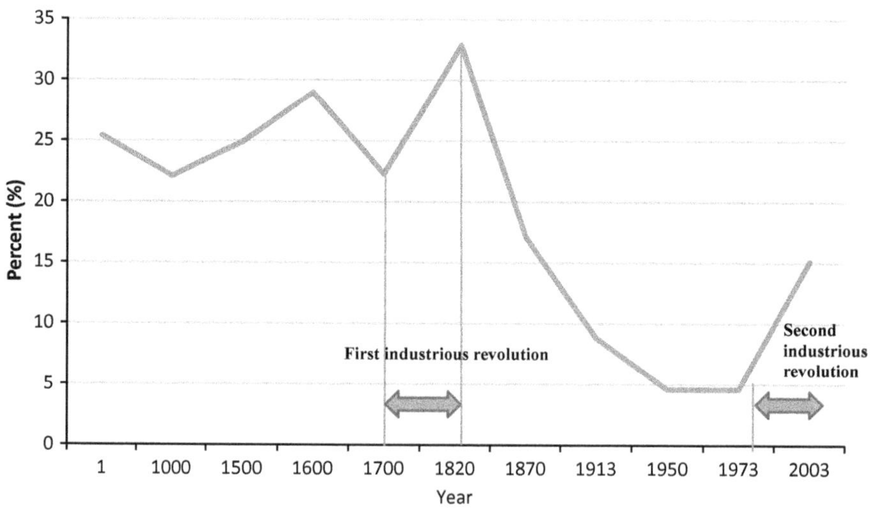

Figure I.2 China's share of world GDP (AD 1–2003) and the two industrious revolutions.
Data source: Maddison (2007, 381).

First, the land question in China is critical to the choice of development between agrarian capitalism and the path of industrious revolution. While the concentration of land can increase labor productivity and improve agricultural income for a small number of large-scale farmers, it undermines the foundation of the industrious revolution and places the livelihood of peasants and rural migrants at grave risks.

Second, the land question should not be limited to the issues of agriculture. One of the main characteristics of an industrious revolution is that land will be used for both farm and nonfarm activities. This is to absorb more laborers into the land-based rural activities as well as to avoid the involution of labor. The recent industrious revolution in China was associated with a remarkable expansion of rural industry in many provinces.

Finally, urbanization and the expansion of capitalist sectors in the city can lessen population pressure in rural areas, but the informalization of production and the rising precarity of urban employment, a sign of urban capitalism's inability to absorb labor, entail the development of the rural economy along the path of industrious revolution. The absorption of labor into rural sectors will also reduce competition among workers for urban jobs, thus increasing the bargaining power of urban workers. For instance, the recent wage increase for city-based migrant workers has occurred against the background of the improvement of rural conditions in China in the past decade. Thus, a foolhardy push for land concentration would further weaken the bargaining power of urban workers and turn Chinese cities into a ground of unemployment, precarious work, and social instability, moving China away from East Asian development, while drawing it closer to the case of South Africa.

State, market, and community: conditions for an industrious revolution

Broad access to land among rural producers is a necessary condition for the emergence of an industrious revolution, but not a sufficient one. According to Henry Bernstein, "… who got land, what land, how much land, and what they were able to do with it …" are all key questions in agrarian studies (2006, 453; 2010, 22–4). Thus, while the issue of land ownership or land use rights is important, it is equally important to ask how much produce or income rural producers can get from the land. Two examples from my own research shine a light on this aspect. In Changzhou Prefecture of Jiangsu Province, one of the most-developed regions in China, rural residents used land to build factories. In 2010, when I was there doing fieldwork, one *mu* of land (667 square meters, or one-fifteenth of a hectare) used for a textile factory could produce 300,000 yuan (about 48,000 US dollars) of surplus value (inclusive of wages and profits) in a year. In Chifeng Prefecture of Inner Mongolia, where land is mainly used for agriculture, one *mu* of tobacco, the most profitable crop in the area, could at most produce 3,000 yuan (480 US dollars), given that the land has access to good irrigation. In most cases, one *mu* of agricultural land in Chifeng could only produce a surplus of 500 to 1,000 yuan, and in the case of poor-quality land, the surplus value was as low as 200 yuan per *mu*. Thus the difference in surplus value generated from the same size of land could be hundreds of times. In an area where the returns of agriculture are low, access to a small piece of land would not be able to provide a sufficient livelihood for a rural family.

The surplus-generating capacity of land is affected by many factors, including, but not limited to, soil quality, ecology, irrigation, technology, and methods of land use. Given the same natural conditions, the surplus-generating capacity of land in a large region (e.g., a country) reflects the key difference between an industrious revolution and a subsistence economy. In the latter, the surplus from the land can only support the simple reproduction of the rural population, whereas in the former land-based farm and nonfarm activities not only supports social reproduction but also provides a source of economic growth as surplus is accumulated and reinvested. The capacity of land to generate surplus for peasants in China has had much to do with external factors including state intervention, market conditions, and their interactions with rural communities.

The Chinese state has intervened in land institutions for centuries. Conventional wisdom holds that the state, in imperial times, was a despotic, repressive apparatus that wanted to extract surplus from the peasant population (Wittfogel 1957). The official ideology of the Chinese Communists suggests that the imperial state represented the interests of the landlord class, and thus it functioned to extract surplus for landlords while suppressing the resistance of peasants. While this was certainly the case, it was also found that the extraction of surplus was sometimes paired with measures to protect peasants' land rights and to develop the rural economy, because a well-to-do peasantry provided a sustainable source of taxation. In the eighteenth century, the taxes from the rural population accounted for more than two-thirds of state revenue, and the Qing state was extremely cautious with raising taxes for fear that it would undermine peasants' livelihoods (Wong 1997, 129–35). The alliance between the state and the landlord class was also a fragile one. Although the imperial state relied on landlords to rule, particularly at the local level, it was suspicious of the latter's power and intention to cheat the bureaucracy and to squeeze the peasantry for self-interest. This led to the imperial state periodically taking action to curb the power of landlords and local elites, particularly when it was capable of doing so.

The complex relations between the state, landlords, and peasants shaped interventions in land relations. Rather than encouraging the concentration of land, the imperial state often enacted edicts to call for the protection of land rights for peasants and tenants. In the mid-eighteenth century, the emperor had seriously considered placing a cap on landholding among large-scale landlords, although the plan was dropped due to practical difficulties (Gao 2012, 87–93). This long tradition of "land to the tiller" culminated in the land reform carried out by the Chinese Communists in the early 1950s, which gave rise to a highly equal land system. Seen from this long-term perspective, the recent push for land concentration by the Chinese state is rather exceptional as it deviates from a long-held ideology and practice in China.

The role of the imperial state was not limited to regulating land relations but extended to raising the surplus-generating capacity of land, such as building irrigation infrastructure and disseminating agricultural and handicraft technologies. This became evident in the eighteenth century, when land reclamation reached its limit while the population was still growing rapidly. As I will show in Chapter 1, the emperors and officials of the Qing dynasty were conscious of population pressures and land constraints, and they were taking active measures to introduce labor-absorbing technologies and practices so that the limited land could support a larger population. The critical role of the state was also evident in the decades after 1949, which saw the doubling of the Chinese population from 500 million to one billion. The socialist-period Chinese state, like its Qing predecessor, made great efforts to disseminate agricultural technologies and to improve irrigation infrastructure. The transfer of urban industrial knowledge to the countryside in this period also contributed to the rise of rural industry.

The market affects how much surplus rural producers can derive from the land. The issue has been at the forefront of agrarian studies in recent decades, as small commodity rural producers have been increasingly integrated into national and global markets. Agrarian capital does not have to directly control land and agricultural production to exploit peasants and small farmers; it can do so by controlling the upstream and downstream of commodity chains. For example, the monopoly of seed supply provides a powerful mechanism for large transnational corporations such as Monsanto to exploit small farmers in the world (Kloppenburg 2005; Otero 2012). The current literature of agrarian studies generally views the market as unfavorable to small rural producers.

Seen from the perspective of an industrious revolution, however, the market provides a crucial avenue for small producers to realize the value of their labor. Small producers are usually located in geographically bounded communities and have access to limited natural resources. To increase the surplus from land, they must specialize in certain products and engage in market exchange. The eighteenth-century industrious revolution in China is a good example. Although China had yet to transition into a capitalist economy, it witnessed the rapid expansion of the market, with peasants and artisans being deeply involved in market exchange. This led the historian William Skinner to contend that social structure of rural China must be understood through an analysis of the marketing system (Skinner 1964). It is useful here to refer to Fernand Braudel and Giovanni Arrighi for distinguishing between capitalism and a market economy. In a market economy, competition and free entry would lead to market expansion and economic growth while at the same time driving down the rates of profit. Large capital under capitalism, however, tries to slow down or to avoid the trend of falling profit rates by restricting entry and reducing competition, particularly when it has the support of the state (Arrighi 1994; Braudel 1977; see also Wallerstein 1991). Students of late imperial China usually described the economy as a Smithian market, rather than a capitalist one (Arrighi 2007; Hamilton and Chang 2003; Wong 1997; Pomeranz 2000).

The separation of the market economy from capitalism is meaningful because it allows us to see the contradictory role of the market. It can be *a channel* for small producers to realize the value of their labor by participating in market transactions, as well as *a mechanism* for large capital to exploit small producers. A key condition for an industrious revolution is to create market conditions that are favorable to small producers and allow them to benefit from market exchange. This is why Giovanni Arrighi (2007) emphasizes the importance of a Smithian market in the historical resurgence of the Chinese economy. The state, with all the power and resources, no doubt plays a vital role. It can either support large agribusiness companies or create conducive conditions for small rural producers in the market. As I will show in Chapter 3, the rise of the industrious revolution in the 1980s had much to do with market conditions in China at the time, in which large producers were either non-existent or restricted, providing a golden opportunity for small rural enterprises to flourish. Over the past four decades, however, the Chinese state has shifted support from peasants and small enterprises to large agribusiness companies, which has facilitated the rise of agrarian capitalism in China (Xu 2017; Yan and Chen 2015; Zhang, Oya, and Ye 2015). It should also be noted that the distribution of land would affect market conditions. Market conditions are generally more favorable for small producers in a country where land is equally distributed than in one where land is concentrated with large farms dominating agricultural production and trade. This can be seen from the comparison with South Africa in Chapter 5.

The discussion of the market draws our attention to the cooperative movement. A main goal of rural cooperation is to improve market conditions for small producers, as they are individually too weak to resist the power of agrarian capital or take risks in the market. Rural cooperatives can help small producers achieve vertical integration and exert a certain degree of control over the upstream and downstream of commodity chains (Chayanov 1991; Huang 2011). The earliest cooperative movement in China can be traced to the 1930s. Between 1978 and 1983, the rural reform broke up collective farms and eastablished a household economy. And yet, the rural cooperative movement reemerged in the past two decades (Yan and Chen 2013). In 2006, the Chinese state enacted a law to support villages to establish rural economic cooperatives. However, the goal of the policy was not so much to encourage cooperation among rural producers as to integrate rural households into the commodity chains dominated by agribusiness companies. A study discovered that most of officially registered rural cooperatives, whose number reached 1.9 million in 2017 (Dong and Hong 2017), were not genuine cooperatives, and that many of them were used as pawns to serve the interests of agribusiness and large farms (Hu, Zhang, and Donaldson 2017). Nevertheless, there have been some real efforts to create rural cooperatives for the interests of peasants among intellectuals and local practitioners (Day and Schneider 2017). My own fieldwork in Chifeng in Inner Mongolia found that some cooperatives served peasants' interests, although they may not fit into the strict scholarly definition of a rural cooperative.

In addition to rural cooperatives, other forms of village-based cooperation also helped peasants and rural enterprises utilize resources and strengthen their position in the market. Tiejun Wen (2011) argues that informal cooperation among rural households within villages give rise to a village welfare system (*cunshe lixing*, literally, "village rationality"), which protects village members from the worst impact in the market. Xuefeng He (2012) argues that rural administrative organizations, including villages (former brigades) and production teams, which are inherited from the socialist era, continue to play a significant role in organizing peasants in production and public affairs. My own study on rural industry in southern Jiangsu found that the community boundary protected rural enterprises from market forces while at the same time subjecting them to competition, creating a "community-based market dynamic" (Zhan 2015a). It should be noted that these forms of cooperation are also based on broad access to land among members within the village community. They would disappear or considerably weaken should peasants be displaced from the land.

Given widespread formal and informal cooperation among rural producers, this book categorizes rural producers according to their relationship with the rural community. The main force in an industrious revolution consists of community-based producers, which include peasants (rural households), small farmers, small rural enterprises, rural cooperatives, and collective enterprises. These producers are rooted in the rural community and utilize community resources such as land and labor. Although some rural cooperatives or collective enterprises are of large scale, their development is beneficial rather than harmful to small producers. By contrast, capitalist producers such as agribusiness companies and large farms are not rooted in a particular community, and their expansion would displace small rural producers. This classification is different from the conventional Marxist classification based on the relations of production. In a Chinese village community, class positions, particularly relations to land, cannot fully reflect one's socioeconomic status because of the diversification of economic activities (Zhang 2015). The issue of class also fails to capture cooperative relations, both in and across classes, within the community. Furthermore, the key issue of agrarian change in contemporary China, as well as in many other countries, might no longer be the differentiation of rural classes, though the issue is still important, but the intrusion of large agrarian capital from outside, which seeks to grab land and displace all occupants on land. The contemporary relevance of the industrious revolution, with its great capacity to absorb labor, should be located in this context.

The East Asian development path and Chinese experience

The remarkable rise of East Asia (Japan, South Korea, Taiwan, Singapore, and Hong Kong) in the second half of the twentieth century has led to the formulation of the East Asian development path (other terminologies include "East Asian model," "East Asian miracle," and "East Asian development"). However, scholars differ on what constitutes the East Asian development path. There have been at least three main interpretations.

The first interpretation attributes the success of East Asia to a new model of industrialization – the export-oriented industrialization (EOI), in contrast to the import-substitution industrialization (ISI). The strategy of ISI, which replaces foreign imports with domestic industrial production, was widely practiced in developing countries in the 1950s and '60s, particularly in Latin America. EOI, formulated based on East Asian experiences and as an opposite of ISI, referred to a strategy exporting industrial goods in comparative advantage and using the returns from exports to accelerate domestic industrialization. The EOI model was hailed as outward looking and an efficient way of allocating resources (Corbo *et al.* 1985; Krueger 1978). This interpretation has met criticisms, however. Gary Gereffi (1989), in comparing East Asia and Latin America, shows that both regions had combined inward-oriented and outward-oriented strategies and that the success of East Asia should not be attributed to exports alone, but also to other factors such as transnational economic linkages and the ability of domestic institutions in managing these linkages. William Cline (1982) argues that the EOI model could not be generalized because of the fallacy of composition, that is, while the model may work well if pursued by a limited number of countries, it would break down if all developing countries seek to do the same.

The second interpretation looks at the interventions of the state in the economy, particularly domestic industrial policy. It argues that the common factor in the success of East Asian economies is the enabling role of a developmental state, which directly intervened in the development process and set the pace and direction of industrialization and overall economic development rather than only relying on market forces to allocate resources (Chang 1993; Evans 1995; Johnson 1982; Wade 1990). The developmental state argument is a direct rebuttal to neoliberal prescriptions that have been advocated by international donors and financial institutions such as the International Monetary Fund and the World Bank since the 1970s. For instance, Amsden argues that one of the keys to South Korea's economic success was not to "get prices right," but to deliberately get prices "wrong" (1989, 139). The World Bank's report on the Asian miracle was also criticized for paying insufficient attention to the interventionist state in East Asia (Lall 1996; World Bank 1993). The developmental state argument has not gone without challenges. Dwight Perkins (1994) contends that there were at least three different models of state intervention in East Asia: generalized state interventions in Japan, South Korea and Taiwan, the mixed model of free markets and state intervention in Singapore, and a laissez-faire free-market approach in Hong Kong. The more serious challenge came after the 1997 Asian Financial Crisis. The previous enabling developmental state was accused of not adapting to the new situation of globalization and of accommodating crony capitalism (Beeson 2004; Stubbs 2009).

The third interpretation focuses on the inclusiveness of East Asian development, that is, economic growth is shared widely among nearly all social classes and groups, particularly the poor through job creation, redistribution, and land reform. It also emphasizes the role of the state, as the state is the main actor to implement inclusive policies. The interpretation is both historical and contemporary. Kaoru Sugihara's arguments on "industrious revolution" and "labor-intensive industrialization" examined, from a long-term historical perspective, how labor was absorbed rather than excluded from economic development in East Asia (Sugihara 2003, 2013). In the contemporary period, it is found that the three major East Asian economies – Japan, South Korea, and Taiwan – all successfully implemented land reforms prior to economic takeoff. Christóbal Kay (2002) argued that successful agrarian reforms in South Korea and Taiwan had a great redistributive impact on social equity and consequently a positive impact on their industrialization. During Japan's early industrialization in the prewar period, later in South Korea and Taiwan as well, rural industry had played a crucial role and absorbed a large number of laborers in the countryside. And the rural-based and labor-intensive industries continued even after the Second World War (Francks 2002; Ho 1982; Hayami 1998). The third interpretation has also been met with critiques. The relatively equal distribution of income should not belie the fact that there was also inequality and poverty in these countries, particularly in large cities such as Hong Kong and Singapore. With an economic slowdown over the past two decades, the problems such as working poor, inequality, precarization of work and even urban poverty have been on the rise in East Asian cities, where the most population now lives (Ahuja *et al.* 1997; Kalleberg and Hewison 2013). Kenneth Pomeranz (2001) is skeptical of the existence of a labor-intensive East Asian model, showing that East Asian economies have been moving in the direction of capital-intensive and resource-intensive development since the nineteenth century.

This book defines the East Asian development path as closest to the third interpretation and focuses on land rights and rural-based economic development. It refers to a model of vigorous rural development based on broad access to land before labor is fully absorbed into urban industrial sectors; that is, the model contains key elements of an industrious revolution. Such a model contrasts with the displacement of small farmers and the eviction of tenants for cities before urban sectors are able to absorb them.

Does China fit into this East Asian development path? The answer is both yes and no. China's rapid economic growth over the past four decades was preceded by a thorough land reform and infrastructure buildup in the socialist period, and was pioneered with rural economic takeoff in the 1980s.[4] Broad access to land, small-scale farming, and the rapid expansion of labor-intensive rural industry all fit into the model. However, China is a continent-sized country with a huge rural population, and rural conditions vary widely from locality to locality. While coastal provinces saw the rapid expansion of rural industry, there was a very low level of rural industrialization in interior provinces. While agricultural production was greatly increased in eastern and central provinces, small-sized farmland in mountainous areas in western provinces could not even support the subsistence of rural households in some cases. Rural development also fluctuated over time. The 1980s saw a great expansion of the rural economy, but it was followed by a severe rural crisis in the late 1990s and early 2000s (Wen 2001). More importantly, other East Asian economies were able to transfer the majority of the rural population to the city, but this process in China has been much longer and incomplete. Although the rate of urbanization has surpassed 50 percent, more than 150 million urban workers are rural migrants while the problems of urban poverty and precarious employment are widespread (Lee 2016; Swider 2015; Zhou 2013). In this respect, China looks like most developing countries in the global South. It is not unreasonable to extrapolate that China would never be able to urbanize the population with a living wage to the same degree as did other East Asian countries. This is due to China's huge population and resource constraints as well as to the unequal capitalist world system being incapable of supporting the majority of proletarians with a living wage (Arrighi and Silver 2001). The land question in China and the significance of the industrious revolution should be situated in this multifaceted and sometimes contradictory context.

The data in this book is derived from a variety of sources. I have drawn on historical archives, national statistics, policy documents, and secondary sources for the analysis of national changes in both the late imperial and contemporary periods. In addition, I carried out extensive fieldwork in a number of provincial regions over the past two decades, including in Jiangsu, Hunan, Henan, Beijing, Heilongjiang, Inner Mongolia, Sichuan, Chongqing, and Yunnan. I also conducted two in-depth case studies of two counties: Wujin County in Jiangsu and Aohan County in Inner Mongolia. I visited the two counties about every other year (Aohan since 2005; Wujin since 2010) and conducted about 260 interviews with local officials, farmers, migrant workers, and rural entrepreneurs. I will use data of these two case studies extensively in the book. Figure I.3 shows the locations of the two cases and my other field sites.

Figure I.3 My research sites including Aohan and Wujin.

The following six chapters are organized into three parts: Part I (Chapters 1 and 2) examines the conditions for the emergence of the two industrious revolutions. One was in the eighteenth century, and the other was in the early reform period. The chapters will particularly focus on land institutions, government interventions, and market conditions. Part II (Chapters 3 and 4) describes how two different forces have undermined the conditions for the industrious revolution in China since the 1990s: one is the urban-centric development that drains resources from rural areas, which either undermines the surplus-generating capacity of rural land or displaces villagers from the land; the other is the rise of agrarian capitalism that has not only extracted surplus from rural areas through contract farming and the control of commodity chains, but has also sought to concentrate land by displacing small farmers. Part III (Chapters 5 and 6) is devoted to cross-national comparisons. Chapter 5 compares China with South Africa, where land has been highly concentrated after the black peasantry was displaced from most of the land. Chapter 6 examines land institutions and rural changes in three East Asian economies – Japan, South Korea, and Taiwan – and highlights the importance of land against the rising precarity of urban employment and the welfare crisis due to economic slowdown and neoliberal structural reforms in the past two decades.

Notes

1 The rural lands targeted in the new land reform also include residential land (*zhaijidi*) and construction land (*jianshe yongdi*), that is, the lands used to build houses, factories, and public facilities. The reforms aim to create a market for these lands (Box I.1 and Figure I.1).

2 The precarization of urban employment refers to the process in which an increasing number of urban workers hold precarious and insecure jobs with no or low welfare protection (Standing 2011).

3 Chinese official documents renamed use rights "operating rights" (*jingying quan*).

4 China is also characterized by a strong tradition of state developmentalism, as are other East Asian economies (So 2009).

Part I

Historical perspective

1 The Ming–Qing transition, land, and China's first industrious revolution

China in the Qing dynasty (1644–1911) has been portrayed rather negatively in scholarship and popular narratives due to its repeated defeats in wars with Western powers and Japan – its economy was stagnant and backward, and its bureaucracy corrupt, incompetent, and inward-looking (Cohen 1984; Hung 2003). In addition, the fact that it was ruled by Manchus, an ethnic minority that originated from outside China proper,[1] fueled Chinese nationalist sentiment and the debate over ethnic relations.

Over the past two decades, a growing number of scholars began to view late imperial China in a more positive light. They drew attention to the considerable market expansion and economic growth that took place in the late Ming period through the mid-Qing period (1550–1800). For instance, Andre Gunder Frank (1998), by charting the flows of silver, argued that China continued to be the center of the world economy until the early nineteenth century. Kenneth Pomeranz (2000) contended that China and West Europe both experienced similar economic expansion from the sixteenth century to the eighteenth century and that the divergence between them did not occur until the early nineteenth century. More recently, William Rowe noted:

> … from the mid-sixteenth century to the end of the eighteenth, the empire underwent a second commercial revolution even more transformative than the first.[2] This period saw the development of what historians sometimes call a "circulation economy" or "commodity economy" in which commercialization penetrated local rural society to an unprecedented degree. For the first time, a large percentage of China's farm households began to produce a significant percentage of their crop for sale and to rely on market exchange for items of daily consumption … by the end of the eighteenth century more than a tenth of the empire's grain, more than a quarter of its raw cotton, more than half of its cotton cloth, over nine-tenths of its raw silk, and nearly all of its tea was produced for sale in the marketplace.
>
> (2009, 123)

A question thus arises: In a period when China had yet to transition into capitalism, what drove this impressive economic growth? This question takes on great importance because many contemporary scholars, including Marxist scholars who are critical of capitalism believe that only capitalism can lead to *real* economic development. The literature of late imperial China attributed economic prosperity in late imperial periods to the Smithian dynamics, characterized by specialization and market expansion (Feuerwerker 1992; Wong 1997). The working of this dynamics in China was stimulated by the influx of American silver and empire-wide peace and stability – except for the disruption of the Ming–Qing transition in the mid-seventeenth century. As noted in the Introduction, the notion of separating the market economy and capitalism originated from Fernand Braudel. Drawing on Braudel and the literature of late imperial China, Giovanni Arrighi (2007) argues that the economic theory of Adam Smith could be best applied to imperial China, rather than to Western capitalist economies as conventionally perceived.

This chapter looks at land relations as an important dimension of the market economy in late imperial China. It presents three main findings: First, the relative position of small producers (tenants, peasants and small-scale landlords) versus large-scale landowners in land relations was strengthened after the Ming–Qing transition, giving rise to a market economy of smallholders. This was another (perhaps more important) divergence between China and England, in which the latter saw the empowering of large-scale landowners in a period of commercial expansion (Brenner 1982). This finding also provides a nuanced interpretation of China's late imperial economy, differing from the existing literature that tends to see the period between 1550 and 1800 as a continuum. Second, the predominance of smallholders allowed the market economy to absorb a large rural population, which led to the emergence of the first industrious revolution. The Qing state played an enabling role in this change. It protected land rights of tenants and peasants and took efforts to disseminate technologies and farming methods among rural households. Finally, the weakening of China in the nineteenth century was preceded by the decline of the industrious revolution. The continuous growth of the population, the weakening of state capacity and a lack of technological breakthroughs all played a role in this decline. Nevertheless, the legacy of the industrious revolution had carried on, shielding smallholders in some regions (not all) from the worst impact of the tumults of the nineteenth and early twentieth centuries. The following sections discuss these three findings in turn.

Changing status of smallholders: 1550–1800

The influx of silver after the mid-sixteenth century, resulting from the expansion of international trade, transformed the late Ming dynasty into a monetized economy. Agriculture and handicraft production were increasingly oriented toward the market, rather than self-consumption, hence producing a wide range of commodities including rice, cotton, silk, tea, timber, cloth, paper, and porcelain (Atwell 1982; Lufrano 1997). The commercial revolution created opportunities for some societal sections, particularly the elite groups, to improve social and economic status. But the majority of smallholders continued to suffer oppressive social relations and poor economic conditions.

Expanding serfdom and elite power in the late Ming dynasty

There would be no better phenomenon than expanding serfdom to demonstrate the worsening conditions of smallholders after the mid-sixteenth century. This led some scholars to draw an analogy between late-Ming China and Eastern Europe, which saw a "second serfdom with commercial expansion over the same period (Walker 1999, 8–9; Wallerstein 2011[1974], 66–131).

The expansion of serfdom in the late Ming dynasty was characterized by the increased use of bondservants (*nupu* in Chinese). Bondservants were registered in their masters' households and had no legal land rights. Among other things, they had to pay exorbitant rents and manual services to their masters. They were also legally considered "mean or base people," and were prohibited from marrying commoners or participating in civil examinations (Wiens 1980, 5; Ye 1983). In the early Ming dynasty (fourteenth–fifteenth century), the use of bondservants was limited to a small number of powerful elites. By the late sixteenth century, however, it had become a widespread practice among landlords, merchants, and official households (Niu 2002). This suggests extreme social polarization with an increase in elite power and the worsening-off of smallholders such as peasants, tenants, and hired laborers, who were the main source of bondservants. It was found that poor peasants and landless laborers often had no choice but to turn themselves into bondservants due to indebtedness, bankruptcy, coercion, or the excessive burden of taxation (Fu 1957, 31–2, 60–2).

Bondservants were not only used for personal services, but also for profit-making endeavors. The Yangtze delta, the most commercialized region, was among the places where the use of bondservants was most widespread. Agricultural books written during this period suggested that the number of large managerial landlords who hired dozens to hundreds of agricultural laborers including bondservants was on the rise, and these landlords had developed new methods of labor control for the purpose of profit maximization (Fu 1957, 54–66).[3]

The number of bondservants owned by an elite household in the region could reach thousands (McDermott 1981; Xu and Wu 1985, 59). The exact figure of the bondservant population remains unknown, but it probably reached very high levels in some areas. For example, it was estimated that bondservants in Macheng County, Hubei Province toward the end of the Ming dynasty (1630s) accounted for 20 to 50 percent of the population (*Macheng xianzhi* 1993, 71; Niu 2002; Rowe 2007, 109–35). The expansion of servitude met resistance, and millions of bondservants joined domestic rebellions in the early seventeenth century, contributing directly to the fall of the late Ming regime (Walker 1999; Yang and Chen 1993, 433–72).

Peasants and tenants also fared poorly in the late sixteenth century. Peasants were losing land to landlords and powerful elites. It was estimated that more than 60 percent of peasant families owned none or very little land (less than one *mu* per person) toward the end of the sixteenth century,[4] while in the eighteenth century, nearly half of peasant families owned land. Permanent tenancy, if it existed in the late Ming dynasty, was a rare phenomenon and much more limited than that in the eighteenth century (Naquin and Rawski 1987, 100; Xu and Wu 1985, 58–68). With no land or secure land rights, tenants in the late Ming dynasty had to pay high rates of rent to landlords, which could be 50 to 60 percent of land output (Fu 2007, 80–9).

Land relations and the market in the eighteenth century

While large-scale landlords, particularly those with official degrees, were still very powerful in the eighteenth century, their control over land and labor had somewhat diminished. For example, large-scale landlords tended to share land rights with tenants while permitting rent negotiation in the event of natural disasters and poor harvests. It was difficult to evict tenants, either because tenants held permanent tenancy or because it must go through a long legal or customary process, thus tenants would often make excuses to avoid paying the full amount of rent. Taking all these factors into account, Wangling Gao (2005a, 76) estimates that the actual rent paid to landlords in the late eighteenth century could be as low as 30 percent of land output.

After taking power in 1723, the Yongzheng emperor announced a series of emancipatory policies liberating outcast social/occupational groups, including musician households (*yuehu*), debased people (*duomin*), hereditary servants (*shipu*), tenant bondservants (*tianpu*), the Tankas (*tanmin*), beggar households (*gaihu*), banner slavers (*Qinu*), and shelter people (*pengmin*) (Huang 1974, 226–7). The policies were so radical and their effects so profound that historians called the change the "Yongzheng's emancipation" (Rowe 2002, 500). The use of bondservants had virtually disappeared, and the tenant–landlord relationship was bound by contract rather than by personal dependence. The subsequent Qianlong reign (1735–96) continued these policies and further cleared legal and social discriminations against the lower social classes. As a result, the inequality in social status in the eighteenth century had been considerably leveled (Mann 1997, 21–2; Wakeman 1985, 1056–7).

While peasants and tenants were still subjected to the power of landlords and elites, they as a whole had gained unprecedented independence. William Rowe (2002, 529) argues that the eighteenth century should be regarded as "the age of triumph of the freestanding commoner household (*hu*) as the basic feature of the Chinese landscape." This change had led to the rise of a smallholder market, a new market where smallholders emerged as an important force of market expansion and economic growth.

With secure land rights and improved social status, smallholders developed a strong incentive to improve agricultural conditions, and they were able to adopt new seeds and new methods of cultivation, particularly those that would absorb more labor (Fang 1997; Perdue 1987, 93–135; Yan 2005). Francesca Bray shows that the rice economy and handicraft industry in China provided technological and material bases for household production, allowing them to make full use of labor, particularly female labor (1994, 5–61, 1997, 206–72). The standards of consumption of the lower social classes also increased. The gaps in consumption between tenants, middle peasants, rich peasants, and small-scale landlords diminished and were converging to middle peasants. This suggested intense competition among rural households for socioeconomic status and a high level of social mobility (Zhang 2006).

The improved status of smallholders was not limited to land and agriculture, but also extended to other economic sectors, such as handicraft industry and commerce. Bozhong Li documented how it was households and small workshops rather than large factories that drove the expansion of handicraft industries in the Yangtze delta in the eighteenth century. According to him, small producers, who were connected through specialization and division of labor, were "the main propeller of industrial growth in the age" (2000, 58). With regard to commerce, while long-distance, large-volume trades had to be organized by large merchants, numerous small merchants usually operated local trades. The large number of merchants, often up to thousands in a prefecture, suggested intense competition and a low degree of monopolization (Myers and Wang 2002, 590).

Peasant households often combined multiple activities to expand income sources and to reduce the risk of harvest failure. Consider a middle peasant household in the Yangtze delta in 1750 with two main laborers: husband and wife.[5] A household owned three *mu* of land and leased seven *mu* of land from a landlord. The husband worked on the land to grow rice (in the summer), wheat (in the winter), and other commercial crops. During slack seasons, he would work in the nearby town as a temporary laborer. The wife took cotton from a merchant and spun and wove it into cloth, which was then sold back to the merchant. There were dozens of merchants in the nearby area, thus the household could switch to another were it not satisfied with the merchant. With income from weaving, farming and wage work, the household could live a modest life and even send their children to school. The landlord and the market were of crucial importance to the livelihood, but the household could negotiate, to a certain degree, on land rights, rent payment and prices.

The transition to a small-producer market in the eighteenth century had expanded the economy rather than shrunk it. Wangling Gao (1999) showed that economic growth and market expansion in the eighteenth century were not limited to the Yangtze delta and a few coastal provinces, as they were in the late Ming dynasty, but extended to all provinces in China proper. The case of interregional grain trade, which was an indicator of regional division of labor and market expansion, lent credence to his argument. The trade was often cited as the evidence of China's vast national market and economic prosperity (Pomeranz 2000, 34; Wong 1997, 211–13). The geographical reach of the trade was limited in the sixteenth century. The main places that imported grains included the Yangtze delta, Fujian, and Huizhou of southern Anhui, and the total volume of grains traded did not exceed five million *shi* (one *shi* equals approximately 103 liters). However, by the mid-eighteenth century, grain trade had expanded to all regions in China proper. A conservative estimate suggested that the total volume of long-distance grain trade reached at least 30 million *shi*, six times that of the late Ming period (Dai 1992, 317; Wu 1983, 277).

Peasant households usually lived together, clustering into rural communities (villages). Built on common residence, kinship, and family lineages, Chinese villages contained dense social networks and various social organizations, providing the communal basis for social recognition, reciprocal behavior and cultural activities (Cohen 2005). Many villages owned common assets that could be used for collective purposes such as village schools, public infrastructure works, and philanthropic granaries. These communities had a stratified structure – at the top were gentry members and degree-holders, who owned land, but did not engage in production. Below them were farming landlords, small merchants, rich peasants, middle peasants, tenants, and landless laborers, in descending order based on economic status. Neither the functional roles nor intra-stratification was unique to Chinese villages, as observed in peasant communities across various parts of the world (Ostrom 1990; Scott 1977). What distinguished Chinese villages in the eighteenth century from others might have been their incorporation into a highly developed market economy. Thus, the social and economic life of the peasant household was not only shaped by the village community, but also by the larger market system (Skinner 1964).

1.2 The role of the Qing state

The rise of the industrious revolution in the eighteenth century was a result of multiple factors. For example, peasant rebellions and wars during the Ming–Qing transition eliminated a large number of landlords and powerful elites (Wakeman 1985, 1054–6; Walker 1999). In addition, the family inheritance system that divided family assets among all of the sons contributed to the fragmentation of lands and assets (Chao 1986). However, these were also true in other historical periods, but they did not led to an industrious revolution as was seen in the eighteenth century. This section will show how the Qing state's support for smallholders in land relations and livelihoods played a crucial role.

The scholarly views on the Qing state have also shifted in recent decades. Previously, Marxist scholars saw the Qing state as representing the interests of the landlord class (Xu and Wu 1985). In the Cold War era, it was portrayed as a despotic oriental regime (Wittfogel 1957). A more popular view was that the ruling Manchus were sinicized after they conquered China proper – they inherited the Chinese political system, adopted Confucianism, and were assimilated into the Chinese society. Therefore, the Qing state was another ruling house in Chinese history (Ho 1967). Recent scholarship of the Qing state revised these views in two important aspects: state-market relations and the Manchu identity of the ruling class.

On state-market relations, it was argued that the Qing state was actually pro-commercial and pro-market. It promoted the free circulation of commodities for the sake of popular livelihoods and prohibited the obstruction of grain circulation in times of natural disasters (Dunstan 1996; Hung 2011, 31; Wong 1982). With regard to the Manchu identity, the school of New Qing History, which emerged in the United States in the past two decades, argued for the distinctiveness of the Qing regime. It contends that the ruling Manchus had not been fully assimilated into the Han society or culture. Rather, they deliberately maintained or created a Manchu identity via political arrangements and cultural practices (Rawski 1996; Crossley 1999; Elliott 2001). Both the pro-market stance and ethnic identity shaped the Qing state's political will and capacity to enact and implement supportive policies for smallholders.

Political will

The manifested political will of the ruling class may have originated from three sources. First, it was derived from the need to consolidate its rule in China proper. As an external nomadic power, the Manchus were possibly more willing than Han Chinese rulers to improve the well-being of the populace in order to win the broad consent to its rule (Gao 1995, 97; Hung 2011, 30). Throughout the Kangxi (1669–1722), Yongzheng (1723–35), and Qianlong (1735–96) reigns, improving the conditions of commoners and lower classes was a common concern in policymaking. Commerce was encouraged and promoted because it was an important way to improve popular livelihoods. Thus, "the Qing was more energetically solicitous of trade than nearly any of China's preceding empires" (Rowe 2009, 132).

Second, the Qing rulers may have also learnt the lessons from the fall of the preceding Ming dynasty. Peasants, tenants, and bondservants joined in domestic rebellions en masse in the early seventeenth century and became a major force in toppling the Ming regime. The Qing ruling house wanted to avoid this fate, and this motivated it to improve popular livelihoods, particularly for the lower classes (Walker 1999).

Finally, the political will supporting smallholders had to do with sources of state revenue. Agrarian taxes constituted a major part of state revenue, which allowed the Qing state to be relatively independent of the influence of commercial capital. Agricultural taxes accounted for more than two-thirds of imperial revenue in the eighteenth century, while commercial taxes, even including mandatory "contributions" from large merchants, made up no more than a quarter. This contrasts with the situation in Western Europe, where the states relied heavily on commercial taxes and sought to expand the tax base by providing protection, support and privileges for large merchants (Wong 1997, 129–35). A notable success of the Qing state in the eighteenth century was that it raised revenue not by increasing tax rates but by expanding the economy. Although it collected taxes mainly from small producers such as peasants and tenants, it did not increase their tax burden.

State capacity

The political will was a necessary, but not a sufficient, condition because the state must possess the ability to carry out policies. In the late seventeenth and eighteenth centuries, the Qing state was relatively capable. This was partly contingent on the personal ability of the Kangxi, Yongzheng, and Qianlong emperors, who were among the most able and diligent emperors in Chinese history. Their reigns together lasted for more than a century. Nevertheless, it also had much to do with state autonomy and successful mobilization of the bureaucracy.

Developmental state literature has stressed the importance of state autonomy in economic development. Being autonomous from class interests or special interests allows the state to pursue broad development goals and prevents officials from colluding with interest groups (Evans, Rueschemeyer, and Skocpol 1985; Evans 1995). The Manchu identity helped the Qing state maintain a certain degree of autonomy. For example, many important documents for political and military communications were only written in Manchu language, with the intention of bypassing Han bureaucrats (Crossley and Rawski 1993). More importantly, the Qing state staffed key positions with Manchus who supervised Han bureaucrats and communicated directly with the emperor. The Grand Council, the most important decision-making institution in the Yongzheng and Qianlong reigns, was staffed predominately with Manchus. The number of Manchu officials in the Grand Council exceeded Han Chinese by 73 percent during the Qianlong reign (Bartlett 1991, 178). While provincial governors were usually Han Chinese, governor-generals, who supervised provincial governors, were mostly Manchus and Bannermen. It should be noted that these measures were less for ethnic reasons than for political and ruling considerations. Han Chinese bureaucrats were supervised and disciplined, so were Manchu officials and aristocrats. During the Kangxi reign, previously powerful Manchu aristocrats were significantly weakened after the emperor eliminated the Oboi clique in 1669. During the Yongzheng reign, the newly instituted Grand Council rendered the Deliberative Council of Princes and Ministers (*yizhengwang dachen huiyi*), which was previously an institution for Manchu nobles to influence political decisions and state affairs, insignificant. The Yongzheng emperor also reformed the banner system to reduce the power of Banner nobles (Huang 1974, 16–17; Feng 1985, 272–80).

In addition, the law of avoidance, which the Qing rulers forcefully implemented, increased the autonomy of bureaucrats from the influence of interest groups, particularly at the local level. The Qing state did not allow officials to serve in their home prefecture or even province. In addition, it deliberately separated officials of common kinship and native origin, and mixed officials of different ethnic backgrounds (Han, Manchu, and Mongolian) when assigning posts. The purpose of the Qing state was to build a system of checks and balances to prevent officials from forming factions and interest groups (Rowe 2009, 38–9).

State capacity was also enhanced through the successful mobilization of the bureaucracy. For example, provincial governors in the Ming dynasty were irregularly appointed and their roles ill defined. In the Qing dynasty, in contrast, they assumed a variety of clearly defined military and civilian responsibilities. As a result, provincial governance reached an unprecedented level of effectiveness and perhaps outstripped any preceding dynasty in terms of bureaucratic capacity and official competence (Guy 2010, 3–18). In addition, the Qing state, particularly during the Yongzheng and Qianlong reigns, established and implemented a problem-solving, goal-oriented evaluation system, which helped the government select the most competent and experienced officials to staff provincial and sub-provincial positions (X. Gao 1995). The officials were also socially "embedded" in the eighteenth century, most Qing officials including provincial governors and county magistrates could be called "field officials," who got out to the grassroots levels, "being seen, being heard, and being perceived as listening and approachable" (Rowe 2001, 71; Will 1997). As such, the Qing state was able to hold the bureaucracy together for common governance goals and prevent factional fights (Dai 1992, 34–135; X. Gao 1995, 108–411).

The capacity of the Qing state was also built on its information-collecting system. The collection of population data and timely information, regarded by some scholars as an important feature of modern nation-states in the West (e.g., Giddens 1985), allowed the Qing state to evaluate officials' performance and make informed decisions on national and local matters. The palace memorial system (*zouzhe zhidu*), which was created in the Kangxi reign and formalized in the Yongzheng reign, was an important channel for the emperors to receive information and communicate with officials at the provincial level or higher (Bartlett 1991, 50–65; Feng 1985, 250–72; Huang 1974, 14–15). The Qing state had also gradually established or improved the systems of reporting natural disasters, food prices, local protests and population numbers in the eighteenth century (Will 1990, 97–126; Will and Wong 1991, 25–7; Hung 2011, 51–7).

Supportive policies for smallholders

Land relations

The improved status of peasants and tenants had much to do with the land policy of the Qing state. For example, the state supported permanent tenancy, and mandated that the landlord should not take away tenancy rights or change tenants at will. In addition, it recognized two ownerships of a piece of farmland: surface ownership (*tianmian quan*) and sub-surface ownership (*tiandi quan*). Many tenants had surface ownership, and they could transfer it or sell it to others (Li and Li 1999; Rowe 2002, 520). The surface ownership bears some resemblance to land use rights in contemporary China.

While land transactions were widespread in the eighteenth century, the law on land sale protected smallholders' land rights. For example, the statutes on land sale in 1740 and 1756 supported the customary claim that the land seller retained the right to redeeming the land if it was not specified as an outright final sale. The land seller could claim the right of redemption within a period of 30 years, according to the 1756 statute (Buoye 1993, 48–9; S. Li 2000). These laws ensured that small-scale landowners would not lose all land rights when they were forced to sell land.

The Qing state also supported rent reduction and negotiation. It issued edicts urging landlords to reduce rents in years of natural disasters, and not to raise rents. For tenants who deliberately delayed or evaded the payment of rent, the punishment was not too harsh. The 1712 imperial edict that the state would never raise tax rates (see below) also empowered tenants, who often used the policy to resist rent increase. As a result, rent arrears and evasion became a common phenomenon in the eighteenth century, leading to the decrease in actual rates of rent (Gao 2005a, 149–69).

Qing officials regarded the security of smallholders' land rights as the bedrock of popular livelihood and social stability. The reports sent from field officials to the emperor showed that provincial and county officials believed that smallholders could cultivate the land most efficiently and provide sufficient livelihoods for a growing population (Gao 2005b). Chen Hongmou, who served as governor-general, governor, and other provincial posts between 1733 and 1963, was a good example. According to William Rowe,

> … Chen fits comfortably into the mainstream of early and mid-Qing economic policy making; which repeatedly specified as its object the sustainability of the small-producer household. As Chen himself asserted, it was this unit that was best able to facilitate not only popular subsistence but also economic development.…
>
> (Rowe 2001, 193)

Under this consensus, the Qianlong emperor encouraged the debate among high-level officials over the feasibility to cap the amount of land held by each large-scale landlord, for example, at 30 hectares. The debate lasted from 1736 to 1743, and the emperor finally concluded that the policy was not feasible because landlords could register land under the name of their relatives, thus eliminating the effect of the policy (Gao 2012, 87–91).

The Qing state also issued laws to reduce status inequality between tenants and landlords, and between hired laborers (*gugongren*) and their employers, ruling that these relationships were contractual rather than dependent. In the Ming dynasty, hired laborers were socially subject to their employers, and their status was between commoners and bondservants. In the eighteenth century, the Qing state issued statements (in 1727, 1742, and 1788) to clarify that employers and hired laborers were equal in legal terms (Huang 1988; Liu 1980; Mann 1997, 38). The laws also upgraded the status of tenants to the extent that they were no longer subject to landlords, in legal terms, as servants. Partly as a result of these policies, tenants and hired laborers enjoyed a much more equal relationship with landlords and employers than their counterparts in the Ming dynasty (Fu 2007, 172; Liu 1980).

The support for smallholders was also reflected in land reclamation policy. Under the pressure of a growing population, the Qing state was eager to reclaim new lands. By 1723, the beginning of the Yongzheng reign, farmland across the country reached 900 million *mu* (60 million hectares), exceeding the 700-million-*mu* record in the Ming dynasty by a significant margin (Gao 1995, 14–16). The Qing government offered seeds, livestock, and farm tools for free or as loans in land reclamation, and exempted the newly reclaimed land from taxation for three to five years (Rowe 2001, 56–7; Wang 2001, 133–4). These policies were made to benefit poor farmers and landless tenants rather than large-scale landowners (Huang 1974, 241–3). For example, Chen Hongmou believed that land reclamation "should be accompanied by the emergence of new local societies based on the orthodox model of autonomous small-producer households living harmoniously in village communities," and thus reclamation should not be "large-scale state projects or handed over to large private developers" (Rowe 2001, 193, 219).

Finally, the granary system in the Qing dynasty shielded smallholders from becoming dependent on powerful elites or going bankrupt in the event of harvest failures or natural disasters; otherwise they would subject themselves to large-scale landowners, usurers, or gentry households in exchange for subsistence, a common phenomenon in the late Ming period (Will 1990, 5). The system also protected small-scale landowners by controlling the fluctuation of food prices in the market (Gao 1999, 86–7; Will and Wong 1991, 43–73). The granary system existed long before the Qing dynasty, but it was not until the eighteenth century that it became a well-functioning, state-sponsored system (Will and Wong 1991). The system was based on three types of granaries: ever-normal granaries (*changping cang*), public granaries (*yi cang*), and community granaries (*she cang*). The operation of ever-normal granaries was the responsibility of the state. Public and community granaries were supposed to depend on voluntary donations and be managed by local elites and merchants. However, voluntary actions were often not enough. The Yongzheng emperor solved the problem by supplementing them with government revenue (Huang 1974, 258–67).

Taxation

The Qing state held a policy of low taxes on the population in the eighteenth century. Comparing tax rates in Europe and Qing-era China, Rosenthal and Wong showed that tax rates in Europe were much higher than those in China during the eighteenth century (2011, 16, 175). The Qing state managed to lower tax rates in three ways.

First, the Qing state froze labor service levy (*ding shui*) at a low level. In 1712, the Kangxi emperor declared that the total labor service levy would be fixed. This policy, called "no labor service levy for the added population" (*shengshi ziding, yongbu jiafu*), mandated that the Qing government only collected the same amount of labor service levy as that in 1711 every year thereafter. In 1711, the government collected labor-service levy from a population of 24.62 million male adults. The population had grown steadily thereafter, thus the levy per head had progressively decreased.

Second, after the freezing of labor service levy, the Qing state further merged it into the land tax. As a result, peasants who did not own any land did not need to pay any labor service levy. The policy effectively reduced the tax burden on poor peasants and small-scale landowners. The merging started in the Kangxi reign, but it was the Yongzheng emperor who made it a national policy and enforced it in most provinces. The Qianlong emperor continued the policy and completed the merging throughout China proper (Feng 1985, 172–80; Huang 1974, 263–4). The policy to some extent resembled the "Single Whip" (*yitiao bianfa*) tax reform in the late Ming era. However, the result differed as the Ming state was unable to effectively implement the reform, which eventually worked in the interest of large-scale landlords and powerful elites (Feuerwerker 1984, 310; Ye 1983, 140).

Last, the Qing state frequently lowered tax rates and offered tax holidays for the entire country or areas that were struck by natural disasters or rebellions. Throughout the eighteenth century, tax reductions and exemptions were routinely offered, contributing to the lightening of tax burden. For example, the amount of taxes in Sichuan Province in the eighteenth century accounted for only about 3 percent of a household's total income. From the late seventeenth to the eighteenth century, the imperial state reduced seven years' land tax in total for the province (Wang 2001, 422–37). Sichuan was not an exceptional case, and tax reduction and exemption were widely offered across the country.

Dissemination of technologies and good practices

The industrious revolution had driven the economy to grow in the eighteenth century. While the total acreage of farmland only increased by about 30 percent, the population that fed on the land had more than doubled (Shi 2017, 142). This success should be attributed to a significant increase in agricultural output of per unit of land (land productivity). According to Zhihong Shi's recent estimates, the grain output per hectare had increased from 1,822.5 kilograms in 1600 to 2,325 kilograms in 1766, up 27.6 percent (2017, 71). Dwight Perkins showed that land productivity in China was among the highest in the world, even though her estimate was at the lower end of all estimates (Perkins 1969; Shi and Ma 2010). In any case, the total grain output was not only sufficient to feed the population in the eighteenth century, but there was also a sizeable surplus. As a result, a significant amount of land was allocated to grow non-grain crops such as cotton, mulberry trees, sugarcane, and tea.

Most studies agreed that the productivity of agricultural labor, however, had stagnated or decreased. This was because the increase in labor input in the fixed amount of land resulted in the diminishing returns of labor. Philip Huang's involution theory was built on this assumption (Huang 1985). This way of calculating labor productivity only took into account farming, but rural laborers in China not only worked on the farm, but also engaged in *more* profitable nonfarm activities, particularly in developed regions such as the Yangtze delta. Thus it could not explain why the Yangtze delta, where the population density was the highest, was the most developed region in China. Bozhong Li (1998) employed a different method to calculate labor productivity. He used the peasant household instead of the individual worker as a unit of analysis, and took into account both farming and nonfarm activities. In addition, he calculated labor productivity on a yearly basis rather than on the hourly or daily basis. Thus his definition of labor productivity was the surplus value of a peasant household creating in farming and nonfarm activities in a year. Using this definition, Li found that labor productivity in the Yangtze delta had increased rather than decreased in the eighteenth century, although the household had to mobilize more labor resources (women and the elderly) and devote more days to work (Li 2008). Li's definition seems more suitable than the conventional one for the analysis of an industrious revolution, the main feature of which is to absorb more labor into the production process with limited land resources.

The increase in both land and labor productivity should be attributed to the popularization of labor-intensive agricultural and handicraft technologies, in which the Qing state played a significant role.

The ruling house of the Qing dynasty was aware of the problem of growing population pressure from very early on. In 1709, the Kangxi emperor noted that the rapid population growth at the time would lower living standards, and by the end of the eighteenth century, most government officials recognized population pressure as a serious issue (Gao 2012, 23). However, to solve the problem the Qing rulers did not resort to the control of population growth – as a large population was seen as a sign of prosperity – but to economic development. They made great efforts to introduce and disseminate agricultural technologies and practices. In both the Yongzheng and Qianlong reigns, the state issued sweeping edicts to call on bureaucratic officials to promote agriculture (*quannong*) in their jurisdictions. The government either introduced new crops or seeds in areas where they had not yet been attempted, or it promoted new methods of labor-intensive cultivation such as deep plowing, fertilization, and multiple cropping. These were particularly aimed at less-developed regions. For instance, cotton planting was limited to the Yangtze delta and a few northern provinces in the late Ming dynasty. The Qing state consistently promoted its planting in less-developed provinces such as Shannxi, Gansu, Sichuan and Guizhou. As a result, Sichuan and Shannxi became main areas of cotton planting in the late eighteenth century. In addition to cotton, Qing officials promoted silkworms, mulberry trees, sweet potato, cereals, vegetables, fruit trees, and animal husbandry in less-developed regions. In developed regions such as the Yangtze delta, local governments encouraged multiple cropping and high-value commercial crops. As a result, regional inequality was mitigated, and new crops and cultivation methods spread to a much larger geographical area (Gao 1999).

The Qing state also promoted handicraft industry. Officials in the eighteenth century placed much emphasis on teaching women to spin and weave (*jiaozhi*), as it was seen as a vital source of livelihood (Mann 1997, 28–9; Will 1997, 42). As a result of state support, home handicraft activities, most importantly spinning and weaving, had spread to nearly every province in China proper in the eighteenth century. Pomeranz suggested that the Qing state's success in rural industry was to introduce best practices from one region to another (Pomeranz 2001, 333). The wide spread of handicraft activities in China would be impossible, or at least much slower than it was, without the intervention of the state. With regard to handicraft technologies, Bozhong LI (2000) documented that a variety of new devices and methods, most of which were for small-scale production, had been innovated or improved in the eighteenth century, leading to the growth in the productivity of labor.

Qing officials, who would be transferred to a new place after serving in a locality for a few years due to the law of avoidance, played a role in technological dissemination. For example, Chen Yudian, a Shandong native, introduced silk worms to Zunyi of Guizhou Province, a less-developed region in the Southwest, after he became its prefectural magistrate in 1738, turning Zunyi into one of the richest areas in the province (Gao 1995, 104–5). Chen Hongmou served in more than ten provinces. Whenever he arrived in a new jurisdiction, his first agenda was to encourage peasants to plant cotton and new commercial crops, as well as teaching women how to spin and weave (Gao 1995, 187–8; Rowe 2001, 231–3). In the mid-eighteenth century, officials in northern and western provinces had successfully introduced the sweet potato to their jurisdictions, which previously was grown only in the south (Dai 1992, 287–90).

The Qing state also devoted effort to popular education. In the early eighteenth century, officials in the Yangzi delta pushed to establish at least one school in every township (B. Li 2000, 445). The state during the Yongzheng and Qianlong reigns went further to use government revenue to finance public schools (*yixue*) and academies (*shuyuan*) (Rowe 2001, 409–10). In 1733, the Yongzheng emperor ordered to build with government funds at least one academy in each province, resulting in the swift establishment of 21 academies (Huang 1974, 204). Government support and funds led to the flourishing of schools and academies. As a result, literacy in the mid-eighteenth century reached a level comparable to Western European societies at the time (Rawski 1979).

The unraveling and legacy of China's first industrious revolution

The industrious revolution started to unravel in the late eighteenth century. A main cause was that the continuous growth of the population placed great pressure on smallholders (Naquin and Rawski 1987, 106–7). Without significant technological breakthroughs, it had become increasingly difficult for them to maintain the standard of living. Population growth also shifted the balance of power in favor of landlords as land had become more scarce and valuable (Marks and Chen 1995; Rowe 2009, 149–200). This may suggest that the industrious revolution had reached its limit at the time. After all, it could not bear the burden of unlimited population growth, though it enabled the economy to support a much larger population than it would otherwise. It should be noted that, although the industrious revolution in China did not lead to technological breakthroughs that were seen in the Industrial Revolution, it does not imply that smallholders would be averse to technological change (Elvin 1973). As I will show in the next chapter, smallholders were highly adaptable to technological change, and the diffusion of modern technologies also stimulated small-scale production in rural areas as limited land resources could generate more surplus.

Aside from population growth and technology, declining state capacity since the late eighteenth century was another important factor. At the national level, the emperor was aging and lost his moral legitimacy after the 1770s, and the bureaucracy lost dynamism and gave in to a culture of corruption and factional fights (Hung 2011, 39–43; Perdue 2005, 547–50; Will and Wong 1991, 76).

The more serious problems lay at the local level. The Qing government relied heavily on local elites for local governance below the county level: these elites, such as gentry members and landlords, collected taxes, coordinated the construction of public projects, and arbitrated local disputes. This made it difficult to enforce the policies that would harm their interests (Naquin and Rawski 1987, 15–6). For example, the Yongzheng emperor stepped up tough measures against gentry members by clearing up tax arrears and abolishing their privileges in the 1720s. This met strong resistance from the latter (Zelin 1984, 220–64). After Qianlong took power in 1735, he quickly abandoned his father's tough policies and made concessions to gentry members. The reversal appeased local elites, but it also strengthened their power at the expense of smallholders. Partly because of this, the concentration of land wealth accelerated after the mid-eighteenth century (Rowe 2001, 45–7).

In addition, the Qing state did not have an effective county administration system. The county was the lowest level of formal administration in the Qing dynasty, and the population of a county could reach one million by the late eighteenth century. However, the county government was severely understaffed: the county magistrate, who was the head of the administration system, was supposed to be responsible for everything in his jurisdiction, including, but not limited to, local defense, policing, public projects, disaster relief, tax collection, education, and civil litigation. However, the number of officially appointed clerks who assisted the magistrate was very small, usually ten to 20 people. With such a small group of personnel, even maintaining routine work was a challenge. Therefore, the county magistrate had to rely on informally hired clerks and runners, whose numbers could be as high as the hundreds, to do most of administration work. These clerks and runners were not paid out of government coffers, but relied on customary fees collected from their clients, most notably from the parties who were involved in legal cases. Therefore, the tendency for corruption was built into the county-level administration (Reed 1995; Rowe 2009, 48–52; Zhang 1998, 615–22).

The decline of state capacity undermined and in some cases reversed previous policies. The situation went from bad to worse in the nineteenth century when

China had to put down domestic rebellions and fight wars with Western powers. The granary system nearly broke down while the concentration of land was on the rise, pushing up grain prices at the expense of poor peasants (Will and Wong 1991; Zelin 1984, 295–7). To fund military campaigns, the Qing state had to increase the rates of agricultural and commercial taxes. In addition, local governments imposed an increasing number of unsanctioned surtaxes, which could be multiple times as much as formal taxes in the nineteenth century (Jones and Kuhn 1978, 121–9; Wang 2001, 432; Wong 1997, 155–6). Local elites, particularly lower-degree-holders, also penetrated and even controlled the formal tax collection process and benefited through illegal tax farming at the expense of common households (Jones and Kuhn 1978, 112; Hung 2011, 31).

The outcome of these changes was the unraveling of the industrious revolution and the increase in social instability. As more and more smallholders such as peasants, tenants, and landless laborers were unable to maintain their livelihoods, they were drawn to domestic rebellions, which the Qing military had to put down. In the meantime, elites, such as large-scale landlords, merchants, and rural gentry, were expanding their power in the military campaigns against domestic rebellions (Jones and Kuhn 1978; Kuhn 1980). The increasing incidence of violence in the late Qing period caused the disruption of transportation and commerce, a crucial condition for a smallholder market. The productivity of agriculture also declined and had not recovered until the early 1950s (Rowe 2007, 30; Shi 2017, 138–9).

Although the first industrious revolution unraveled, it left an indelible legacy for later periods. The high proportion of smallholders carried on in some regions in the nineteenth and early twentieth centuries, despite frequent wars, rebellions, and social turbulences. This might have shielded a great number of peasants from the worst impact. By the time of the communist takeover of national power in 1949, the landlord class, whose population was about 5 percent of the total at the time, owned only 30 to 40 percent of the land (Gao 2005a, 8–12). The majority of the rural population in some regions was landholding small peasants. In Wujin County in Jiangsu, one of my main field sites, 2.8 percent of the population was classified as landlords in 1950, who owned 18.2 percent of the land, and 3.0 percent as rich households, which owned 6.1 percent of the land. That is, the landlords and rich households, who together made up 5.8 percent of the population, owned only 24.3 percent of the land. Moreover, the average size of landholding was only 44.4 *mu* (about three hectares) per household among landlords and 12.2 *mu* (0.8 hectare) among rich households. In other words, they would not be classified as landlords or rich households by any Western standards. It should be noted that the distribution of land ownership was uneven across the country. The land owned by the landlord would be more than 50 percent in some southern provinces such as Jiangxi and Hunan (Tawney 1932, 34–5).

The first industrious revolution also left China with a rural population that demanded equal land rights. This was a main reason why Chinese Communists used land reform as a slogan to mobilize peasants in the revolution and the civil war, which eventually helped them win national power in 1949. Although the distribution of land ownership in China should not be considered particularly unequal as compared with many other countries, land reform was still popular among rural dwellers that demanded the further equalization of land rights. By redistributing the land from landlords to poor peasants, Chinese Communists continued and pushed further the policy of the Qing state on land relations.

Notes

1 China proper refers to the eighteen provinces, which constituted the core of China and was governed differently from the frontier areas in the Qing empire. The discussion of Qing policies in this chapter is confined to China proper.
2 The first was the commercial revolution of the Song dynasty, from roughly the eleventh century to the thirteenth century. This footnote was not in the original text quoted.
3 Two famous agricultural books in the late Ming period – *Shenshi nongshu* (*Shen Family's Agricultural Book*) and *Bu nongshu* (*Supplements to the Agricultural Book*), whose authors were both landlords, discussed in detail how landlords could supervise rural laborers to achieve maximum labor output.
4 One *mu* is equivalent to one-fifteenth of a hectare.
5 The construction of the household is based on Fu (1957, 45), Li (1998), Mann (1997, 32–4, 174–7; 2002, 450), and Zhang (2006).

2 Socialism, market reform, and the long road to the second industrious revolution

From a purely economic point of view, the reason for the communist revolution and its victory in China might not be poor economic performance in general, but rather the disruption of economic life in peripheral hinterland regions, particularly in rural areas. Nothing could illustrate this better than the differences between Wujin and Aohan – two counties in which I conducted fieldwork – in the decades leading up to the communist victory in 1949. Wujin, a county in southern Jiangsu Province, is located in the Yangtze delta, the most developed region in China, whereas Aohan is a part of eastern Inner Mongolia lying to the north of the Great Wall and at the margin of the larger North China. Kenneth Pomeranz (2000) classified the Yangtze delta as the core area of China and North China as the periphery in terms of economic development.

In Wujin, grain production (rice and wheat) reached 298.4 million kilograms in 1949, sufficient to feed the county's 1.03 million people, though without much surplus. One hectare of farmland produced 3,855 kilograms of grain in a year, which increased slightly from the late Qing dynasty (Shi 2017, 81). More significant progress was made on industry. Wujin established its first modern cloth factory as early as 1906. By 1950, there were 47 factories in the county hiring 766 workers and 1,980 small household workshops employing 3,131 persons (Wujin County Gazetteer 1988, 326–31). Most of the factories and workshops were in the textile industry, producing cloth and apparels. Other industries include oil crushing, rice processing, comb making, and so on. These factories had started to use modern technologies and materials such as steam-powered machines, fossil fuels, and electricity. In addition, rural households owned thousands of weaving looms, which were upgraded to produce much better cloth than those in the nineteenth century. The industrial output was estimated to account for as much as 25 percent of total economic output in 1949 (Wujin County Gazetteer 1988, 326–31). In short, both agriculture and industry in the county saw some progress in the first half of the twentieth century, despite several economic ups and downs due to wars and market fluctuations.

The situation in Aohan was starkly different. The county is located in a transitory area from farming to pasturage. Ethnic Mongolians previously populated it, but Han farmers started to move in and transformed the pastures into farms in the eighteenth century. Immigration accelerated in the late nineteenth century, as it was encouraged by the Qing government to counter Russian encroachment from the north. The waves of immigration continued until the 1930s, raising the population to 253,000 in 1939. The influx of Han farmers led to the large-scale reclamation of pastures and the clearing of shrubs and trees, which resulted in more natural disasters such as droughts, floods, and sand storms. Food shortages and famines became increasingly common after the 1920s. The year of 1943 was a normal year, but grain production in the county was only 45.9 million kilograms, 185 kilograms per capita, which was below the famine line (200 kilograms). There was little industry in the county. The local population also suffered a number of epidemics. The biggest threat was bubonic plague, which broke out nearly every year in the 1930s and 1940s and claimed thousands of lives. The area was also a fertile ground for rebellions and local violence since the late Qing dynasty, and fighting became increasingly frequent and intense after the 1920s. In short, prior to the communist takeover the county had degenerated into a chaotic situation, both socially and economically (Aohan Banner Gazetteer 1991, 155–8, 192, 262, 1038–42).

Aohan is an example of many Chinese hinterland regions, where agriculture depends on a delicate balance between the vulnerable ecology, man-made infrastructure (for example, irrigation) and social organizations. The economy would be easily disrupted and degenerate into a vicious cycle if a lack of effective local governance led to the breakdown of agricultural infrastructure in the event of natural disaster, causing hungers, famines, and social instability. Based on his study of a hinterland area in North China in the period between 1853 and 1937, Kenneth Pomeranz (1993) noted:

> The government's major failures appear to have been in its traditional tasks – maintaining public order and providing water control, famine relief, military defense – and to have been concentrated in specific hinterland regions …, these failure may have had limited impact on long-term growth rates. Nonetheless, they had great impact on popular welfare and people's lives. Most likely, they also compromised the government's legitimacy in the eyes of ordinary people far more than its limited success in modern tasks did … it was in (these) regions … that peasants abandoned the regime in droves, many eventually supporting the Communist revolution.
>
> (21–2)

This chapter examines the transformation of land relations from the socialist era (1949–76) to the early reform period (1980s) and the efforts to increase the surplus-generating capacity of land in the two counties. The economic trajectories of the two counties continued on different paths, with Wujin emerging as a major rural industrial county and Aohan regaining (not fully) ecological balance and increasing agricultural productivity. Neither path was a smooth transition as they were full of serious challenges and painful setbacks. The road to the second industrious revolution was long and rocky, even more so if taking into account the nineteenth century and the first half of the twentieth century. Economically,

Wujin was much more successful than Aohan, but the change in the latter was no less significant as peripheral regions such as Aohan were crucial to supporting the livelihoods of a growing population as well as striking a delicate balance between the environment and intensive farming.

Land reform, collectivization, and market reform

The land reform redistributed 47 million hectares, or 46.5 percent of total farmland, from landlords to peasants in China between 1947 and 1952. It also confiscated and redistributed landlords' draft animals, farm implements, houses, and grains, while abolishing the debts of peasants owing to landlords (CCP Archival Research Office 1993a, 336; CASS 1992, 403–4). As a result, the landlord class was eliminated, and former landlords were denigrated and targeted as "class enemies" in subsequent political campaigns. Nevertheless, the reform did not redistribute the land of all rich peasants, and the structure of land ownership after the reform was not completely egalitarian, though much more equal than it was. The moderation of land reform was intended not to harm the incentive of rich peasants who would play a crucial role in recovering the rural economy (Bramall 2009, 94–5; Selden 1988, 3–30; Unger 2002, 29–48).

Wujin implemented land reform in 1951. As noted in Chapter 1, the distribution of land in the county was not highly unequal before the reform. Landlords accounted for 2.9 percent of the total population and 18.2 percent of the land. Poor peasants accounted for 54.3 percent of the population, but they also held 31.1 percent of the land. Nevertheless, the reform further leveled the inequality in land ownership by redistributing 24,000 hectares of land, 22.6 percent of the total, from landlords and rich peasants to poor peasants (Wujin County Gazetteer 1988, 248).

Land reform in Aohan was more radical. On the one hand, it was because the distribution of land was highly unequal, with landlords and rich peasants occupying two-thirds of the land; on the other hand, Aohan was an area where the communists wanted to win and control in the early phase of the civil war (1946–9). Communist troops arrived in the county right after the Japanese surrendered in 1945, but the county was in a tug-of-war between communists and nationalists during the following two years. To win more popular support, the communists launched land reform in some parts of the county in 1946, and carried out a very radical reform at the end of 1947 after the entire county was under control. The land reform was dubbed "big storm" (*dafengbao*), indicating a sweeping destruction of the old structure. Before the reform, the average landholding of landlords and rich peasants was 3.2 hectares per person while that of poor peasants was only 0.1 hectare. The reform redistributed half of the land and 31,000 large animals (about one-quarter of the total) from landlords and rich peasants to poor peasants, in addition to agricultural implements, houses, and grains (Aohan Banner Gazetteer 1991, 207–8, 249–50; Wang 2010).

Nationwide, the land reform transferred land rights to millions of rural households. This enhanced the incentive of rural smallholders, and partly as a result, the rural economy swiftly recovered and surpassed the historical record level in the early 1950s (Selden 1988, 10). However, a smallholder economy was never the communist ideal, and it was only regarded as a transitory phase to large collective farms. In addition, the ultimate goal of the Chinese state was to build a modern economy and catch up with Western developed countries. This entailed developing modern industries, particularly heavy industry. Without much support of foreign investment during the Cold War era (except for the aid from the Soviet Union in the 1950s), the state had to transfer rural surplus to fund urban industries. The smallholder economy presented a problem to the policy of transferring rural surplus because it was very difficult for the state to collect taxes or procure grains from over 100 million rural households (Wen 2000, 157).

To follow the socialist ideal and solve the problem of surplus transfer, the Chinese state organized peasants into agricultural cooperatives. By 1955, the majority of rural households (about 65 percent) had formed proto-cooperatives (*chuji hezuoshe*), in which households still retained most of their rights to land and assets. In 1956, the state urged the countryside to form advanced cooperatives (*gaoji hezuoshe*), and more than 90 percent of rural households joined within two years. Advanced cooperatives were very different from proto-cooperatives, in that rural households in the former must forgo the rights to land and assets, such as draft animals and farm implements. It was a process of collectivization, in which peasants lost their ownership of land and became the members of cooperatives (Bo 1991, 342–65; Schurmann 1968, 453–63; Wen 2000, 191–8). After the collectivization, the task of grain procurement was much simplified: the state had to purchase from over 100 million households previously. But after the collectivization, it only dealt with less than one million cooperatives (Bo 1991, 255–83; Wen 2000, 141–202).

The communists regarded collectivization as a progressive move toward building communism and developing a modern economy, as the large collective farms it created would increase productivity (Schurmann 1968, 453–63; Hinton 1983). The rapid nationwide collectivization, however, produced two negative results: one was the radicalization of class relations and the other communization in the late 1950s. The policy to expand advanced cooperatives met peasant resistance. To achieve this goal, the communists singled out rich peasants, and sometimes even upper-middle peasants, to be the targets of political campaigns, and forced them to accept collectivization. Rapid collectivization in 1956–7 also gave the communists, particularly Mao, unfounded confidence on the pace of advancement to so-called communism. In 1958, the state launched the Great Leap Forward, in which advanced cooperatives were further merged into 23,400 People's Communes. The commune was a much larger unit (usually 30 times larger) than the advanced cooperative. Due to the lack of effective coordination and supervision, the Great Leap Forward's commune system created a chaotic situation in production and distribution (Bo 1991, 727–65; Lin 1990; Wen 2000, 198–207). The outcome was a huge famine in 1959–61 and a sharp contraction of the national economy, including urban industry.

Between 1961 and 1962, the Chinese state downsized the units of the commune system, which was divided into three tiers: commune, brigade, and production team. Production team, each of which comprised only 20 to 30 households, became the basic unit of economic organization. In addition, every rural household was given a very small plot of land (*ziliudi*) to grow grain crops and vegetables (CCP Archival Research Office 1993b, 176–92; Wen 2000, 214–20). The three-tier commune system had remained in place throughout the rest of the socialist period (1960s and 1970s).

Both Wujin and Aohan went through collectivization and policy adjustment, as did the rest of the country. In Wujin, at the height of collectivization, 2,423 households protested and wanted to leave advanced agricultural cooperatives in 1957. The establishment of the People's Communes and the Great Leap Forward negatively impacted grain production in the county, which decreased from 429 million kilograms in 1958 to 325 million kilograms per year in the following three years (Wujin County Gazetteer 1988, 250–5). Mr. Wu Daohuan, born in 1945 and graduated from middle school in 1960, still remembered the hungry years when I interviewed him in October 2010.[1] He was upset at Jiangsu's radical collectivization policy during the Great Leap Forward and suggested that the policies in neighboring provinces, such as Zhejiang and Jiangxi, were much less strict. Due to shortages of food, the mortality rate was high among the elderly, while the birth rate was low, and there were families in his village sending children to relatives in Jiangxi Province. The situation was improved in 1962, and the county had no longer suffered food shortages thereafter. Mr. Wu was employed in a township textile factory and retired at the time of interview. He was very knowledgeable on the local history, particularly the development of rural industry. He was the author of the gazetteer of his village, *Bridge Village*, where I conducted most of my village-level fieldwork.[2]

In Aohan, more than 90 percent of the households joined advanced cooperatives in 1956; the last 10 percent joined in 1957. An advanced cooperative in Aohan consisted of 190 rural households on average and farmed about 680 hectares of land. During the Great Leap Forward, the county government organized these cooperatives into 12 communes in 1959. After the Great Leap Forward, the county reduced the size of communes, whose number increased to 24. In addition, the county government partially restored the economic role of household: it allocated 5 percent of total farmland to rural households (called *ziliudi*, literally "self-retaining land"), about 0.02 hectare per person, and another 0.1 hectare of hilly land per person for households to plant trees. It also allowed rural households to raise their own animals (called *ziliuxu*, "self-retaining animals"). In 1966, the proportion of domestic animals owned by rural households reached as high as 45.2 percent, while it was only 11.4 percent in 1959. Although the Great Leap Forward affected agricultural production in the county, which slightly decreased in 1959 between 1961, natural disasters were a much bigger threat. For instance, the 1962 summer flood reduced grain production in the county to 200 kilograms per capita, near the famine level (Aohan Banner Gazetteer 1991, 250–2). Thus the local memory of the socialist period is very different from that in Wujin. My informants in Aohan had a much deeper memory of hunger caused by natural disasters than the impact of the Great Leap Forward.

The Chinese state launched the market reform in 1978, replacing the commune system with the Household Responsibility System (HRS). Collective farms were divided and contracted to rural households on an equal basis within the village. Under the HRS, peasants held the use rights of the land, but the ownership belonged to the village collective. The new system granted peasants much autonomy in farming and nonfarm activities (Unger 2002, 95–118). The three tiers – commune, brigade, and production team – were changed into township, village, and production team, respectively. The importance of production team declined markedly because it no longer assigned work tasks or distributed benefits to peasants (Stockman 2000, 137–8; Wen 2000, 282–9). The village and township levels continued to be important, particularly in regions where the rural collective economy was strong. The reform also reopened the market, and as a result, peasants and rural enterprises were able to purchase farm inputs and sell produce in the market. Furthermore, peasants could move to cities to look for wage jobs and business opportunities after the control of migration was relaxed in 1984, though the *hukou* system was still in place, regulating population movements (Andreas and Zhan 2016; Cheng and Selden 1994; Zhan 2011). The market reform met no resistance, if not support, from peasants in Wujin and Aohan. The former implemented the reform in 1981 and the latter in 1983, and as I will discuss below, strong evidence showed that the reform accelerated economic growth in the two counties.

From the land reform to the market reform, land relations in the Chinese countryside underwent profound changes. First, land was distributed more equally among peasants, while the inequality in land rights diminished. This laid the foundation for the second industrious revolution to emerge. Second, besides land ownership, the use rights of land were also adjusted. Under the commune system, the state often intervened in production and regulated crop types and nonfarm activities, whereas under the household system, peasants and villages could make decisions in response to the market. Finally, although collectivization restricted the role of the household, it strengthened the capacity of rural communities to take collective action, for example, in infrastructure building and rural industry.

However, land relations were only one dimension of the land question in China, albeit an important one. Another crucial issue was to increase the surplus-generating capacity of land. With the doubling of the population, the very small size of landholding, and a vulnerable environment, this presented a more daunting task to the communists than land reform. The next two sections describe the successes and failures of Wujin and Aohan in rural industry and agriculture respectively.

Rural industry in Wujin: 1949–90

There was not much room for Wujin to make progress on agriculture due to the small size of landholding. The county was already densely populated in 1949, and landholding was only 1.25 *mu* (0.08 hectare) per person. In the socialist period (1949–78), the population grew from 84,500 (excluding the population in the area that was designated as Changzhou city) to 130,500, up 54.4 percent, and as a result, landholding had decreased to 0.05 hectare per person. Nevertheless, the county managed to double grain production from 330 million kilograms in 1949 to 685 million kilograms in 1977/8 (Wujin County Gazetteer 1988, 198, 255–6). In other words, grain production outgrew the population, and the county was able to feed itself, even with some surplus. The growth in grain production should be attributed to irrigation improvement, the application of new cultivation methods, and new inputs such as better seeds and chemical fertilizers.

The economic potential of the county lies in industrial production. As noted in Chapter 1, peasants in the Yangtze delta relied on the handicraft industry for a major source of income at least from the eighteenth century onward. The rural handicraft industry, particularly cotton spinning and weaving, declined in the first half of the twentieth century under the impact of modern factories and textile imports. However, there were still as many as 20,000 looms in rural areas of Wujin in the 1940s, about one loom for every ten households (Wujin County Gazetteer 344–5). Bridge Village is located in a township where the textile industry was most developed. The rate was one loom for every three households in the village in the 1940s. A small number of households engaged in other handicraft activities in the county, such as tailoring, haircutting, carpentry, house building, and iron forging, which were collectively called the "Small Five Handicrafts" (*xiao wu jiang*).

In 1952, Wujin organized rural households with looms into cotton-weaving cooperatives. My informants called this policy *daiji rushe* ("join the cooperative with your loom"), usually one loom in exchange for one or two memberships. These cooperatives were merged into four textile factories in 1958, and peasant weavers thus became factory workers. The number of factories in Wujin increased rapidly from 33 (another 24 factories were located in the area designated as Changzhou city) in 1950 to 109 in 1957. The growth was mainly due to the county government either organizing individual peasant artisans into industrial cooperatives or creating new factories. In 1958, following the call of the Great Leap Forward, the communes in the county established 730 new industrial enterprises (Wujin Country Gazetteer, 317–30). These enterprises were not limited to traditional handicraft industries, but also ventured into many modern industries such as chemical industry, machinery, electronics, metallurgy, and electric motors. The reason why the county was able to establish these factories had much to do with its location. The county is located near Shanghai and Nanjing, two of the largest industrial centers in China at the time, and many people in the county had either worked in these cities or had relatives, friends, or fellow villagers working there. Thus they had access to relevant information and technologies.

However, due to the failure of the Great Leap Forward and the ensuing famine, most of the enterprises were closed. The central government also prohibited brigades and communes from running rural enterprises, for it would take peasants' efforts away from grain production. By 1963, there were only 35 commune enterprises left in the county, and the total number of enterprises was down to 144. About 6,000 workers were dismissed and went back to agriculture. However, rural industry was not a product of the Great Leap Forward, but rather a major source of livelihood and economic growth in the county. As soon as the hungry years were gone, the communes started to reestablish the enterprises. For example, the commune where Bridge Village was located established three rural industrial cooperatives in 1962, making cloth, combs, and brushes, and employing about 2,500 peasants. In 1966, Mao openly supported rural industry, which further motivated communes and brigades to establish enterprises. By 1969, the number of enterprises in Wujin increased to 325, while the total industrial output exceeded the highest level during the Great Leap Forward (Wujin County Gazetteer 1988, 317–30).

The impacts of the failure of the Great Leap Forward on rural industry were not all negative. Due to the contraction of urban industry, a large number of urban workers, cadres, and technicians were sent down (*xiafang*) to the countryside, and a similar policy was implemented during the Cultural Revolution (1966–76). Their arrival injected valuable skills and technical know-how into the countryside, and helped communes and brigades set up rural enterprises with urban technologies (Whiting 2000, 50–1; Xu 1996, 49; Zhang and Zhang 2001, 43–4). Bridge Village was a good example. Mr. Zhou Xing, who was working in a machine-making factory in Shanghai, was sent to the village in 1962. With the help of Mr. Zhou, the brigade was able to set up a plate factory in 1966 manufacturing badges and metal plates used on machines. The factory was the first rural plate factory in Wujin. It was highly successful due to the great demand for badges in the first two years of the Cultural Revolution and demand for machine plates after that. It was the most profitable enterprise in the village between 1966 and 1978. The village also relied on a *xiafang* couple to set up a factory for making paper boxes in 1962.

The rural industry grew rapidly in the 1970s as communes and brigades established more enterprises and ventured into new industries. The number of enterprises in Wujin increased from 325 in 1969 to 1,852 in 1979, of which communes and brigades established 1,646. In the meantime, the gross industrial output grew from 123.5 million yuan to 692.4 million yuan (at 1980 prices), up 4.6 times. Nationwide, the annual growth rate of rural industry averaged more than 20 percent (Table 2.1). By 1978, rural enterprises employed 35 million rural workers and produced 51.4 billion yuan of industrial output.

The market reform gave rural industry a further push. The reform played a positive role in many respects. Most importantly, it opened the market as an

Table 2.1 Annual growth rates of rural industry in China in the 1970s, percent

Year	*1970*	*1971*	*1972*	*1973*	*1974*	*1975*	*1976*	*1977*	*1978*	*1979*
Growth rate (%)	20.7	36.1	19.6	16.4	20.3	39.6	26.5	43.9	25.6	2.5

Sources: Wong (1988, 3–4) and Zhang and Zhang (2001, 45).

important avenue for rural enterprises, which was renamed Township and Village Enterprises (TVEs), to allocate resources. In the socialist era when the market was restricted, rural enterprises depended heavily on urban enterprises for subcontracts, sales, raw materials, and technologies (Oi 1989, 13–42). The opening of the market lessened this dependence since it allowed rural enterprises to obtain raw materials and sell products through market channels. In the 1980s, rural enterprises dispatched hundreds of thousands of rural workers to seek resources from the market. These workers, called *gongxiaoyuan* (literally, "supply and sales persons"), traveled nationwide to find raw materials and markets for their enterprises. Mr. Wei Lin in Bridge Village, who was the head of the village committee when I interviewed him in 2010, told me that, as a *gongxiaoyuan*, he traveled to more than 20 provinces in the early 1980s to find raw materials for the enterprises of his village.[3]

The market reform also released economic potential of rural households. In addition to farming, households took up sideline activities such as digging fish-ponds, raising animals, driving trucks, and opening small shops. In Wujin, rural households also started to establish small factories. In Bridge Village, about 20 households were running small textile factories in 1990. These factories usually operated fewer than ten looms and employed family members, but they generated more income than factory jobs. Running a household enterprise required primary investment, business skills, and market networks. In the 1980s, most of these household enterprises in Wujin depended on collective TVEs: they used skills learned from collective enterprises, produced for them, and made sales through their market networks. In Wujin, about 140,000 rural laborers were engaged in nonagricultural household enterprises in the county in 1989, accounting for one-fifth of the rural labor force (Wujin Yearbook Committee 1990, 233).

The rapid growth of rural industry in the 1980s was regarded as a miracle of the Chinese rural economy, and it also marked the emergence of the second industrious revolution. In Wujin, industrial output grew from 831 million yuan in 1978 to 9.6 billion yuan in 1990 (at 1990 prices), up 10.6 times. Rural industry and other nonfarm sectors employed 57.2 percent of the rural labor force (Wujin Yearbook Committee 1992, 310–7). The data might have excluded many household enterprises, as my fieldwork found that a higher proportion of the rural laborers employed in nonfarm sectors and that the rural enterprises started to confront the shortage of supply of workers in the county at the end of the 1980s. Nationwide, rural enterprises employed 92.6 million rural laborers in 1990, and produced 978 billion yuan of gross output, accounting for 58.9 percent of total rural output (Ministry of Agriculture 2003, 9; National Bureau of Statistics 1991, 45).

The development of rural industry was uneven. Coastal regions and areas near large cities were growing faster than others. Three large municipalities (Shanghai, Tianjin, and Beijing) and seven coastal provinces (Zhejiang, Jiangsu, Guangdong, Fujian, Hebei, Shandong, and Liaoning) had per capita output (calculated by dividing gross output of rural enterprises by the rural population in a province) in excess of 1,000 yuan in 1990 (Figure 2.1). Taken together, they

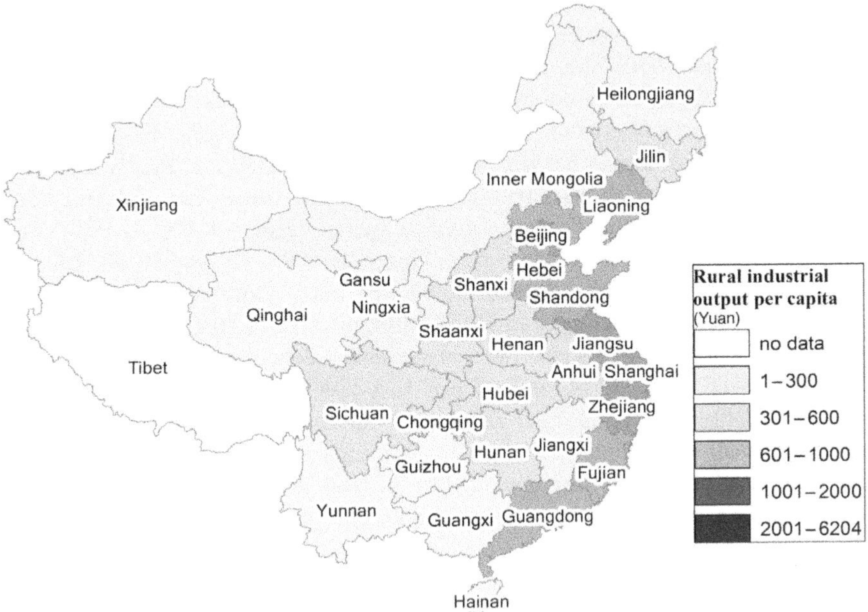

Figure 2.1 Rural industrial output per capita in China in 1990.

Data source: Ministry of Agriculture (2003, 172).

accounted for 49.1 percent of rural nonfarm output. The strong performance of these regions demonstrates the importance of the flows of resources from urban to rural areas, particularly urban technologies and market information. It should also be noted that a number of inland provinces were moving forward. Four populous central provinces (Henan, Hubei, Hunan, and Anhui), three western provinces (Sichuan, Shanxi, and Shaanxi), and Jilin in the northeast had a per capita output between 600 yuan and 1,000 yuan. The development of rural industry was slow in the rest of regions, including Inner Mongolia, where Aohan is located.

Agriculture and environment in Aohan

The biggest challenge for Aohan was to increase agricultural production while restoring the ecological balance. This task became more difficult when the county's population doubled from 250,000 to 500,000 in the socialist period. Population growth, as was in the rest of the country, was due to high birth rates and low mortality rates, resulting from social stability and improved health care. My fieldwork in the county found that it was common that peasants in their forties and fifties had four to six siblings.

The rapid population growth placed enormous pressure on the environment, which had already deteriorated to a bad situation in the 1940s. The land that was suitable for farming in the county had been over-reclaimed, thus the reclamation campaigns in the 1950s only extended the farmland from 190,000 hectares to a little more than 200,000. In the 1960s and 1970s, environmental problems, such as desertification and soil erosion, caused arable land to shrink, and the acreage fell below 140,000 hectares in the late 1970s. In addition, the rapid increase in livestock population also added stress on pasturelands. There were 136,000 large domestic animals in 1949, and the number increased to 560,000 in 1981, four times the original amount (Aohan Banner Gazetteer 1991, 155–8, 219–21, 262–5).

Population growth and farmland contraction made food supply a huge challenge in the county. As compared with Wujin, the size of landholding in Aohan was much larger, 0.76 hectare per person and 4.2 hectares per household in 1949. However, the yield of the land was very low because most of land was of poor soil quality and did not have access to irrigation. By introducing new seeds, using chemical fertilizers, adopting new farming methods, and building irrigation infrastructure, the county managed to increase grain production from about 300 kilograms per hectare to 1,279.5 kilograms in the socialist period. As a result, gross grain production increased from 43,500 tons to 125,300 tons, up 1.9 times (Aohan Banner Gazetteer 1991, 265). However, the increase had not freed the local population from the threat of hunger. Natural disasters, particularly droughts, were frequent due to ecological deterioration and periodically pushed grain production down to the hunger level. Figure 2.2 shows that between 1949 and 1984, there were ten years when per capita grain production dropped to below 250 kilograms, a situation in which food shortages and hunger would

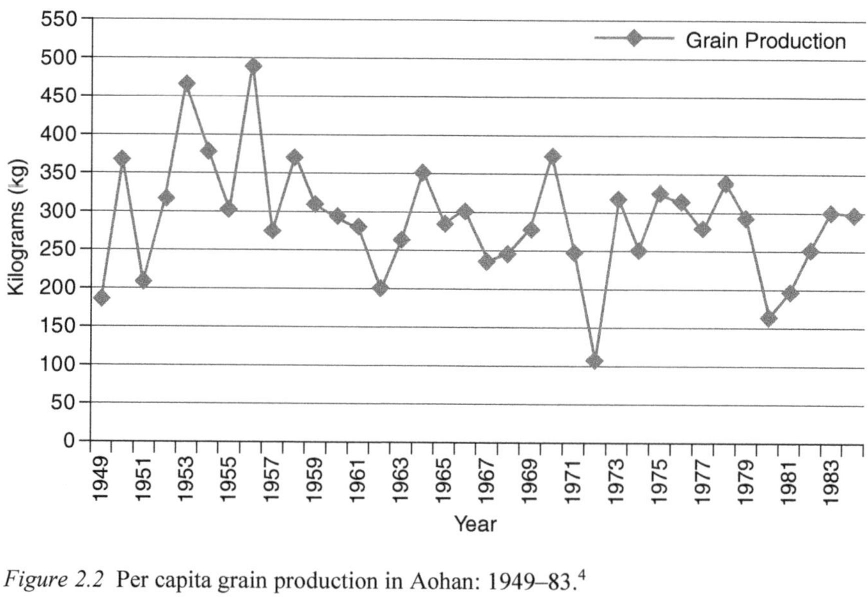

Figure 2.2 Per capita grain production in Aohan: 1949–83.[4]

ensue. In the years of 1949, 1962, 1972, 1980, and 1981, per capita grain production was near and even below 200 kilograms, which would lead to serious hunger and even famine.

My interviews with peasants in Grass Village, one of five villages in the county that I conducted village-level investigation, found that they still remembered food shortages in the socialist period. According to Mr. Bai Qing, who was a production team leader in the 1970s and the village's party secretary from 1988 to 1994, the village often failed to produce enough grain for itself in the 1960s and early 1970s, and had to purchase grain from the government. The problem was partly caused by the summer flood in 1962, which sand-washed the fertile farmland along the river. The flood affected 44,400 hectares of farmland in the county, 22.5 percent of the total, lowering grain production to near 200 kilograms per capita (Aohan Banner Gazetteer 1991, 102).

Droughts were even bigger a threat than floods because most of the farmland in the county was rain-fed, and annual precipitation in the county is below 450 mm. Figure 2.5 shows that the droughts in 1972 and 1980/1981 had greatly reduced grain production and created the near-hunger situation. In 1972, a serious drought reduced grain production per capita to the lowest since 1949, causing food shortages for 270,000 people, or 60 percent of the total. The situation became so bad that more than 10,000 people had to leave the county to seek food (Aohan Banner Gazetteer 1991, 99). Peasants in Grass Village still remembered the difficult years of 1972 and 1973, when they had to endure hunger and relied on disaster relief for food supply.

The productivity of land started to increase markedly in the late 1970s, and this continued after the market reform. The main factors behind the increase were the use of chemical fertilizers and the introduction of high-yield seeds, but the reform also played a significant role. According to my interviews with peasants, the market reform, carried out in the county in 1983, marked a line between the periods of food shortage and food sufficiency. In 1985, per capita grain production reached 423 kilograms, much higher than the lowest standard of food sufficiency: 250 kilograms (Aohan Banner Gazetteer 1991, 263). After 1985, peasants were no longer worried about food shortages. The structure of food consumption was also altered. In the 1970s, peasants fed on sorghum, corn, and sometimes millet. Only on holidays did they cook wheat flour and rice, which were their favorite staple foods (but not produced locally). The prices of wheat and rice were usually higher than locally produced grains. In the late 1980s, however, peasants in the county could afford to eat wheat flour and rice for one-third of each year, a sign of food sufficiency since they had to sell more local grains in exchange for a smaller amount of flour and rice.

The reform also led to the diversification of economic activities, with rural households diverting their resources from grain production to more profitable undertakings, such as cash crop growing, animal husbandry, and nonagricultural activities. The acreage of cash crops in the county increased from 15,100 hectares in 1983 to 33,100 in 1985, more than doubled, while the land used for grain crops contracted from 110,000 to 97,700 (Aohan Banner Gazetteer 1991, 265).

Another important change was ecological improvement in the county. The battle to restore the environment was not an easy one, and it has not been completely won even today. The local government was aware of ecological deterioration and started to reforest and restore desertified pastures as early as 1949. It took three major measures. First, it closed off tens of thousands of hectares of degraded pastures. Second, it started to sow grass seeds in these pastures. By the mid-1960s, the acreage of the seed-sowing area amounted to 2,800 hectares. After that, however, the policy discontinued and the previously sown areas were reclaimed for farming. Last, the local government mobilized peasants to plant trees in barren mountains and around farmlands. During the Great Leap Forward and thereafter, the government organized a number of campaigns to plant trees. The areas where trees were planted in this period totaled 236,500 hectares. If all the trees had survived, the rate of forestation would reach more than 30 percent in the county. However, the survival rate of these trees was extremely low. By the end of the socialist period, the areas covered with trees only accounted for 11.2 percent of the total (Aohan Banner Gazetteer 1991, 210–4, 297–310; Aohan Bureau of Forestry 1985).

Population pressure and natural disasters were two major factors constraining the efforts to restore pastures and forests. The pressure to feed more people drove peasants to farm unsuitable lands, raise more animals, and extract resources as much as possible from an already-fragile ecological system. Mr. Liu Chang, the party secretary of Grass Village in the 1970s, told me that the government forbade peasants to graze animals and collect firewood in the areas closed for restoration and reforestation, but peasants surreptitiously grazed sheep in the hills after the dark, slashed bushes in the winter for firewood, and dug out grass roots if they were edible or could be exchanged for money.[5] In addition, the natural disasters such as sandstorms, droughts, and floods often neutralized restoration and reforestation efforts.

In 1978, Aohan became a part of the national project of reforestation and thus received more funding from the central government than before. After households replaced the production teams as the basic unit of organization in 1983, the local government could no longer rely on the collective system to mobilize peasants. Thus it followed the principles of the reform and assigned the tree-planting task to each household. It even went as far as to declare that households held the private ownership of the trees that they planted. It also offered seedlings, fertilizers, and training classes to rural households, and asked local officials at all levels to supervise and coordinate the work of tree planting. The lands that were not suitable for trees were sown with grass seeds. The new strategy, which was based on a combination of governmental efforts and households' incentives, proved to be very successful. By 1994, the rate of forestation in the county reached 35.3 percent (Aohan Bureau of Forestry 1995). The county thus received a number of awards from the central government and even an environment award from the United Nations in 2002.

The progress in reforestation improved the conditions of agricultural production and the quality of life. Both the quantity and severity of sand storms in the area had subsided. In the 1970s, sandstorms in the worst cases would blanket the newly planted crops in early summer, forcing peasants to replant the crops, sometimes several times in a year. The trees also slowed down the speed of strong wind and thus provided protection for crops, animals, and humans. The progress in reforestation also stopped desertification, reduced the severity of floods, prevented soil erosion, increased air humidity, improved water conservancy, and brought more precipitation to the county (Wang and Liu 2003).

Peasants in Aohan were still poor in the 1980s compared with their counterparts in Wujin. As a matter of fact, the county was designated by the central government as one of the 331 poorest counties in 1986, suggesting its low level of economic development. However, under the condition of rapid population growth, the fact that the county was able to restore the ecological balance, raise agricultural output, and achieve food self-sufficiency should be considered a significant achievement. It not only provided livelihoods for a growing population but also contributed to national economic development. As I will show in Chapter 4, Aohan and other inland regions have become key sites of grain production to meet the growing demand for food in China in the past two decades (also see Zhan and Huang 2017).

Socialism and the industrious revolution

Scholars who are interested in the question of whether China fits into East Asian development often skip its socialist period or regard it as a deviation. Their story of a rising China started after China implemented the market reform and opened up to the global capitalist economy in the 1980s (e.g., Baek 2005). Those who connected China's recent economic success to the prosperous age in the eighteenth century also glossed over the socialist period and even argued that socialism delayed the resurgence of China (Brandt, Ma, and Rawski 2014). However, my research of Wujin and Aohan, as well as of other areas in rural China, showed that the socialist period played a crucial role in the emergence of the second industrious revolution. On the one hand, the Chinese state had played a strong developmental role in agriculture and industry, which was similar to other East Asian states. On the other hand, the socialist practices, including collectivization, greatly enhanced the capacity of rural communities in taking collective actions, which had facilitated the growth of rural collective enterprises and the improvement of agricultural infrastructure.

Socialist developmental state

The existence of a developmental state was regarded as a key characteristic of East Asian development. The states in Japan, South Korea, Taiwan, and Singapore had all played an enabling role in industrial transformation by inducing and helping enterprises invest in new sectors and upgrade technologies and products (Chang 1993; Evans 1995; Johnson 1982; Wade 1990). The Chinese state in the socialist period had made similar efforts to create new industrial enterprises in rural areas and disseminate agricultural technologies (Bramall 2009; Schmalzer 2016).

During the Great Leap Forward, Wujin established hundreds of rural enterprises. Nationwide, the number of commune enterprises surged to 700,000 in 1959, producing 6.7 percent of national industrial output (Zhang and Zhang 2001, 34). The initial push for rural industry faltered, but the efforts, particularly at county and commune levels, had persisted in the 1960s. By the end of the decade, most provinces had regained the peak level of rural industry during the Great Leap Forward, including Jiangsu where Wujin is located (Bramall 2007, 22). The rural industries that the Chinese state aimed to develop were much more than a traditional handicraft industry but including many modern industries that did not exist in the countryside previously. There were two types of rural industries: those built on traditional handicraft industries and new modern rural industries.[6] In the case of traditional industries, local governments or communes had also upgraded technologies and installed modern production lines. The New Light Textile Factory in Wujin is a good example.

In 1965, the commune where Bridge Village was located coordinated seven brigades to establish weaving cooperatives, one cooperative in each brigade. These cooperatives started with 275 looms and 605 workers (members). Peasants joined the cooperatives with their loom, and those who did not own a loom contributed 50 yuan. The loom in use was the "foot-operated steel-wooden loom" (*jiaota tiemu buji*), which was already an improvement from the previous hand-operated wooden loom. In 1966–7, the cooperatives built a partnership with a state-owned enterprise in Shanghai and several enterprises in Zhejiang Province. In 1967, the cooperatives started to take orders from a foreign trade enterprise and produce cloth for export. The scale of production had expanded rapidly to 24 cooperatives and 650 looms, of which 213 were electronic looms. The commune combined all cooperatives into a factory in 1972 and started to use the 1511M weaving loom, one of the most advanced looms at the time. In 1975, the factory received investment and support from the county's industrial bureau, and changed its name to "New Light Factory." By the end of the 1970s, the New Light Factory owned 648 advanced looms, including 260 advanced manual looms (1511M) and 388 automatic looms (1515M-56 and1511M-52), and the number of workers had increased to 1,500. The establishment of the factory came from grassroots initiatives (peasant weavers and brigades), but the commune and later the county government played a crucial role in its expansion. They helped the factory secure loans from the bank, recruit the most talented technicians among peasants, and upgrade its technology and equipment. Several former workers of the factory I interviewed in 2010 spoke proudly of the advanced weaving technologies and machines they adopted in the 1970s and '80s. The New Light Factory was just one example of many. There were at least a dozen of textile factories in the county.

The county government and communes had also taken initiatives to establish rural enterprises in modern industries that were previously absent in the county.

They established the first agricultural machinery factory, the first electric motor factory, and the first plastic factory in 1958, the first diesel engine factory in 1959, the first light bulb factory in 1960, the first telecommunications parts factory in 1963, the first large chemical fertilizer plant in 1964, the first musical instrument factory in 1966, the first tractor factory in 1968, the first textile machinery factory in 1970, the first chemical fiber factory in 1971, the first steel gear factory in 1975, the first aluminum factory in 1976, the first hydraulic hoist factory in 1977, the first synthetic fiber in 1979, and the list goes on (Wujin County Gazetteer 1988; Wujin County Industrial Gazetteer 1990). As the Chinese state was eager to pursue modernization and catch up with industrialized countries, the incentive of top-down initiatives was understandable. They were also in harmony with grassroots interests, as rural areas such as Wujin relied on nonagricultural activities to provide livelihoods for a growing population.

The socialist developmental state also took effort to introduce and popularize new agricultural technologies, which were particularly beneficial to peripheral regions like Aohan. Prior to 1949, millet and sorghum were major grain crops in Aohan. However, the yields were very low: one hectare of land yielded 348 kilograms of millet or sorghum on average in 1949. In the 1960s, the local government introduced high-yield varieties of these two crops, and as a result, the average yield of millet increased to about 1,000 kilograms per hectare while that of sorghum to more than 2,000 kilograms. The local government also experimented with new crops. Maize was a good example. The soil and climate in the county were unsuitable for conventional maize seeds, thus maize was rarely grown in the county before 1949. The change came in the 1960s when the government introduced new hybrid varieties, after which the planting area for maize expanded from 6,000 hectares to 23,000 in the late 1970s, almost quadrupled. The yield of maize reached up to more than 3,000 kilograms per hectare in the late 1970s, higher than both millet and sorghum (Aohan Banner Gazetteer 1991, 263–5). In addition to high-yield seeds, the county had also introduced new farming methods and materials (e.g., seed disinfection, and the use of chemical fertilizers and agricultural machines), and experimented with new breeds of sheep and other animals suitable for the local environment. These measures had all increased grain production and animal population.

A crucial difference between socialist China and other East Asian countries was the absence of the market in the former. Without the market, the Chinese state had to rely on collective organizations such as communes, brigades and production teams and bureaucrats to mobilize resources to sectors that it intended to develop. This is the issue to which we will now turn.

Cadres and collective organizations

The establishment of rural collective organizations, first rural cooperatives, and then the three-tier commune system allowed the Chinese state to extend its influence to the village level. In the eighteenth century, as noted in Chapter 1, formal state organizations did not go below the county level. This intensive bureaucratization down to the village level, which Theda Skocpol (1979, 263–5) regarded as a crucial consequence of the social revolution in China, greatly strengthened the capacity of the Chinese state in mobilizing human and material resources in rural areas. The collective organizations also enhanced the ability of rural communities to take coordinated action. In Wujin, for example, communes and brigades were able to pool community resources and establish collective enterprises. In addition, collective organizations could reduce the risk of enterprise failure and thus take initiatives to venture into new industries and sectors, as compared with individual households. Another area that collective organizations had played a great role was infrastructure building, most importantly when it came to irrigation. Aohan was a good example in this respect.

There were only a few ditches irrigating several hundred hectares of land in Aohan before 1949. Between 1949 and 1978, the county constructed six medium-sized reservoirs and 15 small reservoirs. Connected with canals and ditches, these reservoirs and the rivers formed into ten large irrigation zones. In addition, the county built two large and 22 small pumping stations irrigating hilly lands with river water. It also started to dig wells and equip them with motors and pipelines in the 1960s and 1970s. By 1980, there were 2,119 equipped wells in the county, irrigating 8,500 hectares of farmland. Irrigation efforts expanded the irrigated area in the county from a few hundred hectares to 24,000 hectares, 16.4 percent of the total farmland (Aohan Banner Gazetteer 1991, 7–8; Aohan Banner Irrigation Gazetteer 1988, chapter 9).

The county government invested in irrigation projects, but the main factor behind irrigation expansion was labor contributions from peasants, who devoted 59 million labor days to irrigation projects between 1951 and 1978, 2.1 million labor days per year on average. Rural cadres of collective organizations were the main organizers of the labor-intensive irrigation projects. The ups and downs in labor contribution in the county suggested the importance of their role. There were three spikes in labor contribution to irrigation in the county: the Great Leap Forward, the 1965–7 period, and the late years of the Cultural Revolution (Figure 2.3). During the Great Leap Forward, rural cadres were all-out to mobilize peasants to construct irrigation and other public projects, but the ensuing famine and policy adjustment led them to reduce the effort. At the beginning of the Cultural Revolution, Mao called on rural cadres again to build irrigation projects so as to increase grain production, leading to the second spike. Between 1967 and 1972, the initial years of the Cultural Revolution, however, many rural cadres in the county were criticized, removed, and sent into labor camps. The labor contribution of peasants to irrigation thus dropped. Most of these cadres resumed their positions after 1972, leading to another spike in peasants' participation in irrigation projects.

The experiences of Aohan reflected the national trend of irrigation expansion. China was able to organize more than ten million peasants every year in the early 1950s to construct water works, and this increased to 100 million during the Great Leap Forward. In the 1960s, 30 to 50 million people were mobilized every year, and this again increased to 100 million in the 1970s. According to

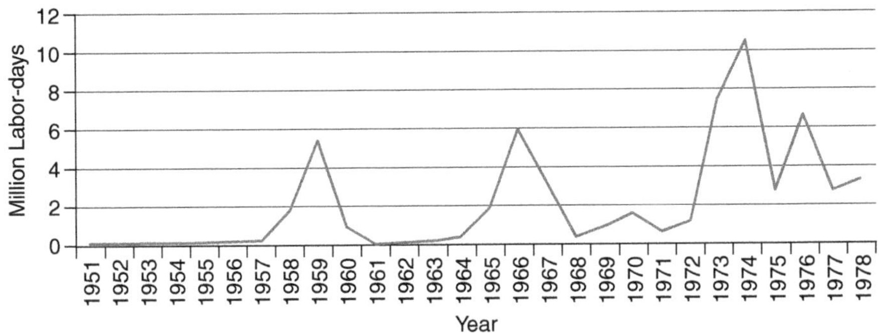

Figure 2.3 Peasants' labor contribution to irrigation projects in Aohan: 1951–78.

Data source: Aohan Banner Irrigation Gazetteer (1988, 6–7 and Chapter 9).

James Nickum's estimates, each rural laborer contributed 30 days a year on average, thus the total number of labor days that peasants contributed was massive (Nickum 1978). The result was the rapid expansion of irrigation infrastructure. Between 1949 and 1978, the country had completed more than 50,000 large-scale water projects, including 311 large reservoirs and 20 million small-scale irrigation works, and established 5,600 large irrigated zones. Irrigated area had tripled from 16 million hectares in 1949 to 48.1 million in 1978 (Ministry of Finance 2007; Ministry of Water Resources 1990, 633, 1999, 19).

Market, community, and the importance of land

The market reform has been regarded as a radical change to the course of Chinese economic development. For liberal economists, the reform corrected distortions of a planned economy and brought the economy back to the right track (e.g., Zhu 2012). For scholars who cherished socialism and collectivism, the market reform was a reversal of progress (Hinton 1990). The experiences of Wujin and Aohan showed, however, that there was much continuity before and after the reform. In Wujin, the rural industry, including collective enterprises, had carried on the trend of expansion after the reform. In Aohan, the growth of agricultural production had already started to accelerate in the 1970s and it continued in the 1980s. Furthermore, the progress in infrastructure, technology and rural industry in the socialist period laid the foundation for the market economy in the reform period.

Seen from the perspective of an industrious revolution, the market reform did bring several important changes. First, the market offers another avenue for peasants and rural enterprises to allocate resources and specialize in market-oriented economic activities. As noted in Chapter 1, the development of a Smithian market allowed the Chinese economy to absorb a large and growing population in the eighteenth century. Second, the reform eased restrictions on the role of the rural household as an economic organization, one that possesses great potential in intensive farming, running small enterprises, and extending economic scope (rather than scale) by combining farm and nonfarm activities. A third change, which has so far received little attention in scholarship, and probably more important than the first two, was that the market reform created a market structure that was favorable to smallholders. This is reflected in at least two respects. One is that the reform had initially restricted large enterprises, thus creating the space for small, community-based rural enterprises to expand, particularly in the case of rural industry. This might be a key difference between China and other former socialist economies in transition to a market economy. The other is that the relatively equal distribution of land rights restricted large farms to emerge, thus small-scale household farms faced little competition from large farms in the market of agricultural produce. Both respects attest to the importance of land relations in influencing market conditions.

Community-based market dynamics

Previous writings suggested that the rural market was immature in the 1980s. For example, Byrd and Zhu (1990) pointed out that the mobility of capital was low, that is, enterprises rarely moved to invest in another locality. Naughton (1994) argued that the land market in the countryside was virtually absent. My research found, however, that low capital mobility and the absence of a land market were the evidence that large capital was restricted.

The state-owned enterprises (SOE) might be the most powerful economic players in the 1980s. However, it was difficult for SOEs to move to the countryside to take advantage of cheap rural resources due to the regulations of land and labor inherited from the socialist period. If a SOE took land and resources from peasants, it must hire those peasants as urban workers who were entitled to a range of welfare benefits, including housing, medical care, children's education, and pension. Rural enterprises, however, were not subject to these regulations. On the one hand, rural enterprises were usually rooted in rural communities, thus they had relatively easy access to land. For example, if township governments and villages took land from peasants to build collective factories, they would also have to hire the occupants on the land. However, the wages for these peasant workers were much lower than urban wages, partly because they stayed in their own houses and many of them still cultivated some land. In other words, the production costs of SOEs were much higher than those of rural enterprises. As a result, rural enterprises held advantages over urban enterprises in market competition even though the latter may be more financially powerful.

In the 1980s, it was rural enterprises that sought to take advantage of urban enterprises rather than the other way around. For example, urban wages had been rising in the 1980s, but at a slow pace due to the delay of urban market reforms. Rural enterprises thus invited urban technicians to help establish factories or solve technological problems, and paid them with a handsome amount of consultation fees. This was particularly common in the Yangtze delta where it took only a few hours to travel from large cities such as Shanghai and Nanjing to the countryside. Many urban technicians came to work for rural enterprises on Sundays, when they did not work in the city. They were called "Sunday engineers" (*xingqitian gongchengshi*) in Wujin. In many cases, the consultation fees for four days could be as much as one month's urban salary, thus many came to the countryside despite urban enterprises trying repeatedly to prevent the practice. Bridge Village built a small hotel in the village specifically for these Sunday engineers.

Rural markets of industrial goods were by no means immature if measured by the degree of market competition. Almost all my respondents in Wujin pointed out that the competition in the 1980s was highly intense. This was also found in other studies (Byrd and Lin 1990). The intensity of competition was partly derived from the local-based character of rural industry. Rural enterprises, though most of them collectively owned in the 1980s, were clear in terms of the geographical boundary: township enterprises were attached to a particular township; and village enterprises belonged to a particular village. As a result, rural enterprises in one village or township often faced competition from those in other villages and townships. Unlike large and mobile capitalist corporations that could move geographically to take over or merge with their competitors, rural enterprises had no way to fend off market competition. Thus they had to lower prices, improve product quality, or shift to less-competitive new products. I coined the term "community-based market dynamics" to capture this phenomenon:

> The community-based market dynamics is a unique combination of two different principles: the community principle that gives enterprises exclusive access to community resources but requires their activities to involve and benefit community members, and the market principle that forces these enterprises to compete on the open market. The first principle lowers production costs for village enterprises and increases community welfare, while the second principle compels these enterprises to improve performance for maintaining market competitiveness.
>
> (Zhan 2015a, 108)

The community principle is based on access to land, which allowed rural communities and households to establish enterprises at very low costs. In Bridge Village, all collective enterprises were built on land within the village while rural households built small factories in their own houses. Township enterprises obtained land through the township government (communes in the socialist period), which usually took land from villages within its jurisdiction, but the enterprises must offer employment to peasants in return when it took village land. In other words, it must acknowledge land rights of the village and peasants. In addition to land, community-based rural enterprises could also have access to low-cost labor and social resources, which would make rural enterprises very competitive in the market. As I will show in the next chapter, land expropriations in the late 1990s and 2000s had taken large tracts of land away from rural communities, and this undermined the foundation of the community-based market dynamics, leading to the closing of large numbers of rural enterprises.

Land rights and small-scale farming

The rural reform broke up collective farms and created millions of small household farms. Despite the growth of grain production and agricultural output in the 1980s, many observers worried that the small size would render household farms vulnerable in the market. This concern deserves serious attention. According to the first rural census in 1996, 193 million households were farming land, with 30.3 percent farming less than 0.2 hectare, 50.1 percent between 0.2 and 0.6 hectare, and 9.8 percent between 0.6 and 1.0 hectare (Figure 2.4). In other words, 93.2 percent of farming households cultivated less than one hectare of land. Many households that farmed more than one hectare might be located in areas such as Aohan, where the productivity of land is low due to poor soil quality and low levels of precipitation. In other words, almost all farms were very small in size, and large farms were virtually absent in the Chinese countryside in the 1980s and early 1990s.

The first constraint of small size of landholding is that farming would not be able to provide rural families with a sufficient livelihood, although it could produce sufficient food. In Wujin, farming could not generate an adequate income or provide enough employment opportunities for rural laborers. Thus peasants in Wujin had to engage in rural industry and other nonfarm activities.

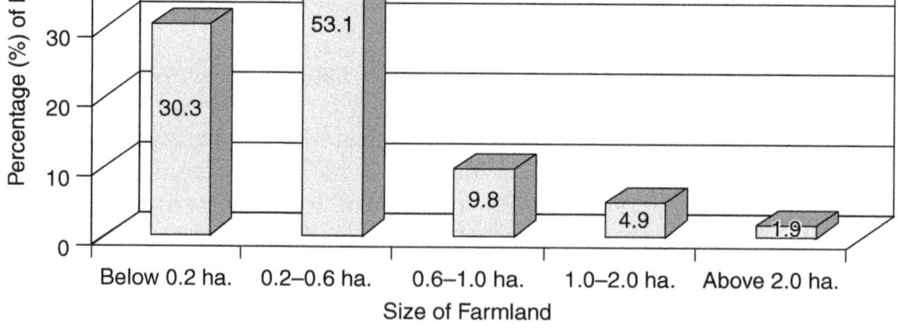

Figure 2.4 Size of household farms in China in 1996.

Data source: Ministry of Agriculture (1998, 3–5).

Across China, 34.4 percent of farming households engaged in nonfarm activities in 1996 (Ministry of Agriculture 1998, 3). This excluded the households whose members took up temporary nonfarm employment; otherwise, the proportion would be even higher. Therefore, it should be acknowledged that the rural reform, by encouraging peasants to engage in sideline and nonfarm activities and allowing them to migrate to cities in search of jobs, had effectively lessened this constraint and made a positive impact on rural livelihoods.

The second constraint is that farming households are at a disadvantage in the markets of agricultural inputs such as fertilizers, seeds, pesticides, and farm implements. The supply of these inputs is controlled by agricultural enterprises. In the 1980s, agricultural enterprises in China were mostly state-owned, and the prices of these inputs were subject to state regulations. With the further marketization of agricultural inputs in the 1990s and 2000s, however, the state reduced its control of prices, which often fluctuated in the interest of the enterprises, particularly large enterprises, rather than rural households, as I will show in Chapter 4. It should be noted that the state could still intervene and protect farm households in the markets of agricultural inputs, if there is a political will to do so.

The last constraint is that farm households are subject to the fluctuation of crop prices. Due to the small size of landholding, households have little power in determining crop prices, and the fall of the prices often makes small-scale farming unprofitable. This is also the case in many other countries, even though their farm size may be larger. In the 1980s, the Chinese state set the procurement prices for major crops, particularly grains. This to some extent lessened the impact of the market on farm households by preventing the prices from falling too low in the short term. The Chinese state has maintained the practice to date by setting procurement prices of rice and wheat (sometimes corn as well), which are deemed to be staple foods.

As Chapter 5 will show, which compares China with South Africa, the relatively equal distribution of land in China to some extent helped mitigate the last two constraints for farm households. On the one hand, the absence of large farms gave rural households some breathing space in the market. This contrasts with South Africa, where the absolute dominance of very large farms has crowded out small household farms. On the other hand, the broad access to land by peasants increased the importance of household farming to national food security. This renders it necessary for the Chinese state to support farm households so that the latter are willing and able to produce sufficient grains and agricultural goods for the economy and society (Zhan and Scully 2018). However, with the rise of large farms in the recent decade, which I will show in Chapter 4, farm households have become increasingly disadvantaged in the market, and much of state support has also been shifted from small household farms to large farms and agribusiness enterprises.

In summary, the emergence of the second industrious revolution in the 1980s seemed to revive a tradition that dates back to the eighteenth century. However, it should be noted that the change couldn't be solely attributed to the market reform. Socialist practices and progress made before 1949 paved the way for this long-term change. The second industrious revolution was also much more than the first in terms of labor absorption, livelihood improvement, and productivity increase due to the adoption and diffusion of modern technologies in the countryside. Land relations, particularly broad access to land, had played a crucial role in this process. However, as China has pushed further on transition to capitalism after the 1990s, the forces underpinning the industrious revolution, particularly broad access to land, have been undermined. This will be the topic of the following two chapters.

Notes

1 All informants are pseudonymised. Date of Interview: October 15, 2010.
2 All places below the county level are pseudonymised.
3 Interview date: September 5, 2010.
4 The figure is made based on the Aohan Bureau of Archives (1991), pp. 85–6.
5 Interview date: March 18, 2006.
6 For a similar formulation of rural industrial development, please see Otsuka (2007), who shows that rural industrialization in East Asia transitioned from Stage 1 to Stage 2, during which rural industrial enterprises introduced new technologies, ideas, and information from urban and foreign enterprises.

Part II

Undermining forces

3 Urban bias and rural crisis

The land question beyond the countryside

While the rural reform was successful, the urban reform from 1984 onward created serious problems, such as excessive inflation and official corruption, both of which partly triggered the 1989 Tiananmen Square incident. The Chinese economy went into three years (1989–91) of "adjustment" marked by slow growth and a tight fiscal policy. The market reform appeared at a crossroads, facing the choice of either going further or swinging back. In 1992, Deng Xiaoping, at the age of 88, broke the stalemate during his tours in South China by urging to further marketize and open up the economy at greater speeds. In the meantime, state policy shifted from pro-rural to pro-urban. Dennis Tao Yang and Fang Cai (2003) suggest that the reason for the shift, beside Deng Xiaoping's role, might have been urban unrest in 1989 that prompted the Chinese state to placate urban interest groups, such as managers of the state-owned enterprises. Yasheng Huang (2008, 159–60) argues that the substitution of Zhao Ziyang – a rural reformer – by Shanghai-based politicians (Jiang Zemin and Zhu Rongji) in the central leadership strengthened urban interests in Chinese politics.

This shift in policy gave rise to a number of urban bias policies in the 1990s. Both urban- and foreign-invested enterprises were offered substantial tax reliefs, generous bank credits, and easy access to land. Both the central- and local-level governments invested frenetically in economic development zones in urban areas, while tightening credit supply to rural enterprises (Huang 2008, 109–74). The 1980s urbanization strategy that placed emphasis on small cities and towns was discarded and replaced with the policy to build large cities (Fei 1986; Hsing 2010). The Chinese economy also turned outward. The governments, at every level, promoted exports with tax rebates and subsidies, which gave an edge to urban- and foreign-invested enterprises (Wen 2011).

The urban bias policies had devastating impacts on the rural economy, particularly on inland provinces, where rural industry was still underdeveloped. First, as the engine of economic growth shifted to urban areas, rural savings and migrants' remittances were channeled out of the countryside to the city through the banking system. This made it very difficult for peasants to get bank credits for farm or nonfarm investments. Second, although peasants still had access to land, land use for nonfarm activities by peasants was restricted, whereas local governments accelerated the expropriation of rural land for urban and foreign investors. Third, the 1994 fiscal reform, which gave a larger share of tax income to the central government, led local governments in inland provinces to increase tax rates on farming and other economic activities. Finally, the marketization of rural education and health care added an extra burden on household expenditure (Andreas 2010; Li 2010). As a result, the countryside in inland provinces descended into a crisis in the late 1990s, characterized by the "Three Rural Problems," namely, the problems of rural area, rural people, and rural economy (Day 2013, 95–8; Wen 2001). Changping Li, who was then a township party secretary in Hubei Province (an inland province), summarized the situation in his letter to Premier Zhu Rongji in 2000: "Peasants are so miserable, the countryside is so poor, and agriculture is so in danger" (Li 2002).

The rural crisis in the 1990s was not derived from any substantive change to land relations, as most of the peasants still retained the use rights of farmlands. The key factor was the urban bias policies that concentrated financial and human resources in and transferred rural resources to urban areas. As a result, the surplus-generating capacity of rural land diminished, and access to land could not provide peasants with sufficient livelihoods. However, the rural crisis did not occur in all of the rural areas. In coastal regions, including Wujin, there was no sign of a rural crisis in the 1990s. These areas accumulated enough capital in the 1980s, and the policy shift in the 1990s continued to favor coastal regions, as China intended to turn them into export zones. As urbanization accelerated further, however, a great number of peasants in these areas lost land rights and factories to urban expansion.

This chapter contends that the land question in China cannot be fully understood without looking at factors beyond the countryside. It documents how urban bias policies have affected rural areas in different regions in China since the 1990s. In inland provinces, the concentration of resources in urban areas undermined the surplus-generating capacity of land, forcing peasants to leave farmland, even though they still retained use rights. In coastal regions and areas surrounding cities, the rapid urbanization since the 1990s has motivated local governments to expropriate rural land on a large scale, turning tens of millions into landless peasants without secure livelihoods. Although some of the landless peasants received an acceptable compensation package, a concession made by the state as a result of intense land struggles, they have lost land rights in land expropriation, which converted rural land into state-owned urban land. In both cases, the industrious revolution, which was based on the economic activities of community-based smallholders, was undermined. In what follows, I will first examine the impact of urban bias policies on inland regions based on the findings in Aohan, and then I will reveal how rapid urban expansion has undermined rural industry in Wujin. The last section examines the swelling army of landless peasants and their land struggles.

Impacts of urban bias on rural areas in the hinterland

Deng Xiaoping's speeches spurred a new wave of investments in cities and coastal regions. The fixed capital investment increased from 559.4 billion yuan in 1991 to 2.0 trillion yuan in 1995, up 2.6 times. Figure 3.1 shows that most of the growth took place in urban areas. Although rural areas saw some growth, it was mostly concentrated in coastal regions. Urban bias was also evident in the composition of the Chinese state's infrastructure investment. Agriculture accounted for about 10 percent of the total infrastructure investment in the 1970s, but the proportion decreased to 3 percent in the 1990s (NBS 2009b, 74). The urban bias policies also involved land use, financing, taxation, market regulation, education, and health care, which together placed rural areas at a severe disadvantage (Li 2010).

A direct consequence of urban bias was the widening gap between rural- and urban-household incomes. In 1983, the urban-to-rural income ratio was at its lowest point, 1.82, but it started to increase after the urban reform was initiated in 1984. The widening trend accelerated in the 1990s, with the ratio rising to 2.86 in 1994, and further to 3.23 in 2003 (NBS 2009a, tables 1–23). The urban bias policies struck inland provinces much harder than coastal regions, creating a rural crisis in the former. As a result of the urban bias, in the 1990s, rural industry was further concentrated into coastal regions, where most of the cities were situated. As noted in the previous chapter, ten coastal regions accounted for 49.1 percent of rural nonfarm output in 1990. By 1996, however, they accounted for 63.6 percent of rural nonfarm output and 70.0 percent of rural industrial output (Ministry of Agriculture 2003, 173–81).

Aohan, a county in eastern Mongolia, is a good example to illustrate how the urban bias policies harmed inland rural areas in the 1990s. As noted in the preceding chapter, the county is located in an ecologically vulnerable hinterland. By the 1980s, it had successfully raised grain production and partially restored the

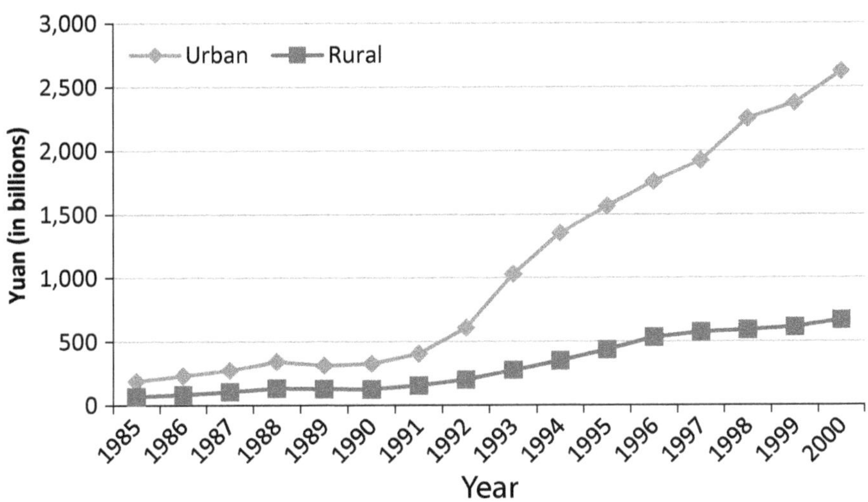

Figure 3.1 Fixed capital investments in rural and urban areas in China: 1985–2000.

Data source: NBS (2009a), tables 1–12.

ecological balance. However, the county's infrastructures – such as electric grids, roads, irrigation facilities, and telecommunication networks – were still underdeveloped. This limited the productive potential of smallholders, because poor infrastructure restricted the application of technologies and increased the costs of market transactions. Up till the 1980s, the central government provided some assistance for the county. For instance, the ecological fund that the county received in the late 1970s and 1980s contributed to its environment's improvement. To achieve a more-balanced development, and to further improve rural livelihoods, the Chinese state should have further increased financial assistance and technological support for the inland regions like Aohan. However, rather than transferring resources to inland rural areas, the urban bias policies put forth in the 1990s did the opposite. The adverse impacts were reflected in many respects, including, but not limited to, taxation, infrastructure, access to bank credit, and the increasing burden of rural education and health care. Below I will examine these impacts in turn.

Growing taxes and fees

In 1994, the Chinese state carried out a major fiscal reform, which significantly enlarged the share of the central government in industrial and commercial tax revenue. However, the reform did not lead to the flow of central resources from urban areas to rural areas; neither did resources flow from developed regions to underdeveloped regions. It was actually the other way around. With insufficient fiscal transfer from the center, local governments in the inland regions sought to collect more taxes from agriculture. The tax revenue from agriculture increased rapidly from 8.8 billion yuan in 1990 to 42.4 billion in 1999, up 3.8 times and much faster than the income growth of rural households (Bernstein and Lü 2003, 50–1). In addition to agricultural taxes, the local governments imposed an increasing amount of township and village levies for public projects and services, surcharges on cash crops and sideline activities, unruly fines for minor infractions, ad-hoc fundraising for large public projects, and compulsory labor services. Taken together, the amount extracted from the peasantry reached 120 billion yuan in 2000 (Bernstein and Lü, 59). It was not an easy task to collect such heavy taxes from peasants. The local governments had to hire extra hands to do the job. This required collecting more taxes to support the extra personnel (Zhao 2004), giving rise to the phenomenon of "state involution," a term that Prasenjit Duara (1988, 73–7) used to characterize North China before 1949.

The growing tax burden not only undercut rural livelihood, but also restricted the economic potential of smallholders. The most pernicious policy might be the imposition of taxes on cash crops and sideline activities, which is literally called "tax on special agricultural products" (*nongye techan shui*). This policy was initiated in 1983, but it was not until the 1990s that local governments widely and forcefully implemented it. According to national statistics, the amount of taxes on commercial agriculture rose rapidly from 6.4 billion yuan in 1994 to 14 billion yuan in 1999 (CCTV 2003). The actual tax revenue of this sort would exceed the figure because local governments tended to underreport their unscrupulous tax collection for fear of possible punishments from the upper-level governments.

Combing through Aohan's official archives, I found that, during the 1990s, the local government was collecting various taxes and fees on agriculture and sideline activities. In addition to cash crops, the government collected the tax on slaughtering domestic animals (*tuzai shui*), the tax on animal husbandry (*muye shui*), the tax on grazing animals on mountains (*dengshan shui*), the fee on raising honeybees (*fangfeng fei*), the fee on animal disease prevention (*fangyi fei*), the tax on fruit trees in household yards (*zhaijidiguoshu shui*), and so on. The wide reach of local taxation reveals that the local government attempted to tax all economic activities that rural households could possibly undertake.

Peasants in the county felt the crushing burden of heavy taxes. Mr. Li Fengwen, who was born in 1957, complained about the collection of taxes and fees in the 1990s when I interviewed him in March 2011,

> The government's policy has become much more benevolent than before. We used to pay all kinds of taxes and fees, and little was left after having paid the government. These taxes and fees were countless: you had to pay the wool tax and the tax on grazing on mountains. Each household paid 10 yuan for slaughtering pigs for the Spring Festival, no matter whether we actually slaughtered a pig or not. Before these taxes and fees were abolished in 2004, the tax burden of each person was at least 100 yuan a year. The tax burden was light in the early years of the rural reform, but it became increasingly heavier.[1]

The efforts to raise tax revenue not only undermined the rural economy, but also alienated local officials from peasants. Taxation was a major source of peasants' grievances in the 1990s, and tax resistance often led to large-scale petitions and protests (Bernstein and Lü 2003, 120–36; O'Brien and Li 2006). It was common in Aohan for peasants to collectively resist taxation or delay the payment. When doing fieldwork in 2006, I found that some villages in the county still owed a substantial amount of taxes from the 1990s.

Insufficient infrastructure investment

Infrastructure projects, such as roads and irrigation facilities, can improve the surplus-generating capacity of land and increase the access of peasants to the market. However, compared with the socialist period, when the county made great progress with infrastructure porjects, the 1990s saw sluggish development on both roads and irrigation facilities. The principal reason was that Aohan, as a rural county in hinterland China, was unable to finance infrastructure projects, and its infrastructure budget could barely cover the costs of maintaining existing facilities. This was a sharp contrast to large cities and coastal regions, where the central government invested heavily in infrastructure during the same period, particularly in economic development zones.

Most roads in the county were not paved. It took 3.5 hours for a peasant to travel from Grass Village to the county town, which was 70 kilometers away. Due to a lack of investment, the 1990s saw little expansion of irrigated areas in the county. In Grass Village, peasants still relied on the pump station that was constructed in the socialist period. In 1995–6, the village received a small fund from the local government, with which it drilled three tube wells. The wells only irrigated about 25 hectares of farmland, too little to significantly change the village's agricultural conditions. Between 1999 and 2002, a serious drought struck Aohan and cut agricultural output nearly in half. The natural disaster made the already-bad rural situation worse, and prompted even more rural laborers to migrate. The drought was also a reminder that the local population lacked necessary means to shield themselves from a major natural disaster.

Drying up of rural credit

In the 1980s, townships and village governments could obtain bank loans to organize collective enterprises and development programs, and rural households could also loan money for household businesses. The main financial institution that provided these services was the rural credit cooperative. In the 1990s, it became difficult for villages and households to get loans from rural credit cooperatives, which shifted most of their financial services to urban areas partly due to the urban bias policies. As some scholars pointed out, the role of rural credit cooperatives had changed from credit suppliers to rural "bloodsuckers" because they used rural savings to invest in urban development (Chen, Liu, and Zhang 2010). Another well-known bloodsucker in rural areas was the postal saving system (*youzheng chuxu xitong*), which provided only saving services in the countryside, and loaned rural savings to urban enterprises and projects in this period.

Rural credit drying up was deeply felt in Aohan. The Women's Federation in the county started a microcredit program in 2001, which gave out loans to women for starting small businesses. The terms of these loans were very strict: the applicant could borrow only 1,000–3,000 yuan a year, and then the applicant had to pay back the loan starting from the second month and pay off the loan in a year, with an interest rate of 10 percent. Nevertheless, the demand for these loans was high. In Grass Village, Mr. Zhang Zhanwei, who was elected the head of the village committee in 2000, became very popular among the villagers. One reason for his popularity was that he loaned his own money to rural households at no interest (or at very low interests). Few households in the village could obtain loans from the local rural credit cooperative in the 1990s. When money was in dire need, for example, in the event of paying medical bills and covering the expenditure of wedding, peasants had to seek help from relatives or loaned money from usurers. Mr. Li Huaqiang and Ms. Zhang Huaying, a couple I interviewed in February 2011, recalled to me that they borrowed 15,000 yuan to build a house in 1997, and they paid more than 3,000 yuan for interest in a year. The interest rate was more than 20 percent.[2] The situation was a reminder of the

1920s and 1930s, when interest rates in the Chinese countryside were exorbitantly high (Tawney 1932, 62).

Marketization of education and health care

In 1985, the central government reformed the rural education system and demanded that the township government be responsible for financing basic education in its jurisdiction, including teachers' salaries and schools (Liao 2004). In actuality, it was peasants who paid for basic education since the township governments' revenue came from collecting taxes and fees from peasants. Rural households that sent children to schools paid tuition, textbooks, and miscellaneous fees (*zafei*). Insofar as rural health care is concerned, the socialist cooperative medical system was dismantled after the reform, and what replaced it was a system based on private clinics and hospitals (Wang 2008).

In the 1980s, the costs of children's education and health care were kept low because the charges on related goods and services such as textbooks, medicine, and hospitalization had not been fully marketized. In the 1990s, however, with the further marketization of these goods and services, the costs of children's education and health care quickly grew and rose beyond affordability of most rural households, particularly in the inland regions. The proportion of expenditure on education and related services in the total household expenditure had risen from 5.4 percent in 1990 to 11.2 percent in 2000 (NBS 2001, 251).

Peasants in Grass Village found the costs of health care and children's education to be a heavy economic burden. Most children only completed middle school. According to the 2010 census data, which I collected from the village committee, among 168 people in the village who were born between 1976 and 1985, only 19 people went to high school or above, which is less than 12 percent. There was a high school near the township, and it was convenient for parents to send children there. However, my interviewees told me that the high costs of education, as well as economic difficulty in this period, forced most of the households to halt their children's education at middle school. Health-care costs were also surging. Many rural households could not even afford daily medical expenses. One of the private clinics in the village became very popular because the owner allowed patients to defer payments. Without medical insurance or government support, rural households would quickly fall into poverty once any of their members caught serious diseases. For example, Mr. Zhou Jianfeng, 44 at the time of the interview, caught a serious heart disease in 1997 and spent more than 50,000 yuan on the surgery. The disease drove his household into poverty. Before the illness, his household owned a truck and raised dozens of sheep, and was relatively better off in the village.[3] Nationally, in 2002, rural households spent 4.03 times as much as in 1992 on hospitalization, and 3.36 times on doctor's visits (Du, Zhang and Huang 2006, 125–31).

Underuse of farmland and rise of a migration-dependent economy

The urban bias policies undercut the profitability of agriculture and other rural economic activities, and as a result, land could not produce much surplus for peasants, even though they held its use rights. In 1994 and 1996, concerned about food security, the Chinese state increased the procurement prices of grain crops (Zhan 2017a). However, it failed to significantly improve rural conditions at a time of extreme urban bias. A useful indicator is the rent of land. In the 1990s, the rent of farmland in Aohan was near zero, which was a sharp contrast to high rents in the recent decade, as I will show in the next chapter. A rent of near zero indicates that there was a very low demand for farmland. Many rural migrants wanted to lease out land in order to participate in migration, but only found that no one wanted to take it. Many farmlands, particularly those without access to irrigation, were left uncultivated. In places with access to irrigation, peasants would still farm the land, but they did not grow crops intensively, as farming could not bring much income anyway. This led to the underuse of farmland in the countryside as peasants abandoned agriculture en masse. Contra William Arthur Lewis (1954), not only had "surplus" rural laborers left the countryside for the city, but those who were not "surplus" per se were also forced out in an urban bias situation.

The result was that the countryside was turned into a migration-dependent economy. As the local economy generated less and less income for rural households, while the government demanded more taxes and fees, peasants in Aohan had no other option but to migrate to cities and coastal regions in search of employment opportunities. The "push" factors in Aohan, as it existed in many other inland regions, coincided with the "pull" factors in large cities and coastal regions. As the Chinese state poured resources into these places, a large number of employment opportunities in construction, manufacturing, and service sectors were created, drawing large numbers of peasants to leave the villages. The number of rural migrant workers in China jumped from fewer than 20 million in 1991 to 40 million in 1992, and further to 60 million in 1994 (Zhan 2004).

Outward labor migration has long existed in Aohan. In the socialist period, many rural laborers worked as temporary workers for factories in Liaoning Province, which was then one of the major industrial bases in China. These workers were recruited through rural collectives such as brigades and communes, and their earnings had to be turned over to their collectives as a part of collective assets (see also Yan 2003). In return, the collectives gave these workers full work points and some extra bonuses. In the 1980s, after the market reform, more peasants migrated to the city, and most of them were seasonal migrants. For example, a number of Grass Viallge peasants went to Panjin, a prefecture in Liaoning, to harvest reeds during the winter season in the late 1980s. With three months of work, each migrant would bring home about 1,000 yuan.

In the 1980s, migration was only a supplement to the local rural economy. In the 1990s, however, its importance rose considerably. The problem became so serious in the late 1990s that parents would not be able to get children married if they did not earn enough cash income from migration. That is to say, Aohan became a migration-dependent economy that could hardly sustain itself without resorting to migration.

The first feature of a migration-dependent rural economy is that local sectors lack the capacity to generate enough surpluses to meet local needs. As such, peasants in Aohan had to earn income through labor migration to purchase agricultural inputs, pay taxes and fees, send children to schools, and pay medical bills. Ms. Chu Xiayun,[4] born in 1951, had two children in the middle school in the 1990s. She suffered a spinal problem and had to take medicine regularly. To pay for her children's education and her medical bills, her husband had to migrate to Panjin to work as a construction worker, earning 2,000 yuan a year. While the household accumulated some debt over the years, it would not have made it through those years without her husband working as a migrant worker. Money from the migration was also used to pay for agricultural inputs such as seeds, fertilizers, and pesticide, because although farming was not profitable, it provided subsistence for household members, particularly the young and the elderly. The earnings from migration were not enough to cover all subsistence costs, thus rural households had to engage in farming and animal husbandry even though these could not generate much income. An important difference between a migration-dependent economy and a local-oriented economy is that agriculture in the former mainly provides subsistence, while it is often regarded as an investment opportunity in the latter variety.

The second feature of a migration-dependent economy is that a large number of talented laborers leave for migration while the least-able laborers are those who take care of the local economy. In the 1980s, about 150 rural laborers in Grass Village, or one-sixth of its labor force, migrated to the city every year. In the late 1990s, however, the number of migrant workers from the village increased to 400 peoples a year, accounting for at least half of the labor force. Young, educated male peasants left the village. Women also joined the migration. Unmarried young girls left for large coastal cities such as Beijing, Tianjin, and Dalian (Liaoning Province) to work in factories or as domestic workers. Some married women joined their husbands as migrants. They took care of cooking or housekeeping and worked some odd jobs. Ms. Shi Xiuli, who was born in 1970 and got married in 1990, went with her husband in 1994 to Shenyang, the capital city of Liaoning. They both worked in an aluminum alloy factory, and thus were able to earn 4,000 yuan a year. In addition to the job in the factory, Ms. Shi also cooked meals and took care of housework for her husband and herself. They left their child and farmland to their parents, who were already over 55 years old at the time.[5] The exodus of talented rural laborers further undermined the local economy, creating a vicious circle. At the extreme, the countryside became a place that peasants wanted to leave behind as long as they could manage to survive in the city (Yan 2003). Young people were pushed out no matter whether they wanted to leave or whether they could find urban employment, because the act of staying in the countryside itself was seen as evidence of failure. Mr. Jia Shuhui, born in 1970, had to follow fellow villagers to Liaoning Province. He worked in a construction site and earned about 2,000 yuan a year. To him, migration was an unpleasant experience, because he had to work on tedious construction work for long hours. He returned home in 2003 and was growing cash crops and raising chicken when I interviewed him in 2006 and 2011.[6]

The last feature of a migration-dependent rural economy is that rural migrant workers have to accept the poor terms when working in the city. They are poorly paid and have to endure unpleasant working and living conditions without safety protection. Migration studies usually attribute the poor treatment of rural migrant workers in Chinese cities to state policy, most importantly, the *hukou* system, which did not provide protection and support for rural migrant workers (Alexander and Chan 2004; Solinger 1999). The systems of regulating migration, such as the *hukou* system, were indeed an important factor, but the miserable conditions that migrant workers had to endure in the 1990s should also be attributed to the migration-dependent economy. Migrant workers had to accept poor terms in the city because they did not have any other option. In other words, they had little marketplace bargaining power (Silver 2003; Wright 2000). A common memory among peasants in Aohan about migration experiences in the 1990s is that working as migrant workers was no better than farming in the countryside in terms of labor intensity and working conditions. Ms. Yang Yingrong, born in 1952, recalled her husband's migration experiences in the 1990s to me in March 2006:

> My husband went to many places and worked on numerous jobs. He worked on railways and in brick-making factories, and even went to a mountainous area working as a lumberjack. The mountain was such a remote place that he could not find any household there for drinking water. He worked there for three months and took home little money. Working on railways and in brick-making factories also did not make much money. Sometimes he labored for a whole year but did not get paid. However, staying home was not an option because farming could not make money at all. Therefore, he still chose to migrate in hopes to earn some extra cash income.[7]

Ms. Yang's husband, Cui Bing, is a skilled carpenter, and he also knows how to drive a truck. With increased job opportunities in the county after 2003, he returned home and worked as a part-time carpenter in the county town. I interviewed him in February 2011. He and his wife grew greenhouse vegetables, farmed sugar beets, and raised sheep. In 2011, growing greenhouse vegetables was less profitable than before due to market competition, but he still preferred it to migration. He told me that, as a migrant worker, he had to work more than 12 hours a day and was strictly supervised by the employer. That was why he did not want to work as a migrant worker anymore.[8]

Migration might have kept the countryside from falling apart, but it did not substantially improve the rural situation. By the early 2000s, after more than a decade of large-scale outward migration, most of rural households in Aohan still lived in a difficult economic situation and were worried about how to make ends meet. This started to change only after the Chinese state adjusted its urban bias policies and transferred more financial resources to rural areas, as I will show in the next chapter. However, many urban bias policies have persisted to date, and a migration dependent economy can still be found in many inland rural areas.

From privatization to land expropriation: rural enterprises in Wujin

There was no sign of rural crisis in Wujin in the 1990s. The county's industrial output, of which nearly 90 percent came from rural enterprises, increased from 17.5 billion yuan in 1992 to 38.1 billion yuan in 1998 (Wujin government 1999, 222). Private enterprises accounted for an increasing share in the local economy. For example, in the township where Bridge Village was located, the number of private industrial enterprises reached 849 in 1998, producing half of industrial output. In the service sector, there were more than 3,000 private enterprises, taking up two-thirds of the market. The expansion of private enterprises presented a challenge to collective enterprises. In the 1980s, private enterprises relied on collective enterprises for technology and the market, but in the 1990s, the former had become increasingly independent of the latter. Furthermore, private enterprises drew resources such as talents from collective enterprises and competed directly with the latter for a larger market share. Large urban and foreign capital also moved to the countryside to establish new factories or take over existing ones, and this further intensified competition on collective enterprises.

A more serious threat to collective enterprises came from the Chinese state, which had increasingly grown hostile toward public ownership after it moved to further dismantle socialist remnants in the economy in the 1990s. In November 1993, the Third Plenary Session of the 14th CCP Central Committee called to reform enterprises of collective ownership, which included both the SOEs and the rural collective enterprises. As early as 1994, the Wujin government started to discuss reforming collective ownership based on the directive from the central government. The ownership reform was a nationwide phenomenon following the order from the central government in this period (Zhang and Yuan 2003). However, this is not to say that the local government did not want to carry out ownership reform. With more and more TVEs running in the red due to market competition and mismanagement, local governments also wanted to reform the poor-performing enterprises because they became more a liability than a revenue source to the government (Oi 1999). The Bridge Village party secretary said to me,

> From the angle of the village collective, we want to reform the ownership of loss-making enterprises if possible, and close them down if no one wants to take them. Otherwise they would become a burden on the village: the benefits go to enterprise managers but the losses are left to the village collective.[9]

In 1999, Wujin started to privatize all collective enterprises. The nature of privatization was to sell collective enterprises to incumbent managers. After that, the enterprises were under the absolute control of former managers. The government compensated workers with a proportion of money from selling the enterprises. After being compensated, workers lost all entitlements to the enterprises. Across the country, the number of collective enterprises reached its peak in 1993, 1.7 million, and it had declined thereafter. In 2003, there were only 292,000 rural collective enterprises (Ministry of Agriculture 2003, 4; Zhan 2015b, 422).

Rural workers suffered most in the privatization as they not only lost job security, but also their share of assets in collective enterprises. Ten years after the mandatory privatization, my interviewees still complained about the policy. Mr. Wu Renrong, a former worker in the New Light factory, explained to me why this was so:

> Workers in the New Light factory were absolutely unhappy about the privatization. The asset of the factory was worth more than 100 million yuan, but it was sold for 30 million yuan to the manager. Workers and their families were cursing the policy. Why? It was because the factory was a joint-share enterprise from the start. The peasant households took their weaving looms together and established the factory. Thus the factory belonged to us, and the process of privatization should be approved by us.[10]

After the New Light Factory was privatized, Mr. Wu left the enterprise and opened a small printing-and-dyeing factory of his own. As noted in Chapter 2, many collective enterprises, including a part of township enterprises and most village enterprises, were created and developed through villagers' collective effort. The mandatory privatization of these enterprises by the government seemed arbitrary and unacceptable to villagers. The shoe accessory factory in Bridge Village was such an example. The villagers attached themselves strongly to the factory and saw it as a symbol representing a collective project since the socialist period. The forced privatization in 1999 came as a shock to villagers in the factory and their families. Their anger grew, and the tension between the buyer (the previous manager) and villagers was high. Most of my interviewees (including all village officials) accused the factory of being sold below its market value. And it was believed that the shoe accessory was worth 30 million yuan, but sold only for ten million yuan. The Bridge Village party secretary also complained to me, "The ownership reform was a national policy. We the village officials, including me, did not think of it as a good policy. The privatization led to collective assets falling into private hands, and it also greatly hurt workers' interests."[11]

After collective enterprises were privatized, the commitment of workers to these enterprises was weakened, while, at the same time, the privatized enterprises started to replace incumbent workers with cheap and easily managed migrant laborers. Many rural workers left the privatized enterprises, and a significant number of them started their own businesses. As a result, the number of small enterprises underwent a new wave of expansion in the early 2000s. The number of rural enterprises in Changzhou Prefecture, where Wujin is located, increased from 10,563 in 1999 to 17,359 in 2005, up 64.3 percent (Zhan 2015b, 423). My fieldwork revealed that many household enterprises were too small to be included in official statistics, thus the actual extent of the growth should be larger than reported. In Bridge Village, the number of industrial enterprises increased from 65 in 1999 to 134 in 2003, and further to 177 in 2006.

Access to land was the main reason why so many households in the village were able to establish small industrial enterprises. In 2000, the township government enclosed 7.3 hectares of farmland in Bridge Village to build an industrial zone for textile printing and dyeing. This deeply alarmed the village leadership. The village party secretary told me that they realized that others would come to grab the rest of the farmland if they did not take action. From 2001 to 2003, the village rented most of the farmland to rural households to build factories. In addition, the village obtained approval to build dozens of factory buildings and rent factories to household enterprises. In retrospect, the party secretary was very proud of this decision:

> From the perspective of the village, it was necessary to control land. Land is money. The township was also grabbing land around. We fight very hard to keep this land to ourselves. If we did not do it, they would come and build their industrial zones. We got the land so that it became the asset of the village, and we could use it to create jobs and increase income for households in the village.... It seems now that we made the right move. Most enterprises in our industrial zone were owned by people of our village.[12]

In addition to land, the surge of small, rural enterprises should also be attributed to the earlier development of rural industry in the region, which provided rural residents with savings, work experience, entrepreneurial skill, and market information. For example, Mr. Wu Xueming, who worked as a salesman in the shoe accessory factory, told me how he had set up his factory:

> My factory was established in 2000. Before that, I worked for the village shoe accessory factory. The ownership reform led me to see things differently because the enterprise was sold to the manger and became private. When the enterprise was collectively owned, I belonged to it, worked for it, and cared about it. In 2000, I used tens of thousands yuan that I saved plus some money that I borrowed from my relatives to start this factory. The money was spent building the factory and purchasing power looms. I bought four looms, which were made in Shanghai, 48,000 yuan a loom. In the beginning, my wife also operated the looms, repaired broken cloth, and cooked meals. We only hired one worker at the time.[13]

However, the prosperity of small rural enterprises did not last long, as the urban bias policies had driven up the speed of urban expansion. As a result, more and more villages lost land to the sprawling city. By 2010, all rural areas between Bridge Village and Changzhou had been turned into urban areas. In August 2010, the village received a notification from the upper government that one-third of its land would be expropriated to build commercial apartments.

Land expropriation was implemented in the name of urbanization. By all academic standards, however, Bridge Village has long been urbanized. According to the village's statistical reports, industry generated more income than agriculture as early as the 1970s. By the 1980s, people who worked in nonagricultural sectors far outnumbered those who worked in agriculture. In 1982, 116 people were counted as agricultural laborers in the village, only 16.0 percent of the labor force, while the majority of laborers, 608 out of 724, worked in nonagricultural sectors, mostly industry. In the late 1990s, most of the land in the village was used for industrial production rather than agriculture. In 2003, the village abandoned agriculture altogether, only leaving small pieces of land for households to grow vegetables.

However, up to my investigation in 2010, it was still called a "village" in policy documents and official statistics, because a village is different from an urban neighborhood (*chengshi shequ*) in terms of land rights. In a village, land is collectively owned, and village members (peasants) are entitled to the benefits generated from the land. After the rural reforms, every household in villages could farm a small size of land and control the products of the land. In Bridge Village, every household received a piece of farmland in the 1980s, but not every household was able to lease a piece of land to establish a factory in the early 2000s. However, all households were shareholders of collective assets of the village, including the benefits generated from leasing out the village land. By contrast, land in urban areas is owned by the state. Thus the nature of land expropriation is to take land away from peasants and turn it into the state-owned urban land.

Land expropriation struck a heavy blow to small, community-based household enterprises. A crucial condition of these enterprises was access to land. Paying very low rent or none at all was the key to their success because it greatly reduced the costs of production. In the 1980s and 1990s, rural households used land to build factories and workers' dormitories and to cultivate farmland to feed families and workers. After losing land to urban expansion, these households lost a crucial condition to run these enterprises.

During my stay in Bridge Village, many households shut down or planned to shut down their factories. In Wujin, thousands of rural enterprises closed doors due to land expropriation. Although industrial output continued to grow in official statistics, the contribution of rural industry had declined remarkably. My interviews with peasants whose villages had been urbanized also confirmed that more than 95 percent of small enterprises in their villages were closed.

Urbanization, landless peasants, and land struggles

On the evening of September 12, 2010, a sharp sound of a gong broke the silence in Bridge Village, and a few hundred villagers quickly gathered. Striking a gong (a traditional Chinese musical instrument) to convene villagers in an emergency is a local tradition, which was frequently used in the late Qing and Republican periods, when villages were under threats from small groups of bandits or wandering soldiers. However, this time, it was not used to fight against bandits, but to deal with local officials and developers who had come to demolish houses and factories. On September 5, dozens local officials, real estate agents, and hired strongmen moved into the village and set up an office to force through land expropriation. The gathering of the villagers was not aimed to halt the land expropriation, as the villagers understood very well that they were not able to counter the government directly. The goal of the gathering was to build solidarity among villagers and negotiate for a good deal on compensation. By 2010, more than 100 villages had been cleared and turned into urban areas in Wujin, making up 40 percent of all of the villages in the county.

Wujin is just one example among the nationwide land expropriations. While national data is unavailable, there is no doubt that millions of peasants have lost land. To gauge the extent of land expropriation, a common method is to estimate the amount of farmland that was converted for nonagricultural uses in official statistics and approximate it with the scale of land expropriation. According to Yulin Zhang (2015), 5.56 million hectares of land had been converted between 1991 and 2013. Based on the average size of landholding in China, one *mu* of land supported 1.5 peasants. Thus he estimated that the number of peasants who had lost land was 127 million for the period. Zhang's approach may not be applicable to Bridge Village, as the land expropriation was industrial land instead of agricultural land. Nevertheless, his analysis reveals the large scale of land expropriations nationwide. This is corroborated by a 2011 Landesa survey that investigated 1,791 villages in 21 provinces. The survey found that 43.1 percent of the villages had experienced land expropriation (Landesa 2012).

The main motivation of local governments for land expropriation has been the revenue generated from the conversion of rural land to urban land. Due to the implementation of urban bias policies, urban land has become much more valuable than rural land. This was so particularly after the urban housing reform in 1998, which created a market for urban real estate. By expropriating rural land and selling the use rights of the land to real estate developers, local governments have reaped an enormous amount of revenue. In 2017, the land revenue reached a record high, 5.2 trillion yuan, accounting for 56.9 percent of all local revenue (Ministry of Finance 2018). Between 2004 and 2015, the land revenue had been hovering around 50 percent of all local revenue, attesting to its crucial importance in local finance (Zhan 2017b, 38).

Villagers were compensated for the loss of land rights. The aforementioned Landesa survey found that 87.3 percent of the respondents whose land was taken had received or were promised compensations. My fieldwork in several provinces rarely found that villagers did not receive any compensation for the loss of land. However, the forms and amounts of compensation vary widely across time and space. The standards of compensation were very low from the late 1990s to the mid-2000s, and only in the recent decade were the standards increased due to intense struggles from peasants. Nevertheless, many villagers saw their standard of living deteriorate after land expropriation. And they lost the security of livelihood and were excluded from the process of land development.

According to the Land Management Law issued in 1998, peasants whose land was expropriated should receive a compensation of ten to 16 times of the annual harvest of agricultural production of the land. Local governments can increase the compensation, but the amount should not exceed 30 times (Kong and Wang 2004). As local governments tended to maximize returns from land expropriation, the compensation was usually set at the minimum, that is, ten times. In addition, the annual harvest of land was calculated based on grain crops, 800 yuan to 1,000 yuan (100 to 130 US dollars) per *mu*, regardless whether some lands were used for commercial crops or even factories (Ong 2014). One *mu* of land, which supported 1.5 persons on average, could only be compensated for 8,000 yuan to 10,000 yuan (1,000 to 1,300 US dollars). Such a small amount could only support a few years of subsistence living. According to a 2003 national survey of landless peasants conducted by the National Bureau of Statistics of China, of 2,942 households, 46 percent reported less income after land expropriation (Mao 2004). In addition, land expropriations had closed millions of small rural enterprises as rural factories were demolished, as was seen in Wujin.

The meager compensation had prompted peasants to protest. In some extreme cases, desperate peasants either committed suicide in public or attacked officials who came to take their land (Sargeson 2013; Walker 2008; Zhang 2015). It was reported that land expropriations accounted for 65 percent of all rural protests or petitions, which totaled tens of thousands a year (Beijing News 2010). Take Sichuan Province as an example, the police had dealt with 1,171 cases related to land expropriation and received 9,946 petitions between 2002 and 2003. The number of participants in some protests reached thousands, and violent clashes often broke out between protesters and the police (Sichuan Public Security Bureau 2004). Peasants demanded higher compensation and the opportunity to participate in land development.

Alarmed by the scale and magnitude of peasant protests, the central government made adjustments to the Land Management Law in 2004. The new policy mandated that the living standard of peasants must not deteriorate after land is expropriated. It also ordered local governments to increase the standards of compensation to 30 times of the annual harvest of land output if necessary. Moreover, it suggested that local governments should take measures to protect the livelihoods of landless peasants. For example, landless peasants should be given newly reclaimed farmland if such land was available. In city fringes where land had been utilized for urban development, peasants should be given shares in land development projects. In April 2006, another document ordered to incorporate landless peasants into social security programs. Local governments could either establish an ad hoc social security program for landless peasants, or include them in existing urban social security programs (Shi, Jin, and Zhuo 2011; Tang 2011).

Pushed from above and resisted from below, local governments started to increase the standards of compensation and create social security programs for landless peasants. In some cities, a small proportion of land was reserved for peasants to run nonfarm businesses. However, the change has been a slow process. Local governments were reluctant to give up their interests, while peasants, in many places, were not satisfied with still-insufficient compensation. Land expropriation continued to be the main source of peasant protests and social conflicts. This further forced the central government to issue another document in 2010 to order local governments to comply with the central policy and increase compensation.[14]

In general, the level of compensation for land expropriation has slowly increased since the early 2000s. However, there have been great variations. Some villagers (but not all) in developed regions or the fringes of large cities were able to receive high-value compensation items, such as multiple flats and even commercial facilities. They were turned into landed proprietors in the city and received a stable rental or business income. In Zhejiang, Guangdong, Hainan, and Shanghai, the local governments issued the policy to return 10 percent of land to villages to use for nonfarm businesses after land is expropriated (Yan 2013). In Bridge Village in Wujin, a family of four whose house was demolished could purchase two subsidized flats with the compensation. However, remodeling and making the flats usable usually cost a lot of money, and the family needed to supplement it with its own savings. The hope was that the family lived in one flat and rented out the other. However, this source of income depended on the rental market. As factories were closed due to land expropriations, large numbers of migrant workers moved to elsewhere or returned to their hometowns, and this reduced the demand for housing, making the source of income unsustainable. A lot of families still hold on to these flats, because their market values are high under the land revenue regime and the real estate bubble. They would be severely affected should the bubble burst.

In small cities and vast inland regions, the compensation for the loss of land is often insufficient to generate a stable livelihood. In some regions, such as Chengdu, where I conducted field research, most of the compensation was used to pay into the land-losing peasant's social security account, but the account only covered very basic pension insurance and health care (Zhan 2017b). In some regions, peasants received all compensations in cash, but this would soon be used up due to the increasing living costs and lack of job and business opportunities. The National Bureau of Statistics conducted a study of 1,500 villages nationwide in 2014 and found that many landless peasants lost the means of livelihood and were in the status of unemployment or underemployment while having to bear the increasing costs of living in urbanized areas (Zhang and Hao 2015). When peasants' houses were demolished, particularly in suburban areas, they would be compensated with urban flats. The value of these flats depended much on location, and the value would be low if they were located in small cities or far away from the city center. It is not rare that the flats built for landless peasants are of poor quality and located distant from the city (He *et al.* 2009; Wu 2017).

The impact of land expropriation was worse on low-income and poor households than on others, because these households used to rely on land for a substantial source of livelihood. This is the case even in developed provinces. A study of landless peasants in Guangdong Province in 2012–14 found that lower-income households reported 20 percent less income after land expropriation, while higher-income households reported 25 percent more income (Liang 2016). Land loss also made a worse impact on vulnerable groups, such as older and disabled peasants (Peng and Zhu 2015; Zhang and Hao 2015). In Wujin, rural industry was the major source of employment and household income before the land was urbanized. Small industrial enterprises in Bridge Village provided employment opportunities for all rural laborers, male and female, young and old, strong and weak. After land was expropriated and factories closed, most of them would not be able to find jobs on the market, particularly the old and the weak. In addition, access to land can significantly lower living costs, which is particularly important to low-income rural households. In Bridge Village, although most of the farmland was turned into factories, the villagers still relied on small pieces of land to grow vegetables and use water from wells for laundry, but land expropriation eliminated all of these benefits.

In summary, the impact of urban bias varies among regions. In coastal regions and areas near cities, it accelerated the pace of urbanization and land expropriation, depriving millions of peasants of land rights and secure livelihoods. In inland provinces, the urban bias policies reduced the inflow of fiscal and financial resources while transferring rural resources out to coastal regions and cities, giving rise to a rural crisis and an economy dependent on out-migration. The rural crisis created serious social and economic problems, including, but not limited to, rural impoverishment, increasing incidence of peasant unrest, and a looming food crisis. These problems prompted the Chinese state to take action and transfer more resources to rural areas in inland provinces since the early 2000s. This is the topic I will examine in the next chapter.

Notes

1 Date of the interview: March 6, 2011.
2 Date of the interview: February 26, 2011.
3 Date of the interview: March 23, 2006.
4 Date of interview: March 11, 2006.
5 Date of the interview: March 20, 2006.
6 Interview dates: March 19, 2006; February 27, 2011;
7 Interview date: March 21, 2006.
8 Interview date: February 25, 2011.
9 Interview date: September 12, 2010.
10 Interview J-28, October 16, 2010.
11 Interview date: September 12, 2010.
12 Interview date: September 12, 2010.
13 Interview date: September 12, 2010.
14 The document can be accessed at website of the Ministry of Land and Resources: www.mlr.gov.cn/zwgk/zytz/201007/t20100713_154433.htm.

4 The rise of agrarian capitalism and the future of the industrious revolution

In 2007, the Aohan government launched a project to turn the county into a vegetable-growing base, supplying large cities such as Beijing and Tianjin with vegetables. To achieve this goal, the government offered bank credit and funds for villages and large farms to build up to 12,500 *mu* (833 hectares) of vegetable greenhouses. It was against this background that Grass Village received a bank loan (3.5 million yuan) and a development fund (200,000 yuan) to construct 160 vegetable greenhouses. The village was the first in its township to take on this project. To increase the chance of success, which would have demonstration effects for other villages, the township government hired a technician (with a monthly salary of 2,500 yuan) from Shandong Province to help the farmers. However, when I visited the village in 2011, the farmers were complaining about this project because the profit rate fell below the initial expectation due to the falling of market prices. All greenhouses were used to grow tomatoes in the village. Mr. Li, the technician from Shandong, told me that the tomato price must be at least 1.2 yuan a kilogram to avoid a loss, and 2.6 yuan a kilogram to make an acceptable profit. However, the prices often fell below 2.0 yuan in 2010, sometimes as low as 1.4 yuan.[1] This led many farmers in the county to give up their greenhouses.

My understanding of the problem is that the county built too many greenhouses, causing the falling of market prices. I conveyed this idea to county and township officials. To my surprise, they did not agree and argued instead that greenhouses were not too many but too few. Their reasoning is as follows:

> Our scale of greenhouse vegetables is too small to attract large merchants from Beijing and Tianjin. Thus we can only supply the local market within Chifeng Prefecture. If we continue to build greenhouses and expand the scale large enough, we will be able to sell our vegetables to Beijing, Shanghai and even large cities in the south. Look, greenhouse vegetables in Shandong province are very successful. Why? It is because their scale is much larger than ours.

The embrace of "large scale" is deeply rooted in official thinking in China. Under the influence of modernization ideology and awed by large-scale, industrialized agriculture in the West, they perceive small-scale, labor-intensive agricultural production as backward and inefficient. In practice, it is also easier for the government to deal with a handful of large agricultural producers than to deal with millions of small farmers. Additionally, large producers can become an important source of revenue, while small farmers contribute little to government revenue.

This chapter examines the rise of agrarian capitalism in rural China in the past two decades, characterized by the emergence and expansion of agribusiness companies and large farms. The rise of agrarian capitalism has resulted from a combination of multiple factors, including, but not limited to, the Chinese state's push for agricultural modernization, the rise of agrarian capital, the expansion of transnational agricultural corporations, the concern over food security, and the growing demand of urban consumers for agricultural produce. The rise of agrarian capitalism has a direct bearing on the land question. The expansion of agribusiness companies and large farms will take away land rights from small farmers. The new land reform, detailed in the Introduction of this book, is aimed to facilitate the transfer of land use rights from farm households to large farms and agribusiness companies. The result would be the weakening of the industrious revolution and the swelling of the rural and the urban poor, who do not have stable employment or secure livelihoods.

In what follows, I will first review the push for agricultural modernization by the Chinese state, followed by an analysis of China's pursuit of grain self-sufficiency and its effects on the growth of agrarian capital. After that, I will examine how the policies of "building a new socialist countryside" have affected small farm households. The last two sections will assess the magnitude of land transfer and assess the impact of the rise of agrarian capitalism on the industrious revolution.

Agricultural modernization and the problematization of "small"

The rural market reform turned collective farms into small household farms. The reform, which started in 1978 and was not completed until 1983, did not go without challenges. A recent article by an insider of the reform reveals that the reform supporters were challenged at both central and local levels (Zhao 2018). Replacing large collective farms with small household farms ran directly against agricultural modernization, the dominant ideology after the Second World War. The belief in agricultural modernization superseded the divide between capitalism and communism as countries in both camps accepted it as the guiding principle for agricultural development (Ye 2015). A key tenet of agricultural modernization is that large farms, by using modern technologies, are more productive and efficient than small farms (van der Ploeg 2009). This ideology was an important factor in agricultural collectivization in China, which consolidated small private farms into large collective farms. It should be noted that there are important differences between capitalist farms and collective farms. For example, the owner in the former exclusively controls profit, while it is shared among community members in the latter.

The partition of collective farms in China was met with the counterargument that it would undercut agricultural productivity and food supply. The rapid increase in grain production and agricultural output, however, helped the reformers overcome opposition and push through the reform in the early 1980s. It should be noted that the increase in agricultural production was not only derived from the switch to the household system. Chapter 2 showed that the use of chemical fertilizers, the adoption of new technologies, and the infrastructure built in the socialist period also contributed to the growth. In the late 1980s, however, the growth of agriculture slowed down, and by the 1990s, the countryside, particularly the regions where peasants mainly relied on agriculture, had descended into a serious crisis.

I have shown in the preceding chapter that the urban bias policies were the main factor behind the rural crisis. The advocates for agricultural modernization, however, used the rural crisis as proof to attack small-scale household farming. They attributed the crisis to the anti-modernist nature of household farming: "small," "scattered," and "weak" (Zhang and Donaldson 2008, 27–8).[2] And they further argued that small household farms lowered agricultural productivity, prevented the application of modern equipment, and was unable to respond effectively to market changes (Dong 1996; Nguyen, Cheng, and Findlay 1996; Fan and Chan-Kang 2005).

In 1993, Weifang Prefecture in Shandong Province reported a new model of agricultural development, and named it *nongye changyehua* (literally, "running agriculture like an industry"), which is often translated into "agricultural industrialization." The new practice was intended to overcome the shortcomings of household production by incorporating farm households into commodity chains. On the one hand, it coordinated hundreds of rural households in an area to grow the same crop or raise the same domestic animal, often in the form of "one village, one product" (*yicun yipin*) or even "one township, one product" (*yixiang yipin*). On the other hand, it linked these rural households to one or more agribusiness companies through contract farming (Guo et al. 2007; Schneider 2014; Zhang 2012).

Agricultural modernists, particularly liberal economists, used Weifang and other local cases to advocate for large-scale agricultural production and the entry of capital into the countryside (Du and Guan 1996; Hu and Wu 2001). This was concurrent with the further marketization of agricultural enterprises in the 1990s. There were basically two kinds of agricultural enterprises in China at the time: One was the state-owned agricultural enterprise that was created in the socialist period, including state-owned farms, the enterprises supplying agricultural inputs to the countryside, and those supplying food products to consumers in the city. The other was the rural enterprise, which was of small scale and did business in local areas. In the 1990s, with the further marketization of the economy, particularly the reform to the state-owned enterprises, the state-owned agricultural enterprises were either privatized or granted a substantial degree of flexibility in the market. Some rural enterprises had grown in scale and had become large private enterprises. A good example is the New Hope Group, which started as a small household enterprise specializing in producing and marketing animal feed. By 1995, it had grown into one of the largest private enterprises in China. To date, it has been transformed into a business conglomerate, doing business not only in agri-food sectors, but also in banking, real estate, energy, and chemical industry.[3]

The further marketization motivated large agricultural enterprises to seek the control of agricultural production and markets. Thus it was in their interest to scale up agriculture and open up the countryside for the inflow of large capital. In February 1996, the Ministry of Agriculture held a national forum to promote agricultural industrialization. Central and local officials, academics, financial institutions, and agricultural enterprises attended the forum (Huang 1996). In September 1997, the resolution of the 15th Party Congress endorsed agricultural industrialization. In October 1998, the CCP Central Committee issued a guideline document on the future development of agriculture, which approved agricultural industrialization as a major measure to achieve agricultural modernization. In addition, the document highlighted the importance of agribusiness companies in agricultural industrialization and called to support these companies.[4] Thereafter, agricultural industrialization has become the guiding principle of Chinese agricultural development and was emphasized in nearly all important official documents.

Agricultural industrialization was first implemented in the form of "company + households" (*gongsi jia nonghu*), that is, agribusiness companies are connected with a large number of farm households, often based on the signing of farming contracts. It is a form of contract farming, which has been practiced in many developing countries (Little 1994). Contract farming seems a middle way to scale up agriculture while preserving peasants' land rights.

To make the policy of contract farming work, two conditions must be met, but the household system makes it a challenge to meet either condition. The first condition is that all or most households in a village or a township should be willing to enter contracts with agribusiness companies. Not all areas meet this condition. For example, the amount of land every household cultivates is so small in some provinces that many do not regard farming as a major source of income but use the land to grow crops for self-consumption or to absorb semi-labor such as the elderly. Their main income is derived from nonfarm businesses or migrant work. Thus these households are not very keen to participate in contract farming.

In addition, contract farming that involves hundreds of rural households requires coordination, but agribusiness companies are often unable or unwilling to take on this task for their lack of authority over the households or the high cost of coordination. Thus, villages or local governments usually did the coordination. In some regions, county and township officials were so eager to promote agricultural industrialization that they forced all rural households into contracts with agribusiness companies. However, such coercive policies would backfire if the project of agricultural industrialization failed because rural households would demand compensation from the local government.

A common solution to the two problems is to transfer land from farm households to large farms or agribusiness companies. It is easier to coordinate a small number of large farms in contract farming. Should the land be transferred to an agribusiness company no external coordination would be needed at all. However, although land transfers were permitted, the Chinese state was reluctant to push hard on it in the 1990s, as land in the countryside provided a source of livelihood for more than 700 million peasants. Any attempt to take away land rights from peasants on a large scale would trigger protests and massive resistance, undermining the rule of the regime. As I will show below, it was not until the recent years that the Chinese state had formally relaxed the restrictions on land transfer.

In a nutshell, the 1990s saw the resurgence of the ideology of agricultural modernization and its growing dominance in the policy-making process. Under this ideology, small household farms are perceived as a hurdle to modernization and must be integrated into the production and trade networks of large agrarian capital, lest they be replaced with large farms. A series of agricultural policies in the 1990s, including land transfer, agricultural industrialization, and support for agribusiness companies, were made according to this ideology. I will further discuss land transfer and agribusiness below. The next section looks at another key factor: grain security.

Grain security: the Sword of Damocles

In 1994, Lester Brown, president of the World Watch Institute, published a report entitled *Who Will Feed China*, triggering a firestorm of skepticism over China's ability to feed its population in the future. Brown's warning appeared credible at least on the surface: China was the most populous country in the world, with a population of 1.2 billion, or 22 percent of the world total, in the early 1990s. However, it must feed this enormous population with only 7 percent of the world's arable land and 6 percent of global freshwater resources. In addition, Brown noted that China had been experiencing rapid industrialization and urbanization, which would reduce the resources for grain production and increase the demand for food (Brown 1994; 1995). Interestingly, Brown's prediction that China would import an enormous quantity of grain was made based on the comparison of China with other East Asian economies such as Japan, South Korea, and Taiwan, which are all major food importers (more details can be found in Chapter 6). This comparative perspective holds the implications for examining the question whether China follows the East Asian development path, an issue to which I will return in the book's Conclusion.

To dissipate the fear and skepticism emanating from Brown's report, the Chinese government repeatedly assured the world that China was able to produce sufficient food. In November 1996, China sent a delegation of senior officials, including the prime minister to Rome, to attend the World Food Summit, and the key message of the delegation was that China could feed itself. Right before the summit, the government released a white paper declaring that China would produce 95 percent of the grain that it consumes (State Council of China 1996).

The paper laid out specific goals and means on how to boost domestic grain production. However, despite the apparent confidence that the paper was intended to project, the Chinese government was actually anxious and uncertain about its ability to meet the goal of grain self-sufficiency. For instance, it was revealed that Chinese top leaders, including Jiang Zemin and Li Peng, were deeply concerned about the problem of grain security (Wen 2016). In the key documents issued between 1996 and 1998, the problem of grain security was given top priority, attesting to the worry over the country's ability in grain production.[5]

The strong reaction of the Chinese government to Brown's report should be understood in the historical context. In the socialist period, due to rapid population growth and the limited productivity of farmland, feeding the huge population had always been a challenge. As Chris Bramall noted,

> One of the main challenges faced by the Chinese state during the twentieth century was that of ensuring food security for its population, and the history of Chinese development during this period is, in many respects, a history of the search for solutions to this overriding problem.
>
> (2009, 213)

The matters were made worse by the famine (1959–61) after the Great Leap Forward. Thereafter, the main goal of agricultural policy was to produce sufficient food for the growing population. The slogan "take grain as the key link" (*yiliang weigang*) during the Cultural Revolution became a guiding principle of agricultural policy at the time. To ensure the sufficient supply of grain, some local governments went as far as to restrict cash crops and sideline activities for fear that these would take land and labor resources away from grain production (Bramall 1993, 193; Friedman, Pickowicz, and Selden 1991). In addition, the US-led embargo against China during and after the Korean War also led Chinese Communists to believe that grain security through domestic production was a strategic national interest and the foundation of the regime (Bramall 2009, 99–100). Such belief has not changed even after the Sino-US relationship thawed and the country opened up its economy.

As noted earlier, the legitimacy of the rural reform was derived from the increase in grain production in the early 1980s. However, grain production stagnated in the late 1980s. The problem was partly attributed to the breakdown of irrigation facilities as the government cut the public irrigation investment nearly in half in the second half of the 1980s (Fan, Zhang, and Zhang 2004). In addition, it was also argued that the dismantling of collective organizations made the matters worse because unorganized peasants could not take collective action on irrigation, which was a public good (Hinton 1990). This prompted the government to enact a new policy in 1991 that mandated that each rural laborer contribute 15 to 30 days in a year to public works such as road construction and irrigation maintenance. The central government also increased public investment in irrigation, although the increase appeared puny as compared with the rapid growth in urban and industrial investments. In short, grain security has been like the Sword of Damocles hanging over the Chinese ruling elites: Any sign of grain shortages or even a discussion of the issue would trigger a strong reaction.

Brown's report came against this background. Grain production declined in 1991 and did not recover until 1993. To increase grain production, the Chinese state raised grain procurement prices in 1994 and 1996, together by 82 percent. In 1995, the Chinese state mandated that the provincial governors must be responsible for the sufficient supply of grain in their provinces, mainly by means of increasing production, purchasing grain from the market, and/or stockpiling enough grain to prepare for possible shortages. This policy was called *midaizi shengzhang fuzezhi*, literally, the "responsibility system of provincial governors for the rice bag" (Zhang, Huang, and Yan 1996). Grain production started to grow in 1995, and it reached a new height in 1996, exceeding 500 million tons (Figure 4.1). The growth of grain production had partly mitigated the fear of food shortages.

Although the Chinese government managed to increase grain production by encouraging farm households to grow grain crops, it did not hold much confidence in these small farmers. Rather, the government placed its bid behind modern farm organizations, including large farms and agribusiness companies, which, the government believed, could meet the challenge of raising grain production in the future (Zhang, Huang and Yan 1996). As a result, grain security was employed as a justification for agricultural modernization. Government officials and academics argue that large farms and agribusiness companies should be supported in order to produce sufficient grain for sake of grain security. From the perspective of agribusiness companies, the government's concern over food security offered a window of opportunity for them to lobby

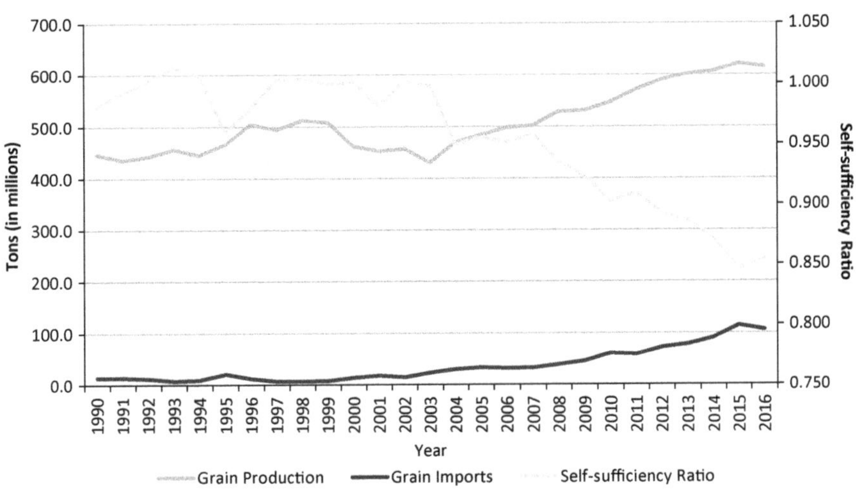

Figure 4.1 China's grain production, grain imports, and grain self-sufficiency ratio.

Sources: China Statistical Yearbooks (1991–2017).

for favorable policies by demonstrating their importance in promoting China's grain production (Zhan 2017a).

Agricultural modernists and agribusiness companies lobbied for land transfer and large-scale farming based on the ideology and grain security, but the policymakers at the top had been cautious on the issues of land in the 1990s, as land provided livelihoods for hundreds of millions. The 1998 guideline document for future agricultural development supported agricultural modernization, but it also reaffirmed the Household Responsibility System as the foundation of agricultural development in China. It went as far as to declare that rural households could adapt to modern agriculture by adopting advanced technologies and means of production. The document showed explicit support for agribusiness companies, but it also encouraged these companies to work with farm households rather than substituting for the latter. Large agribusiness companies were called "dragonhead companies" (*longtou qiye*). In the model of "company + households," the agribusiness company, like the dragon's head, leads a large number of rural households, which consist of the dragon's body, in agriculture. This model was believed to benefit both rural households and agribusiness companies. The document also permitted land transfers, but it held that only a very small number of places were suitable for scaled-up agriculture, thus land transfers must be implemented with the consent of peasants, and no excuse should be made to force peasants to lease out land. The cautious stance was again expressed in a 2001 document on land transfer, which explicitly discouraged the practice of transferring land from households to agribusiness companies. It holds instead that land transfers should mainly occur between farm households.[6]

Thus the change to the land system in China has been a gradual process, and it was only until recently that the Chinese state made substantial changes to the system by permitting and even encouraging the transferring of land from peasants to agribusiness companies and large farms. This is the "new land reform" noted in the Introduction. Nevertheless, the seeds of change were sown in the 1990s. Under the ideology of agricultural modernization and the anxiety over grain security, the Chinese state had greatly increased support for agribusiness companies. As I will show below, the number and the scale of agribusiness companies have grown rapidly over the past two decades, and their influence in agricultural production, commodity trade and policymaking has greatly increased and become a major force behind the new land reform.

The support for agribusiness companies was not limited to domestic enterprises. The government also granted permission to foreign agribusiness companies to run business in China. After the market reform, China was eager to join GATT (General Agreement on Tariffs and Trade [WTO after 1994]). To be accepted as a member, the Chinese government had liberalized its economy at a much faster pace in the 1990s than the preceding decade. Foreign capital poured in, turning it into the largest FDI receiver among developing countries in 1992 and thereafter. To facilitate the acceptance to the WTO, China also voluntarily eased restrictions on foreign agribusiness companies in the mid-1990s. In 1999, it had made significant concessions over agriculture in the negotiation with the

United States. As a result, foreign agribusiness enterprises have gained a growing market share. Large transnational agribusiness corporations such as ADM, Bunge, Cargill, Louis Dreyfus, and Monsanto have exerted an increasing degree of control over agricultural inputs (such as seeds, fertilizers. and pesticide); food processing; and international food trade in China (Wang 2011; Yan, Chen, and Ku 2016).

Raising grain prices in 1994 and 1996 stimulated grain production, but it did not do much to improve peasants' conditions due to the serious urban bias policies. Moreover, the price hikes drove up the prices of agricultural inputs while private grain traders who had political connections could buy cheap from peasants and sell dear to state-owned storage houses (Deng 1994; Pan 1997). As a result, peasants might have gained substantially less than the state intended. The effect of the price stimulation on grain production did not last long. The production started to decline in 1999, and was down to 431 million tons in 2003, which is 15.8 percent less than the highest record of 512 million in 1998 (Figure 4.1). The decline seemed to validate Brown's gloomy prediction, and again stirred up the fear over grain security in the early 2000s.

Building the new socialist countryside, but for whom?

The rural crisis and the declining grain production forced the Chinese state to enact a series of policies after 2003 to promote rural development and grain farming. These policies fall under the banner of "building the new socialist countryside (*jianshe shehui zhuyi xinnongcun*)." This is widely considered a crucial turning point in China's rural policy because the initiative partly mitigated the previous urban bias by allocating more resources to the countryside (Ahlers 2014; Ahlers and Schubert 2009). Some policy changes were already underway even before this comprehensive initiative. In 1999, the central government launched the program of "Develop West" (*xibu dakaifa*), which is aimed to narrow the disparity between eastern (coastal) and western regions by increasing financial support for 12 western inland provinces.

Under the grand strategy of "building the new socialist countryside," the first notable policy is the abolition of nearly all agricultural taxes and fees between 2003 and 2006. Starting from 2004, the central government also offered agricultural subsidies, including direct grain subsidy (*liangshi zhijie butie*), inputs subsidy (*nongzi zonghe butie*), quality seed subsidy (*liangzhong butie*), and agricultural machinery subsidy (*nongji butie*). The first three subsidies were mainly assessed based on the size of landholding and paid directly to the bank accounts of rural households. The agricultural machinery subsidy was paid in the form of reimbursement for actual purchases of machines. In 2015, the four subsidies amounted to 165.2 billion yuan (25.8 billion US dollars). It can be estimated that one *mu* of land (0.067 hectare) received about 80 yuan (12 US dollars) for subsidies in 2014.[7] An average household that farms seven *mu* could thus receive 560 yuan a year. In Aohan, the size of landholding is relatively large, and the average farm size is 24 *mu* per household. Thus an average household could receive 1,920 yuan a year.

In addition, the Chinese state has greatly increased financial support for agriculture and rural areas with various project funds (*xiangmu ziji*). These project funds cover many aspects of the rural economy, including, but not limited to, infrastructure (most importantly roads and irrigation facilities), application of modern technologies, environmental protection, soil improvement, land consolidation, animal husbandry, housing, drinking water, waste disposal, rural cooperatives, agro-tourism, and poverty reduction. According to the Ministry of Finance and the Ministry of Agriculture and Rural Affairs, key areas of financial support for rural development in 2018 included 37 categories.[8] Chinese scholars see the expansion of project funds as the evidence of the emergence of a new form of rural governance: "governing through projects" (*xiangmu zhili*) (Zhe and Chen 2011). The new form of governance is substantively different. For example, the main task of rural officials in the 1990s was to collect taxes, while in the recent decade, they focused on how to secure more project funds from upper governments (Bernstein and Lü 2003; Takeuchi 2014). In 2013, a village party secretary in Hunan Province told me that he spent two-thirds of his time not in the village, but in the cities, as he needed to cultivate relationships with officials in order to get more project funds. The Chinese government also intentionally used project funds to achieve its policy goals, such as social stability and agricultural modernization. The financial resources that have been allocated to the countryside through agricultural subsidies and project funds are enormous. Between 2008 and 2013, the central government provided 5.85 trillion yuan (928 billion US dollars) for rural areas (Liu 2014). In 2012, the financial support for rural areas amounted to 1.1 trillion yuan, and the support has grown every year thereafter (Xiang 2012). Thus it can be estimated that the central government has allocated at least ten trillion yuan to rural areas over the past decade (2008–17). In addition, local governments were required to match central funds with at least equal amounts of financial support. Thus, the total financial support for rural areas from the governments would be more than 20 trillion yuan (3.1 trillion US dollars) in the past decade.

Finally, the Chinese state increased public spending on rural health care and old-age support. It established a new health-care system in the countryside in 2003 – the New Rural Cooperative Medical Care, under which peasants could purchase subsidized over-the-counter drugs and join health insurance that would reimburse a proportion of medical expenses of treating serious diseases. According to the Ministry of Health, the goal of the program is to reimburse the expenses of hospitalization up to six times the local average annual income. By the first quarter of 2009, the program had covered 830 million people, almost the entire rural population (Bai 2009). In 2009, the central government launched an old-age insurance program for rural areas in 2009: the "Rural Residents' Basic Old-age Insurance" (*nongcun jumin jiben yanglao baoxian*). The program covers all rural population aged over 16 (excluding students) (Stepan and Lu 2016). In 2014, it was merged with a similar urban program into the new "Rural–Urban Residents' Basic Old-age Insurance." The program created individual retirement accounts, which are paid from two sources: the government subsidy and the account holder's contribution.

The government subsidy is paid to the basic retirement account, which provides a basic pension every month to the account holders after they reach 60. The basic pension was 70 yuan in 2016, and one would receive more than this amount if he or she made individual contributions to the account.

Peasants have benefited from the policies of "building the new socialist countryside." They are relieved of the burden of paying taxes while receiving subsidies from the state. The increased financial support has also improved rural infrastructure and agricultural conditions. Furthermore, the new programs of health care and old-age support have the effect of mitigating the glaring rural poverty among the sick and the elderly.

The positive effect of the new policies on the rural economy is also evidenced by the growing value of farmland, which indicates the increase in farmland's surplus generating capacity. In Aohan, peasants would give out land for free in the 1990s when they migrated to the city, and the annual rent for irrigated land was only 100 yuan per *mu*. The rent has increased considerably in the recent decade. One *mu* of irrigated farmland was rented out for 500 yuan a year on average when I was doing field work in the county in 2015. According to the head of Grass Village, farmland had become the number-one cause for disputes among rural households in the recent decade. These disputes were usually over the boundaries of farms and the terms of land leasing. In the 1990s, however, peasants rarely disputed over land, since it could not bring much income.[9] The increase in rent has been a general phenomenon that I observed in all of my field sites. In rural areas of Changsha, Hunan Province, one *mu* of rice farm was rented out for 400 yuan a year in 2013. In Chengdu of Sichuan Province, where farmland was used to grow tree saplings, the annual rent reached 1,000 yuan per *mu* in 2015. In Jiamusi of Heilongjiang Province, where farm size is relatively large, a hectare of farmland was rented out for 6,000 yuan a year in 2016 – that is, 400 yuan a *mu*.

While peasants benefited from the new policies, agribusiness companies have benefited even more. My research shows that the agricultural subsidies paid to peasants have been largely eaten away by the growing prices of agricultural inputs such as fertilizers, seeds, and pesticides. Between 2004 and 2014, the costs of agricultural inputs including seeds, fertilizers, pesticides and use of machinery for one *mu* of grain crop increased from 136 yuan to 352 yuan, up 216 yuan or 158.8 percent. As noted above, the subsidy payment was only 80 yuan per *mu* in 2014, far less than the increase in input costs. This has undercut the profit of grain farming. If the costs of land and labor were taken into account, the profit from one *mu* of grain crop had actually declined from 196.5 yuan in 2004 to 124.8 yuan in 2014, down 36.5 percent (National Development and Reform Commission of China 2015, 3–5). By contrast, the agribusiness companies that supplied these inputs had grown rapidly for the same period, with their sales and profits quadrupling or even more (Zhan 2017a, 155).

Additionally, the policies of "building the new socialist countryside" have not lessened but strengthened the ideology and practice of agricultural modernization, which tend to marginalize small farmers and villagers who derive livelihoods from both farm and nonfarm activities. Although no statistics are available, there is no doubt that agribusiness companies and large farms have received the lion's share of agricultural project funds. Influenced by agricultural modernization, the new policies, though pro-rural, are aimed to promote the application of new technologies and the scaling-up of agriculture. Thus the allocation of project funds often favors agribusiness companies and large farms. I have found many cases that the project funds were given to companies and large farms. For example, funds for rural cooperatives were supposed to benefit all rural households in the cooperatives, but in reality large farms in the cooperative often controlled these funds. In some cases, the agribusiness companies, with the help of local officials, set up fake rural cooperatives in order to receive these funds. In recent years, the central government has explicitly stated that more financial support would be given to large farms and agribusiness companies. For example, the first three agricultural subsidies were merged into one subsidy in 2016, which is called "subsidy for agricultural support and protection" (*nongye zhichi baohu butie*). Under the new policy, the subsidy will no longer be evenly distributed; rather, a much larger share will be given to large farms (Zeng 2016; Zhan 2017a, 158). In Wanzhou of Chongqing, for instance, a farm larger than 50 *mu* (3.3 hectares) received the subsidy of 230 yuan per *mu* in 2016, while an ordinary farming household only received 72 yuan per *mu* (Ying 2016).

A more serious consequence is the acceleration of land consolidation and concentration, as the slogan "building the new socialist countryside" has often been used by local government and agrarian capital as an excuse to take land from peasants. After losing land rights to large farms and agribusiness companies, peasants have to move to cities. These peasants are given urban *hukou* and become urban residents, but many of them hold no job or a precarious job. Some would easily fall into poverty once the economy slows down in the future. In this scenario, agribusiness companies and large farms would exclusively reap the benefits of building the new socialist countryside.

Land transfer and the discourse of "who will cultivate the land?"

While the central government was cautious in the late 1990s and early 2000s, local governments and agribusiness companies were less restrained in pushing for land transfer and land concentration. The aforementioned 2001 document on land transfer can be seen as an attempt to rein in the reckless land transfers at the local level. A good example of such cases is the notorious "Lantian Scandal." Lantian Stock was a large agribusiness company in Honghu Prefecture of Hubei Province and was listed in the stock market in 1996. Its main businesses included soft drinks, animal husbandry, aquaculture, and commercial crops such as lotus roots. By colluding with officials, forging accounting reports, and relying on bank loans, its stock value had expanded exponentially until the scandal was exposed in 2001. The company went bankrupt in 2002, and those who were responsible were tried and convicted. It was revealed that the local government helped transfer at least 333 hectares of farmland to the company. The bankruptcy of the company led to more than 7,000 peasants losing livelihoods as the company was unable to pay the rent or provide jobs for these peasants (Chen, Guo, and Li 2002).[10]

Jingzhong Ye (2015) summarized five main models of land transfer in China.[11] The *two-field system* (*liangtian zhi*) is a popular practice that divides land into subsistence land (*kouliang tian*) and responsibility land (*zeren tian*). Subsistence land is typically allocated on the basis of household size to ensure that each household produces enough for its own consumption needs. Responsibility land is allocated to households to engage in large-scale agricultural production. There may be restrictions on how they can use the land and the possibility that some of the land may be taken away and allocated to a large farm and agribusiness company.

The *scaled-up operation* (*guimo jingying*) has been practiced in many places (such as Shunyi County in Beijing Municipality) since 1987. In this system, plots are taken away from peasants prior to the expiration of the contracts and reassigned to fewer selected peasant households in order to increase the scale of operations. In the recent decade, plots that were taken away from peasants were often leased to large farms or agribusiness companies.

Reverse contracting (*fanzu daobao*), a system under which village authorities rent the allocated lands back from peasants, and then lease the land to a third entity. This practice was first found mainly in the southeast coastal provinces, and it has since spread to the whole country.

The *land trust* (*tudi xintuo*), an innovation to develop a local land market where villagers can "deposit" the land rights of their contracted land, and the trust then acts as a broker, actively matching supply with demand, which could come from outside agribusinesses. This practice was first tried in Shaoxing County in Zhejiang Province in 2001, and it was later adopted in the land experiments in Chengdu and Chongqing and became well known through media reports.

Auctioning four wastelands (*sihuang paimai*) is a practice that started from the late 1980s onward in Lüliang Prefecture in Shanxi Province. This is a new path designed to tackle soil erosion on the barren mountains of the Loess Plateau. Instead of land being allocated to peasants on the basis of household size, wasteland use rights are put up for open auction. There are four types of wasteland: waste mountains, waste gullies, waste hills, and waste riverbanks. Many localities auctioned off collective woodland or other collective lands, even though these lands were not *waste*lands.

Among the five models, only auctioning four wastes was unconditionally permitted by the central government, since it did not take away allocated lands from peasants. The 2001 document explicitly prohibited the practice of reverse contracting for it violated peasants' land use rights. The rest of three approaches were allowed only if peasants gave their consent. That is to say, the central government set restrictions on the transfer of land to agribusiness companies and the scaled-up farming in the early 2000s.

Local governments and agribusiness companies have gradually pushed back the restrictions on land transfer. The restriction on large farms was dropped in the mid-2000s, and the central government encouraged agricultural scaling-up as long as peasants agreed to transfer out land. The prohibition of reverse contracting was also dropped in central documents after 2008 (Li 2012). Furthermore, the restriction on land transfers to agribusiness companies was removed in the later documents, and in 2013, the central No. 1 document[12] explicitly supported land transfers to agribusiness companies. In reality, no punitive measures have ever been taken against local officials who transferred land from peasants to agribusiness companies. Local officials would only be scrutinized if the deal of land transfer met peasants' resistance and led to a mass-protest incident. The gradual relaxation of the restrictions in the past decade and a half had to do with the following three changes: the growing strength of agribusiness companies, the policies of building the new socialist countryside, and the rise of the discourse of "who will cultivate farmland" (*shuilai zhongdi*).

With the support of the state, agribusiness companies have expanded rapidly in the past two decades. Large agribusiness companies are called "dragonhead enterprises" (*longtou qiye*), whose numbers grew from 27,000 in 2000 to 129,000 in 2016 (Ministry of Agriculture 2016). This figure only includes those having received official recognition. To qualify as a dragonhead, an enterprise must meet a set of "operational, financial and farm integration criteria," and apply to the government in the region in which it is located for the title (Schneider 2017; Ye 2015, 314–37). The sale of all dragonhead companies reached 9.2 trillion yuan (1.5 trillion US dollars), with a net profit of 550 billion yuan (87 billion US dollars). With growing strength, agribusiness companies exerted increasing influence over central and local governments. In Aohan, the local government offered favorable policies to draw in dragonhead companies, including building production bases and offering long-term land leases. Similar capital-friendly policies have been found in my other field sites. At the central level, the Ministry of Agriculture has been an enthusiastic supporter of large agribusiness companies, and often showcases the rapid expansion of these companies in its reports and documents.

The policies of building the new socialist countryside also facilitated the transfer of land. Many project funds from the central government favored the large-scale operation, thus most of these funds went to large farms and agribusiness companies. After receiving the fund from the central government, local officials would cite the central authority to legitimize their action of transferring land from peasants. Among all project funds, the fund for land consolidation (*tudi zhengli*, or *tudi zhengzhi*) played a particularly important role in facilitating land transfer and concentration. The Ministry of Land Resources made national plans to consolidate farmland in 2003. The purpose of the plans was to reclaim wasteland into farmland, consolidate fragmented lands, and build high-productivity lands.[13] However, the projects of land consolidation have often been used to consolidate household farm plots into a large farm. After the farm plots are consolidated, the previous boundaries are removed and the new farmland would be leased to a few large farms or agribusiness companies instead of previous rural households. In Hunan Province, I found that a county government consolidated 500 *mu* of farmland (33 hectares) and rented the consolidated land to a few households to grow tobacco. In Chengdu of Sichuan Province, the local government launched the project of "golden land" (*jintudi gongcheng*) to consolidate small farm plots. According to the propaganda of the Chengdu government, the project would greatly benefit peasants, who could receive rent for leasing out land and work as workers either for the agribusiness companies or in the city (Xinhua 2008). My field research in Chengdu found, however, that agribusiness companies only hired a very small number of rural laborers. When the agribusiness companies were unable to make an acceptable rate of profit, which was often the case due to market competition, they would leave without paying peasants the rent, leading the latter to seek help from the government (Zhan 2017b).

The rise of the discourse of "who will cultivate land" might be even more effective in pushing the policies toward favoring the concentration of land. As noted earlier, grain security has been the Sword of Damocles over Chinese ruling elites. An important goal of building the new socialist countryside is to increase domestic grain production. In March 2006, Wen Jiabao, the then prime minister, announced that China must maintain a red line of 1.8 billion *mu* of farmland (120 million hectares), that is, the total amount of land must not fall below 120 million hectares. This red line was written into the *Outline of the 11th Five-Year Plan for the National Economic and Social Development*.[14] The red line policy was made against the background that the acreage of farmland had been shrinking due to rapid urban expansion. As I have shown elsewhere, the red line policy has compelled local governments to come up with many "innovative" ways to bypass the restriction on the conversion of farmland to urban land (Zhan 2017b).

While the red line policy concerns land resources for grain production, the discourse of "who will cultivate land" points to the labor force. Due to the massive rural-urban migration, the younger and able-bodied populations have left the countryside for the city. The left-behind populations include women, children, and the elderly. Agriculture, which generates fewer surpluses as compared with nonfarm jobs, is left to women and the elderly, leading to the feminization of agriculture and "ageing farming populations" (*laoren nongye*) (De Brauw *et al.* 2008; Huang 2012). This appears at odds with the policy of agricultural modernization, which requires an agricultural labor force that can adopt modern technologies and take on large-scale production. Against this background, the question of "who will cultivate land" was raised. The implicit answer to the question is that no one would cultivate land in the future, or only the old and the weak would engage in agriculture, if no reforms were made. And this would have disastrous impact on China's grain security. The question was raised in the early 1990s, but it was not until the mid-2000s that it occupied a prominent place in official discussions over grain security. In recent years, the question was brought up time and again in official documents, media reports and social media, suggesting that an agricultural crisis would arrive if no action were taken. Like Lester Brown's "Who will feed China," this scare tactic also seems very effective in setting the agenda of China's agricultural policy. In October

2008, the Third Plenary Session of the 17th CCP Central Committee adopted a guiding document on agriculture and rural areas,[15] which permitted scaled-up agricultural entities such as specialized households, family farms, and rural cooperatives. The 2013 No. 1 document explicitly called to create new types of agricultural entities (*xinxing nongye jingying zhuti*), which included agribusiness companies, in addition to the above three types. In May 2017, the central government issued an ad hoc document on promoting these new entities.[16] The new agricultural entities are characterized as having a young, professional labor force, engaging in large-scale, market-oriented operations, and employing modern technologies.

The discourse of "who will cultivate land" not only overtly discriminates against women and the elderly, but also oversimplifies the complexity of the reality. An apparent irony is that grain production had grown consecutively in official statistics for 12 years from 2004 to 2015 (Figure 4.1 above), when most of the farmland was still cultivated by the members of small farm households, including women and the elderly. In other words, it was the so-called weak and old who contributed to the remarkable increase in grain production. Studies found no significant decrease in the productivity of farms cultivated by the elderly (Hu and Zhong 2012; Ministry of Agriculture 2015). My own research found that the rural elderly could be classified into the young elderly (aged 50–65) and the older elderly (65 or over). The young elderly are often the best farmers, whereas the older elderly tend to reduce the size of farm and engage in subsistence or leisure farming. In addition, I found the emergence of a younger rural labor force in Aohan (Inner Mongolia), Heilongjiang, Hunan, and Sichuan, who aged between 35 and 50, and most of them returned from years of migrant work in the city.

My fieldwork did show that grain farming was undermined in some regions, but the main reason was not the shortage of a labor force, but the relatively low profitability of grain farming in the context of rapid urbanization and rising rural household income (Zhan and Huang 2017). Farmland would be underused or unused for grain farming in two scenarios. One is that the land is farmed to produce grain for self-consumption. In this case, the land use intensity is reduced. For example, I found that many households in a county in Hunan province switched their rice farms from double cropping to single cropping. These housholds earned their income from nonfarm sources while only farming the land to produce grain for self-consumption, for which the single cropping is sufficient. Some farmlands were left uncultivated, but these farms were mostly of low productivity due to poor soil quality or having no access to irrigation. The other scenario is to switch from grain crops to cash crops. The demand for cash crops such as vegetables, fruits, medical herbs, and sugar canes has been rising, and growing labor-intensive cash crops could bring much more income than grain farming, particularly on small plots of land (Zhan, Zhang, and He 2018).

The solution to the problems does not have to be aggressively pushing for scaled-up grain farming. First, rural households have been voluntarily transferring out land to fellow villagers who are willing to take in more land, but in a much more flexible way than the government-forced land transfers. With more government support, these farms can to some extent solve the underuse problem. Second, subsistence farming or the reduced intensity of land use is not necessarily a bad thing as it provides an opportunity to recover the productivity of land, given that much of the farmland in China has been overused, resulting in land pollution and soil degradation. Finally, the current transition to a diet consisting of more meat and resource-intensive food items is neither healthy nor sustainable, and scaling up agriculture can only make such matters worse. The alternative solution would be adopted to promote a healthy diet based on environment-friendly and labor-intensive methods of farming.

The rise of agrarian capitalism and the future of the industrious revolution

In a 2008 article, Qian Forrest Zhang and John Donaldson ascertained that agrarian capitalism had been emerging in China. Based on case studies, they identified several pathways of how rural laborers or small farmers were incorporated into the production process and commodity chains of agribusiness companies. Ten years later, the rise of agrarian capitalism in China has been more evident than ever. Not only have agribusiness companies exercised an increasing degree of control over agricultural production and commodity trade, but also a significant proportion of farmland is transferred to large farms and agribusiness companies.

By 2016, the number of units of agricultural industrialization (*nongye chanyehua zuzhi*), which mainly consist of agribusiness companies, reached 386,000. Among them, 130,300 are dragonhead companies, that is, they received official recognition due to their large size. Through contract farming and land leasing, these companies had incorporated 60 percent of crop production and two-thirds of animal husbandry into their production and marketing networks. The annual sale of all dragonhead companies grew to 9.7 trillion yuan (1.5 trillion US dollars), and their scale also expanded considerably. In 2016, 253 agribusiness companies had a sales income of more than 1.5 billion yuan, and 103 companies earned more than 4.5 billion yuan in sales (Gao and Guo 2018).

The scale of land transfers also grew rapidly in the recent decade. In 2008, 106 million *mu* of land (7 million hectares) was transferred, accounting for 8.7 percent of all land allocated to peasants. By 2016, the acreage of land transferred increased to 471 million *mu*, 35.1 percent of the total, more than quadrupled (Table 4.1). In statistics, only about 10 percent of land was transferred to agribusiness companies. However, my research showed that many agribusiness companies controlled farmland through rural cooperatives, which accounted for more than 20 percent of land transferred. A usual strategy is that the agribusiness company works with local governments or village authorities to create a rural cooperative in the name of households. The company leases farmland from these households and runs the farm directly. The strategy could bypass the restriction on transferring land to agribusiness companies (before 2013) and allow the

Table 4.1 The scale of land transfers in rural China: 2008–16

Year	*Areas of land transferred (million* mu*)*	*The share of transferred land in the total land allocated to peasants (%)*
2008	106	8.7
2009	150	12.0
2010	187	15.0
2011	228	19.0
2012	254	21.2
2013	340	26.0
2014	403	30.3
2015	447	33.3
2016	471	35.1

Sources: Ye (2015, 326) and Chanye xinxi wang (2017).

company to receive project funds in the name of the rural cooperative. I estimated that the land transferred to agribusiness companies could be up to 20 percent of the total transferred land (Zhan 2017b, 159).

Another important change is the emergence of non-corporate large farms, which are usually called "specialized big households" (*zhuanye dahu*), or large family farms in the Chinese context. By 2016, the number of family farms reached 877,000, of which the Ministry of Agriculture recognized 414,000. The average size of ministry-recognized family farms is 170 *mu* (11.3 hectares), about 25 times a common household farm. In addition, there were 1.79 million registered peasant cooperatives (Yu 2017). My research and other studies show that some cooperatives are disguised private large farms. Specialized households or private investors use them to lease land from peasants and to receive project funds from the governments (Hu, Zhang, and Donaldson 2017).

Based on the analysis above, I estimate that the land transferred to large farms would account for at least 20 percent of the total farmland allocated to rural households. Here large farms refer to all farms (including corporate farms) with a size of ten times a common household farm or above in a local area, for example, in a county. Nationwide, the average size of a large farm is five hectares or above.

The rise of agrarian capitalism has far-reaching implications for economic prospects and rural livelihoods in China. The most pessimistic scenario would be that the majority of the rural population is forced off the land and forced to move into the city. However, the urban capitalist economy is not able to absorb such a large population, thus giving rise to a swelling class of urban poor who do not have a stable job or a secure livelihood. The case of South Africa, which will be discussed in the next chapter, is close to the situation in this scenario.

The most optimistic scenario, which is often taken by agricultural modernists as a fact or a natural path of development, is that the urban sectors are able to absorb the rural populations released from land concentrations. As a result, the rural population will fall below 10 percent of the national population while 90 percent of the population is living in the city. Moreover, large farmers are able to earn a good living by producing food and other agricultural produce for the urban sectors. The urban workers hold stable jobs, receive social welfare and earn a secure livelihood. Chinese agricultural modernists often take East Asian economies such as Japan, South Korea, and Taiwan as evidence of this possibility. As I will show in Chapter 6, this scenario is a mirage for the populous countries such as China, and even the three much-smaller East Asian economies have not exactly followed it.

The third scenario is that many of the peasant households are still living in the countryside, but they are completely dominated by agribusiness companies. Although these households have not lost their land rights, they cannot derive much income from farming because the agribusiness companies have taken away most of the profits. These famers constitute the rural poor and are no better off than the urban poor.

The fourth scenario is the emergence of a polarized rural society. Due to land concentration and the penetration of agribusiness companies, a small number of rural elites surge to the top of the rural society, including rich farmers who run large farms with generous subsidies from the state, the managers of agribusiness companies, and rural officials who support these economic elites. Below them are small contract farmers and agricultural laborers working for large farms or corporate farms. There is also a swelling landless rural poor population who could not find any stable job in either rural or urban areas.

The last scenario is a mixture of agrarian capitalism and the industrious revolution. While large farms and agribusiness companies have gained strength in the countryside, many rural households hold on to their land and fight off forced land transfers. They use the land for more remunerative undertakings such as high-value cash crops, small-scale industrial production, e-commerce, and agro-tourism, in addition to food production. They would also combine farm and nonfarm activities such as migrant work in the city.

At the local level, the situations described above could all be found in various parts of the Chinese countryside depending on an array of local factors such as local policy, land struggles, nonfarm opportunities, and the strength of large farms and agribusiness companies. At the national level, the situation would still be close to the last scenario, but it has been moving toward the fourth scenario. If the push for land concentrations continues and even intensifies, it would be moving further toward the most pessimistic scenario.

However, there are good reasons to believe that the most pessimistic scenario would be unlikely in China.[17] After two decades of the push for land transfers and concentrations, more than 70 percent of the farmland is still farmed by farm households. The small-scale production, which often combines farm and nonfarm activities and bases itself in the rural community, has been thriving in many places I visited. The emergence of e-commerce and the massive expansion of the transportation networks (including roads, highways, trains, and even airports) into rural areas have created new opportunities for small rural holders. In other words, the potential for the industrious revolution, though undermined by the rise of agrarian capitalism, is enhanced in some other aspects, particularly with regard to market infrastructure.

As far as state policy is concerned, the push for large-scale production and the ardent support for agribusiness companies are evident in recent policies. However, the concerns over the negative impacts of land concentrations have also grown in policy circles. As Jane Hayward (2017, 539) noted in a recent article, "China's state policies are not governed by a single, coherent logic, and we should avoid drawing broader conclusions by extrapolating from a long-trusted paradigm (of depeasantization)." In October 2017, the 19th CCP National Congress announced the extension of the current farmland policy by another 30 years, to 2053. That is, peasants will continue to hold rights, either nominal or actual, to the allocated lands. The 2018 No. 1 Document laid out a new strategy of "rural revitalization" (*xiangcun zhenxing*).[18] At least three key policy points in the document appear at odds with agrarian capitalism, but more in line with the industrious revolution. First of all, the document calls to support *small* (emphasis added) farm households and to bring them into the track of modern agriculture. Second, the document calls to help rural households engage in all economic sectors, including farming, manufacturing, and services sectors. This is one of the key characteristics of the industrious revolution, but it does not fit into agrarian capitalism, which idealizes the large-scale industrialized monoculture. Last, the document calls to train the rural labor force and encourage the flow of urban talents to the countryside. The follow-up policy specifications have even discussed "reverse urbanization" (*ni chengshihua*). This is at odds with agrarian capitalism, which is conditioned on displacing the majority of rural populations to make way for large-scale agricultural production. Needless to say, to what extent the strategy will be implemented remains to be seen.

The strategy of rural revitalization is made based on the concerns over rural underdevelopment. It appears increasingly clear to some policymakers that the urban sectors are unable to absorb the displaced rural populations. As Chen Xiwen, a former senior agricultural official, pointed out, "There would still be 450 million people in the countryside even if 70 percent of the population is urbanized" (Chen 2018). However, whether the Chinese cities could absorb 70 percent of the population (more than one billion) is highly questionable, given that a significant proportion of the now so-called urban population consists of rural migrants and the urban poor. The tension between agrarian capitalism and the inability of urban capitalist sectors to absorb labor is not a problem limited to China, but a common development problem in the world, particularly in developing countries. The next two chapters will examine South Africa and the three East Asian economies (Japan, South Korea, and Taiwan) to bring in a comparative perspective.

Notes

1 Interview date: November 11, 2010.

2 Qian Forrest Zhang and John Donaldson (2008) document the criticisms of household farming from the perspective of agricultural modernization (pp. 27–8).

3 For more information please see the company's website: www.newhopegroup.com/.

4 The title of the document is "Decisions by the Central Committee of the Chinese Communist Party on Several Key Issues in Rural and Agricultural Works," which was approved by the 3rd Plenary Session of the 15th Party Congress on October 14, 1998.

5 These documents include *Ninth Five-Year Plan for National Economy and Social Development and the Long-Term Target for 2010* (March 5, 1996), *Report of the 15th National Congress of CPC* (September 12, 1997), *CCP Central Committee's Decision on Major Issues Concerning Agriculture and Rural Areas* (October 14, 1998).

6 "Zhonggong zhongyang guanyu zuohao nonghu chengbaodi shiyongquan liuzhuan gongzuo de tongzhi" (Notice of the CCP Central Committee on properly implementing the work of transferring rural households' contracted land). The document serial number is Zhongfa [2001] 18, and the issuance date 30 December 2001. The document can be accessed at http://jiuban.moa.gov.cn/zwllm/zcfg/flfg/200601/t20060123_540896.htm (accessed on April 26, 2018).

7 The Chinese government reported a subsidy payment of 49 yuan for one *mu* of farmland in 2008 when total annual subsidy payment was 103.0 billion yuan. I thus estimated the payment to be 80 yuan per *mu* in 2014 as the total subsidies had increased to 170 billion yuan. See National Development and Reform Commission of China (2009, 3).

8 The Ministry of Agriculture and Rural Affairs and the Ministry of Finance announced key rural support policies in 2018. www.gov.cn/xinwen/2018–04/04/content_5279770.htm (accessed April 27, 2018).

9 Interview IM-85, November 10, 2010.

10 For more information on the scandal, please see http://finance.qq.com/zt2010/fyjjltsh/.

11 I have made some changes to the description of the five models to reflect newest developments.

12 The No. 1 document refers to the first policy document that the central government issues in a year, which provides key guidelines on one or multiple important policy issues.

13 The document was titled *Quanguo tudi kaifa zhengli guihua (2001–2010)* [*The national planning on land development and consolidation (2001–2010)*], which can be accessed at www.china.com.cn/policy/txt/2003–03/17/content_5294768.htm (Accessed on April 30, 2018). The ministry also released the national plans for the periods of 2011–15 and 2016–20.

14 The document can be accessed at http://ghs.ndrc.gov.cn/zttp/ghjd/quanwen/ (accessed on April 30, 2018).

15 The document is titled "Zhonggong zhongyang guanyu tuijin nongcun gaige fazhan ruogan zhongda wenti de jueding" ["The Decision of the CCP Central Committee on several important issues of advancing the rural reform and development"]. Accessed at http://politics.people.com.cn/GB/1026/8194300.html (accessed on April 30, 2018).

16 The document is titled "Guanyu jiakuai goujian zhengce tixi peiyu xinxing nongye jingying zhuti de yijian" ["Opinions on the construction of a policy system to nurture new types of agricultural entities"]. Accessed at www.gov.cn/xinwen/2017–05/31/content_5198567.htm (accessed on April 30, 2018).

17 A useful reference is Jan Douwe van der Ploeg and Jingzhong Ye's book on China's agriculture and rural society (2016).

18 The document can be accessed at www.gov.cn/zhengce/2018–02/04/content_5263807.htm (accessed on May 2, 2018).

Part III

Comparative perspective

5 South Africa in comparison

Dispossession, agrarian capitalism, and struggles for land

South Africa is characteristic of Janus-faced social and economic development. With a GDP per capita of 7,489 US dollars in 2016 (as compared with that of China, 6,894 US dollars),[1] the country sits comfortably within the upper-middle-income countries. It is also a member of the emerging markets – "BRICS." However, the country has been plagued with high unemployment rates, poverty, and social inequality. The unemployment rate reached 27.3 percent in 2017 (World Bank n.d.). This statistic, though already very high, only included those actively seeking jobs. If the "discouraged" work seekers who stopped looking for jobs due to no hope of finding one were included, the unemployment rate would rise to as high as 35 percent (Butler 2017, 81). The population falling below the national poverty line accounted for 55.5 percent in 2015, and the ratio remained very high even after a much lower World Bank standard of poverty (1.9 US dollar per day) was adopted – 18.9 percent (compared with 1.4 percent in China). The country's degree of social inequality has also been among the highest in the world, with a Gini coefficient of 0.63 in 2014 (World Bank n.d.).

The agrarian structure in the countryside shows a similar picture. South Africa has developed a successful capitalist agricultural sector characterized by large commercial farms, high productivity, and substantial exports. The country is rich in farmland, with about 16.7 million hectares of cropland and 83.9 million hectares of grazing land. Given a population of 56 million, the ratio of cropland to population is 0.3 hectare per person, more than three times of that in China. However, most of the farmland, 14.2 million hectares of cropland and 72.0 million hectares of grazing land, has been consolidated into a small number of large, white-owned commercial farms, 39,966 in 2007 (DAFF 2016, 5). Among the commercial farms, the largest 2,000 farms, those that make up approximately 5 percent, produced half of the total commercial farm income (Bernstein 2013, 26). Adjusted for inflation, the gross value of agricultural production increased from 36.5 billion Rands in 1995 to 75.1 billion Rands in 2015 (at 1995 prices),[2] more than doubled, attesting to a successful agricultural sector (DAFF 2016, 75). South Africa has been consistently running a surplus in international agricultural trade. It exports large quantities of commercial crops/products such as fruits (particularly citrus), wine, wool, sugar, and maize, while importing rice, wheat, and meat. The highly developed commercial agriculture, however, only benefits a very small population, primarily tens of thousands of white farmers and agribusinesses. Due to their capital-intensive nature, the commercial farms have employed a declining number of farm workers, from 1.2 million in 1990 to 0.6 million in 2005. Furthermore, permanent farm workers were replaced with seasonal, causal laborers, including cheaper foreign migrants (Helliker 2013). Outside the white commercial farms, 17 million people, about one-third of the population, are concentrated in the former reserves on only 2.5 million hectares of cropland (0.15 hectare per person) and 11.9 million hectares of grazing land (Bernstein 2013). A high proportion of residents in the reserves are living in poverty, suffering malnutrition and food insecurity.

South Africa is an outlier with regard to the history of racial segregation. For decades after the formation of the apartheid regime in 1948, the country was denounced and even ostracized by international organizations, but the apartheid rule, which separated whites from blacks and privileged the former, was not abolished until 1994. Though extreme in racial inequality, the country was not exceptional in capitalist development in terms of dispossession, the use of migrant labor, and industrial transformation. Displacing peasants from farmland while concentrating said land into large farms, also known as primitive accumulation, or accumulation by dispossession, is considered to be a quintessential process of capitalist development in the Marxist literature (Arrighi, Aschoff, and Scully 2010; Glassman 2006; Harvey 2003). While concentrating black Africans in the reserves is outright racial repression, some of its purposes – for instance, to create a reserve army and to maintain a migrant labor system – have been practiced in other countries as a common way for capital to control and exploit labor. Recognizing these commonalities have led to fruitful comparative studies. As Gay Seidman noted, "South Africa has also served as a prism – in part, perhaps, because the extreme character of apartheid lays bare the underlying dynamics of racial capitalism" (1999, 424).

The comparison between China and South Africa in literature has taken two different directions. One is to compare the apartheid with the *hukou* (household registration) system in China with regard to their role in separating rural and urban populations and controlling rural–urban migration. Peter Alexander and Anita Chan (2004) argued that both systems were aimed to create a cheap migrant labor system, which, according to Wolpe (1972) and Burawoy (1976), separated migrant workers and their families. Migrant workers moved to the city and were employed in the capitalist sector on a temporary basis while their families remained in the countryside surviving on subsistence farming. Thus employers in the city could pay lower rates of wages for migrant workers as the countryside subsidized the costs of labor reproduction, such as child rearing and retirement. The theory of the migrant labor system, particularly the argument on state control of migration, however, may be applicable only to a limited period of time. This holds true for both South Africa and China. In South Africa, the influx control was abolished in 1986, but this has not fundamentally improved the conditions of migrant workers and their families (Scully and Webster 2018). In China, the *hukou* system, established in socialist China in 1958, restricted rural-to-urban migration until 1984, and large scales of migration had not emerged until the 1990s. In the recent decade, not only can migrant workers bring families to the city, but also local governments, in many cases, encourage or even force rural residents and migrants to take up urban residence (Cheng and Selden 1994; Chan and Zhang 1999; Solinger 1999; Zhan 2017b). All of these fall beyond the purview of the theory of the migrant labor system.

The other strand of comparison calls attention to the issue of land dispossession. Gillian Hart has been a pioneer in this effort. Other than focusing on the migrant labor system, Hart (1996; 2002) pointed out that a major difference between South Africa and East Asian economies was whether peasants were dispossessed of land. The successful rural industrial transformations in Taiwan and China were preceded by the redistribution of land. This stood in stark contrast to South African experiences of successive racialized dispossessions, which displaced black South Africans from rural "white" South Africa to the densely populated reserves (Hart 2002, 10–12; 201–17). Giovanni Arrighi and his co-authors further argued that the displacement of agricultural producers from the land, commonly considered a successful condition for capitalist development, has created hurdles for economic development in the country, including high costs of reproduction, unemployment, and the narrowness of the domestic market. Thus, the paradigm of accumulation by dispossession, though it may explain the success of advanced capitalist economies a century earlier, shows its limits in lifting economies in the global South after the Second World War (Arrighi, Aschoff, and Scully 2010).

The literature of South Africa–China comparisons, by drawing attention to their differences and similarities in land and labor, laid important groundwork for this chapter. The theory of the migrant labor system has offered insights into the ways in which capital controls and exploits migrant labor, but its explanation for the creation of cheap labor only has limited utility. As noted in the Introduction of this book, the key challenge for contemporary capitalism is not how capital can lower labor costs, but rather about its inability to absorb the labor force. In the Chinese modern history, especially after the population expansion in the eighteenth century, labor has always been abundant, and capital would face little difficulty in finding cheap labor. The key issue is how to incorporate the large labor force into the productive process in order to create sufficient livelihood opportunities. As noted in the previous chapters, the solution in China was the industrious revolution, which occurred both during the eighteenth century and in recent decades. One of the main features of the industrious revolutions is the rise of labor-intensive, community-based small producers, such as peasant households and community enterprises. A necessary (but not sufficient) condition of this, as Gillian Hart and Giovanni Arrighi noted, is that small producers are not displaced from the land, a process that they call *accumulation without dispossession* (Arrighi, Aschoff, and Scully 2010; Hart 2002).

The use of South Africa as a comparative case serves two goals. One is to show that the success of agrarian capitalism, based on the displacement of peasants and the concentration of land in large commercial farms, has brought tremendous social and economic costs in South Africa. The surplus population displaced from the land is unable to be absorbed into the capitalist sector in the city. Given the much higher population-to-land ratio in China, the emulation of South African experiences would produce even worse outcomes. The other goal is to extend the comparison to the recent two decades, when land has emerged as a central issue in South Africa after the end of apartheid. The popular discontent over the sluggish land reform and the pressure from below for land redistribution demonstrate the centrality of land in popular struggles for a secure livelihood. This sheds new light on land struggles in China.

In what follows, I will first recount the history of dispossession in South Africa. The racialized dispossession created conditions for the success of agrarian capitalism, but it also rendered large numbers of Africans as a surplus population, and many of them could neither be employed in the capitalist sector nor have sufficient land to farm. After the end of apartheid, the South African state promised that it would redistribute 30 percent of the land. However, the fear for undermining commercial agriculture, and the resistance from large farms and agribusiness companies, stalled the reform process. The discontent mounted and the pressure intensified on the state to take action in recent years. The last section compares the land question in South Africa and China.

Successive dispossessions: colonialism, segregation, and apartheid

Colonial settlement in South Africa started after the Dutch East Indian Company established the first provision station in the Good Hope Cape in 1652. The settler population was very small during the seventeenth century (less than 2,000), but it grew considerably thereafter (Terreblanche 2002, 157). The Dutch company and white settlers took land from native Africans, by means of wars or coercion, and used the land to produce wheat, wine, and meat, both for local consumption and for export. The white farmers, called *free burghers*, used unfree laborers on their farms, including the indigenous Khoisan people and slaves imported from Indonesia, India, Madagascar, and Mozambique (Terreblanche 2002, 156–7). The colonialists had an insatiable demand for land, and extended the colony continuously to the east and north throughout the eighteenth century.

The British took control of the Cape colony in 1806, and pushed colonial expansion further into the east and the interior north. This led to violent clashes with native Africans. In the 100 years between 1779 and 1879, first the Dutch and then the British waged nine frontier wars with the Xhosa tribes. The result of these wars was the loss of large tracts of land to the colonialists. In addition, the Afrikaners launched the Great Trek in 1836 into the interior and established several Boer republics on the (previously) Africans' land. During the colonial expansions, a great number of Africans were killed, displaced, or forced into being unfree laborers (such as serfs, indentured laborers, and domestic servants), but many were also able to adapt to new circumstances. By adopting new crops and farming methods, a growing numbers of black Africans turned themselves from pastoralist-cultivators into peasants and small farmers who produced for the market. Colin Bundy (1988, 238–9) identified three types of African peasants in the second half of the nineteenth century: (i) peasants who farmed on communally owned land "in areas designated as African reserves or locations" where political and social structures were little altered by colonialism; (ii) "squatter-peasants" who farmed the land nominally owned by whites and paid rent – in cash, kind, or in labor services – to the latter; and (iii) a smaller number of peasants who held individual land tenure and farmed as relatively independent, small-scale commercial famers. These peasant farms were labor-intensive and showed a great degree of economic vitality. White farmers often faced difficulty in competing with them because the latter could tap into family labor (Bundy 1988, 177–8).

The peasant farming, together with the traditional pastoralism-cultivation, provided Africans with subsistence and absorbed a large number of laborers, and this even created labor shortages for large white farms and other sectors in southern Africa (Arrighi 1970; Bundy 1988, 44). While white farmers resented the expansion of the African peasantry, the absentee landlords, the British authority and merchants were tolerant of their existence because of their contributions to rents, taxes and a range of marketable goods. It should be noted that even in this period a series of legislations were enacted to restrict Africans' land rights in both the British colonies and the Boer republics. Sampie Terreblanche noted that peasantization went hand in hand with proletarianization, as "thousands of Africans were proletarianised and forced to enter the labour market as cheap wage labourers" by hut taxes, pass laws and vagrancy laws (2002, 206).

The discovery of gold in South Africa in 1886 led to further land dispossession. The expansion of mines and infrastructure projects greatly increased the demand for African labor. In 1889, gold mines employed about 17,000 African workers, but this number increased to 200,000 in 1909 (Bernstein 1996, 4). As a result, white farmers and mine owners (who had become the most powerful interest group) developed a common interest to further displace African peasants from the land and turned them into workers in farms and mines (Bernstein 1996; Terreblanche 2002, 241). The 1913 Natives Land Act was the culmination of this process. The act reserved only 8 percent of land for Africans, whose number accounted for about 67 percent of the population at the time. The white farmers and private companies, with only 20 percent of the population, were given three-quarters of land. Such a degree of land dispossession in South Africa was "unrivaled in any sub-Saharan African context" (Beinart 2001, 10–11). The land act prohibited Africans from owning land outside the reverses and used anti-squatting provisions to outlaw sharecropping and rent tenancy.

The act made immediate impact on Africans who rented white-owned land (about 1.5 million hectares) and who owned or occupied land outside the reserves (0.5 million hectares) (Klug 1996, 391). According to Sampie Terreblanche, more than one million Africans, out of five million, were abruptly proletarianized (2002, 262). Although many Africans stayed on in the white farms, the act prohibited them from engaging in sharecropping, while white farmers pressed for the change from rent tenancy to labor tenancy. For those who already engaged in labor tenancy, their terms got more onerous. The number of days required to work for the landlord was set at least 90 days a year (Beinart 2001, 56–7). It was argued that the land act was part of the bigger framework to facilitate cheap labor supply to white enterprises as it was preceded by, *inter alias*, the Mines and Works Act and the Native Labour Regulation Act in 1911 (Weideman 2003). A migrant labor system was created based on the condition that black Africans could not derive subsistence from the land and had to work for white enterprises for survival. Thus, historically, the emergence of the migrant labor system in South Africa was not the result of an intentional act to use land to subsidize wages of migrant workers, but to reduce land rights of Africans so that they could not survive on the land. This was fundamentally different from what happened in China where the land reform in the early 1950s was implemented to provide a livelihood for peasants. The policy of segregation was extended to urban areas and the labor market. In 1923, the Natives (Urban Areas) Act established separate residential areas for Africans in the city, and stipulated that they must leave urban areas if not employed. The job color bar, which gave white workers better jobs and a much higher pay, was introduced in the Mines and Works Act in 1911 and reinforced in a series of acts after the white workers' strike in 1922, also known as the Rand Revolt.

In the 1920s and 1930s, the ideology and practice of land dispossession and segregation were further refined. In 1936, the Native Trust and Land Act increased the area of the reserves to 13 percent of the country. However, this increase came with the hardening of forceful removals outside the reserves and the worsening of labor tenants' conditions. In some districts, the labor required from African tenants was increased to 180 days a year. Furthermore, the 1936 land act was aimed to turn labor tenants into wage laborers (servants), that is, to completely deprive them of the means of production (Beinart 2001, 124; Bundy 1988, 231–2). The implementation of this policy on a large scale, however, did not start until the apartheid period.

The National Party, which represented the Afrikaner nationalism and white supremacy, was elected to power in 1948, and this marked the beginning of decades of apartheid until 1994. The apartheid system was among the most discriminatory and rigid racial segregation systems in the world. It segregated blacks from whites in rural and urban areas, in the job market, in schools, in the use of public facilities, in marriages, and in social events. With regard to access to rural land, the apartheid regime further dispossessed black South Africans of land rights by forcefully implementing segregationist policies. Between 1960 and 1982, it was estimated that 1.2 million Africans were evicted from white farms, and a further 614,000 people were removed from the "black spots" that fell outside the territories of the reserves (Weideman 2003). If removals in urban locations, black townships, and the reserves were counted, a total of 3.5 million Africans were affected, accounting for about 17.5 percent of the black population (Platzky and Walker 1985). As a result of these removals, labor tenancy was reduced drastically. The number of labor tenants decreased from perhaps one million in 1936 to 163,000 in 1964, and to only 16,000 in 1973 (Bundy 1988, 235).

The end of apartheid did not halt the eviction of black South Africans from white farms, though the evictions were no longer made based on the segregationist policy, but on the terms of contract. The 1997 Extension of Security of Tenure Act sought to "protect and regulate the tenure rights and security on commercial farms, based on their historical residence and connection to the farm" (Helliker 2013, 85). Nevertheless, 2.35 million people were displaced from farms and close to one million were evicted between 1994 and 2004. Ironically, there were more evictions since 1997 than in any period prior to the establishment of democracy (Helliker 2013, 85). To understand this irony, it is necessary to examine the nature and historical evolution of agrarian capitalism in South Africa.

Agrarian capitalism and the surplus population

In November 2017, a high-level panel, which was tasked to assess the effects of key legislations in South Africa since the end of apartheid, released a report stating that high unemployment, perhaps the most serious social problem in the country, should be attributed to low levels of employment in agriculture. According to the report:

> One of the most important reasons why the level of unemployment in South Africa is so high relative to that of other countries is that, by the standards of the developing world, South Africa's agricultural sector employs very few people: only 5% of employed people work in agriculture, a level similar to that of Europe and far below the much higher rates of agricultural employment in most of the developing world....
>
> (HLP 2017, 116)

This passage captures a fundamental contradiction in agrarian capitalism. Low levels of agricultural employment are usually perceived as the success of agrarian capitalism because it results from the expansion of large-scale and capital-intensive agriculture. However, by reducing the use of labor on the farm, it has created a large "surplus" labor force that urban and industrial sectors are unable to absorb. The problem is most serious in the global South, but it also exists in high-income countries. Ironically, one of the reasons why unemployment rates in South Africa are much higher than in many other developing countries is that it is more successful than others in developing a capitalist agricultural sector. The success of agrarian capitalism contributed not only to high unemployment, but also to widespread poverty in the country.

The triumph of agrarian capitalism in South Africa, as in many other countries, is not a natural result of modernization, but an outcome of state interventions in the interest of large farms and agrarian capital. As noted earlier, the second half of the nineteenth century saw the rise of the African peasantry, which responded vigorously and effectively to the new opportunities: the mineral revolution that increased demand for a variety of agricultural goods, the adoption of new techniques such as the use of plough, and the diversification of crops and farm activities. White farmers, however, were slow in response and often outcompeted by peasants in the market. According to Colin Bundy,

> … the development of a capitalist agriculture in South Africa had not proceeded very far by the mid-eighties. Even more striking is the hiatus after 1886.… A response there was … but what demands attention is the limited and tardy nature of that response.
>
> (1988, 111)

The South African experience is hardly unique, and there are ample records on the persistence and competiveness of peasant farming relative to large capitalist farms in Russia and China, as well as in other countries (e.g., Chayanov 1986; Huang 1985). What may distinguish South Africa from others are consistent political interventions to support white large farms at the expense of black Africans before the end of apartheid. The aforementioned land dispossessions certainly played a key role in this process. By dispossessing peasants of land rights, the South African state removed competitive pressure on large farms while creating a cheap labor force for these farms to use (Legassick 1974).

In addition, South African authorities, one after another, have provided generous financial support for large farms. From 1890 to 1910, the British Cape government implemented a massive program of subsidies, grants, tax relief, and other forms of assistance such as fencing, irrigation, technological advice, and low rail rates to promote the commercialization of white-owned large farms, but none of these were available to African peasants (Bundy 1988, 116; Terreblanche 2002, 259). Between 1910 and 1935, the parliament passed dozens of farm and land bills to provide support for large commercial farms. For example, the Land Bank was established in 1912 to provide the farms with short-term loans for crop harvesting and long-term loans for capital investments. With the growing revenue from gold mines and industry, state support for large farms was increased further in the 1930s and 1940s. In addition to direct grants and loans, the state shielded white commercial farms from market competition with a complex system of price protection. This culminated in the 1937 Marketing Act, under which a series of producer-friendly control boards worked with white farmer cooperatives as sole purchasers of a number of commodities (Beinart 2001, 118; Hall 2009; Terreblanche 2002, 263).

White farmers also benefited from state-sponsored land settlements. Under the 1912 Land Settlement Act and other related acts, white settlers could apply for state lands, and the state also used public funds to buy privately owned land for subdivision into agricultural holdings for white farmers. The state offered generous terms for these land settlements. The lands were initially leased for five years, with low rates of rent, and upon purchase the buyer could pay the price over 20 years, which was later extended to 65 years. Between 1910 and 1936, about 700 farmers were settled every year. As a result of these generous land-settlement programs, the number of white farms had increased from 81,432 in 1921 to 119,556 in 1952 (World Bank 1994, 51–3). The expansion of white farm reduced the farm size, and this held implications for farm employment, as the smaller farm size would allow for the hiring of more workers on the farm. Nevertheless, the size of commercial farms in South Africa remained among the largest in the world, with an average size of 738 hectares per farm in 1953 (World Bank 1994, 26).

State support also accelerated mechanization, which has been considered one of the hallmarks of agricultural modernization, in commercial farms in the postwar period. The mechanization of agriculture has a direct bearing on farm employment. World Bank scholars proposed to divide the process of mechanization in South Africa into two phases: 1950–70 and after 1970. The first phase saw a complementary relationship between farm employment and mechanization, which did not lead to the decrease in the absolute number of farm workers. This was because the introduction of tractors led to an expansion of cultivated areas and output growth, which increased the demand for labor and offset the substitution of labor by machines. As it moved to the second phase, however, the replacement of labor by machines had intensified, leading to a rapid fall in absolute farm employment (World Bank 1994, 106–8).

Nevertheless, the capacity of large commercial farms in labor absorption was limited even in the 1950s and 1960s, and this was evidenced by the forceful removals of black Africans from the white countryside and the concentration of large rural populations in the reserves. In 1951, of a total of 8.6 million black Africans, 3.4 million (39 percent) were living in the reserves, while 3.0 million (35 percent) were living in the areas of white farms. By 1970, the absolute number of Africans living on white farms had increased to 3.7 million (up 23.3 percent). However, the black African population had nearly doubled during this period from 8.6 million to 15.1 million, and this reduced the proportion of Africans living on white farms to 24.4 percent (Beinart 2001, 201, 354; Bernstein 1996, 13). A large number of black Africans, more than seven million in 1970, were concentrated in the reserves, leading to overcrowding, environmental degradation, and absolute poverty. These problems were observed even before the enforcement of apartheid. After the destruction of the independent peasantry and the eviction of sharecroppers and tenants from white farms, the conditions of black Africans had deteriorated dramatically. The Native Economic Commission reported in 1932 that the reserves descended "at a rapid pace toward desert conditions," and that "the process of ruination threatened an appalling problem of Native poverty" (Bundy 1988, 222). Wolpe (1972) argued that the economic decline of the reserves undermined the basis of the migrant labor system, as many areas in the reserves were unable to provide subsistence for migrants' left-behind families.

Economic deterioration in the reserves pushed Africans to migrate to the city. Despite the stringent "influx control," the rate of urbanization had increased steadily among Africans in the 1950s and 1960s. The percentage of the African population in urban areas increased from 27 percent to 33 percent between 1951 and 1970. Due to the rapid population growth in this period, the absolute number of Africans in urban areas had increased from 2.3 million to 5.0 million. The rapid growth of industrial and urban sectors in these two decades had *partially* absorbed the growing surplus population. Manufacturing, commerce, and finance were among the most rapidly expanding sectors, at an average rate of over 7 percent per annum from 1946 to 1975 (Beinart 2001, 172). The three sectors employed 1.9 million workers in 1970, up 132 percent from 830,000 in 1951 (World Bank 1994, 14).

However, economic growth started to lose pace in the 1970s, especially after the Oil Crisis in 1973. This reduced the rate of job creation in urban and industrial sectors. The annual growth rate in employment decreased from 3.2 percent in 1961–5 to 1.42 percent in 1976–80, 0.07 percent in 1981–5, and even negative in 1986–90 (World Bank 1994, 4). Large commercial farms, by further increasing farm size and the degree of mechanization, started to shed workers. The total agricultural employment (including forestry and fishing) increased from 1.5 million to 2.5 million between 1951 and 1970, but it decreased to 1.3 million in 1980, and further down to one million in 1990 (World Bank 1994, 14).

The further scaling-up and mechanization were common measures of capitalist farms to maintain rates of profit, but the South African state also facilitated this process. In addition to subsidies, credits, and grants offered to farmers for land consolidation, the state enacted the 1966 Agricultural Credit Act and the 1970 Subdivision of Agricultural Land Act to consolidate nonviable small farming units into viable units and prohibit the subdivision of large farms. The definition of a viable unit was that the size of the farm must permit the owner to obtain an income level comparable to white workers' income levels in the urban sectors (World Bank 1994, 25). As an interesting comparison, the Chinese state recently issued similar policies to consolidate small farms so that a farmer can earn comparable income of a middle-class urban worker. The number of commercial farms in South Africa decreased rapidly in the 1970s and the first half of the 1980s, down to only 59,960 in 1983, more than halved as compared with the peak in the early 1950s. Consequently, the average size of farm expanded from 738 hectares to 1,435 hectares (World Bank 1994, 176).

The layoffs in large farms, the sluggish economic growth, and the overcrowding in the reserves all contributed to a swelling surplus population and this was made worse by the rapid population growth. The population grew from 21.8 million in 1970 to 29.0 million in 1980 and further to 40.6 million in 1996. Black South Africans were the fastest growing group, and their share in the population increased from 70.4 percent to 76.7 percent between 1970 and 1996 (Beinart 2001, 353). Without any other outlet for the surplus population, many of them had no option but move to urban areas. The rate of urbanization jumped from 33 percent in 1970 to 49 percent in 1980 and further to 58 percent in 1991 (Beinart 2001, 355). The influx control, which was still in place until 1986, was clearly unable to stop the influx. The 1970s and 1980s were also characterized by intense urban struggles of Africans against apartheid policies, partly as a result of a swelling urban population.

The rapid urbanization, other than a sign of progress often glorified in the modernization ideology, largely stemmed from the forcing out of the "surplus" population from the white countryside to make way for agrarian capitalism. Colin Murray coined "displaced urbanization" to refer to, in the apartheid era, "the concentration of black South Africans in huge rural slums which are politically in the Bantustans and economically on the peripheries of the established metropolitan labour markets" (Murray 1987, 312). These rural slums were "urban in respect of their population density and lack of agricultural opportunities, but rural in relation to facilities, services, and employment" (Beinart 2001, 212–4). The application of "displaced urbanization" can easily go beyond the apartheid period and the South African context. The sprawling informal settlements outside the reserves in contemporary South Africa and the global phenomenon of the "planet of slums" can be seen as originating from the same process (Davis 2006). In China, many local governments have also made the efforts to forcefully concentrate rural people in densely populated high-rise buildings in order to consolidate rural lands (Zhan 2017b).

The contraction of farm employment has continued after the end of apartheid in 1994. Between 1993 and 2006, 40 percent of farm workers lost their jobs, and the farm employment was down to 628,200 workers (Bernstein 2013, 34). The situation has not been improved in the past decade, though the pace of contraction might have slowed. According to a recent national agricultural survey, the number of agricultural workers was 723,767 in June 2016. However, the survey adopted a broad definition, which included workers employed in the related agricultural service industry. Thus the actual agricultural employment must be lower than reported (Stats SA 2017). Since the 1980s and especially after the end of apartheid, the adoption of neoliberal policy has led to deregulation and the removal of state subsidies and other supports for commercial farms. This empowered agribusiness corporations and extremely large farms while subjecting smaller farms to greater market competition (Bernstein 2013; Bond 2000; Hall 2009). As a result, commercial farms have been further consolidated, and the number of farms was reduced from about 60,000 in 1994 to less than 40,000 in recent years. The increased use of agricultural machines and the conversion of farms to grazing lands or game farms also contributed to the reduction in the use of agricultural labor (Hall 2009; Helliker 2013).

Struggles for land: land reform, precarious livelihood, and protest

In December 2017, the African National Congress (ANC), the ruling party in South Africa since the advent of democracy in 1994, adopted a resolution that would allow for the "expropriation without compensation" of the land owned by whites. The resolution diverged from the ANC's market-led land reform in the past two decades. This radical change, of course, has much to do with the pressure from below. The majority of Africans, particularly the poor, is frustrated over the sluggish process of land reform, and they have been increasingly drawn to the leftist parties, such as the Economic Freedom Fighters (EFF), which has made the "land expropriation without compensation" a central tenet of its political agenda. As noted, black South Africans experienced three centuries of colonial conquest and land dispossession, thus the redistribution of land is a very popular proposal, as it would redress the unjust legacy from the colonial and apartheid periods. This section will show that land struggles in South Africa are not only about historical injustice, but also about securing a livelihood in contemporary times. In an era of high unemployment and precarity, land plays a very important role in ordinary citizens' livelihood security.

Upon taking national power, the ANC recognized the need for land reform, but it shunned radical measures to take land from white farmers, for it would undermine "white and international confidence" and economic stability (Beinart 2001, 314–22). Based on a proposal of the World Bank, the ANC adopted a market approach to land reform: the state purchases land from "willing sellers" at market prices and sells the land to "willing buyers." The goal was to transfer 30 percent of the land in five years. By 1999, however, less than 1 percent of the land was transferred. The government then extended the time frame for a further 15 years to 2015. However, this target was still not met. According to the aforementioned high-level panel assessment report, only 5.5 percent of commercial farmland or 4.7 million hectares had been redistributed. Furthermore, the implementation of the land reform had abandoned the earlier goals of supporting the livelihoods of the poor and transforming the structure of the rural economy, and instead focused on building "an African commercial farming class" (Hall 2007, 92). Thus it may have largely benefited black commercial farmers and urban-based business people (HLP 2017, 209–12; Hall and Kepe 2017).

While the slow pace of land reform is criticized from the left, the other side questions the necessity of land redistribution. For example, a recent commentary in *The Economist* pointed out that 70 percent of the transferred land lied fallow. Thus, it argued that the government should focus on creating good jobs in the city rather than on redistributing land (*The Economist* 2018; see also Marais 2011, 217–18; Palmer and Sender 2006). As I have shown in this book, the distribution of land is closely associated with the absorption of labor in the rural sectors. The claim that 70 percent of the land was fallow should also be qualified, as much of the land was found to be used for food and livestock production (Chitonge 2013). Nevertheless, the commentary leads us to two important issues. One is that the success of land reform may require more than the redistribution of land, as state support is crucial for small farmers. The other is that the assessment of the land reform should not be limited to agriculture because land assumes multiple roles in poor people's livelihood strategies (Lipton and Lipton 1993).

As I have shown in previous chapters, China has a long tradition of peasant economy, and the Chinese state had made great efforts to support the rural economy such as irrigation development and technological assistance, which laid the foundation for the second industrious revolution in the 1980s. The tradition of a vibrant peasant economy in South Africa, however, was disrupted in the beginning of the twentieth century. As Sampie Terreblanche noted:

> By depriving African farmers of much of their land, and ending share-cropping and tenant farming on white-owned land …, an important agricultural and entrepreneurial tradition and store of indigenous farming knowledge were destroyed. It is difficult to determine the value of this tradition, but it was probably considerable, because it was well adapted to South Africa's weather, land, and labour peculiarities. If this African agricultural tradition had not been destroyed, but given more or less the same government support (both financially and technologically) given to white farmers, South Africa's agricultural and economic history could have been radically different.
>
> (2002, 263–4)

Many factors constrained the development of small-scale farming in contemporary South Africa. The most notable factor might be the absolute dominance of large commercial farms (together with powerful agribusinesses), which crowded out small farms in the market. White commercial farms produced 90 percent of the value added in agriculture and provided nearly all food for urban areas (World Bank 1994, 22–36). In such a context, small farms had little chance to compete with large commercial farms. As a result, rural households in the former reserves have increasingly concentrated on producing food or raising cattle for self-consumption or have given up farming completely. The "willing buyer-willing seller" policy transferred some lands to landless black citizens, but the government provided little support to help these small farmers, who were facing a range of problems, including, but not limited to, poor infrastructure (e.g., lack of irrigation), inadequate farming skills, and a lack of capital for agricultural inputs (Cousins 2013, 2016; Greenberg 2015; O'Laughlin *et al.* 2013). Nevertheless, research found that some land reform beneficiaries experienced improvements in livelihoods (Aliber and Cousins 2013; Chitonge 2013).

In South Africa, as in many other countries, agriculture accounts for a declining share of GDP, only 2.1 percent in 2015 (World Bank n.d.), and only 16.9 percent of African households were involved in agricultural production activities (Stats SA 2016, 18). Thus agriculture contributed only a fraction of household income. However, the importance of land should not only be measured by agricultural income, because land also plays a crucial role in providing livelihood security for rural residents and migrants. Access to land lowers the cost of living and allows migrant families to tap into social resources in rural areas. This is especially important when urban jobs have become precarious in the neoliberal era.

Land, first of all, provides a source of food. Of the households involved in agricultural activities, 8.3 percent used land for the main source of food, while 77.9 percent used land for an additional source of food (Stats SA 2016, 61–2). It was found that migrant or urban workers living in land-occupation sites near the city also cultivated small plots of land for food (Jacobs 2018). In addition, rural land functions as a safety net for migrant workers, as they would have a place to fall back on when they experience possible hazards, such as work injury, illness, and unemployment in the city. Some migrants would return to the city looking for work after recovery, while others had to stay permanently due to the lasting conditions of poor health (Zhan and Scully 2018). Furthermore, access to land and rural residence can amplify the effects of social grants. One of the most progressive policies of the post-apartheid government might be the distribution of social grants, such as the old-age grant, the child-support grant, and the disability grant, to low-income families and vulnerable groups. Nationally, 21.7 percent of households reported social grants as a main source of income in 2015 (Stats SA 2016, 57–8). However, old-age grants (about 112 US dollars a month in 2017) would not be sufficient if one retires in the city without other sources of support. In rural areas, this is a sufficient income given the low cost of living. The retirees can stay in their own houses, engage in crop production, raise livestock and spend much less on utilities such as water and electricity (Neves *et al.* 2009; O'Laughlin *et al.* 2013).

The discussion of the land question should not be limited to agricultural land or rural land as the livelihood of many households is spatially extended to both rural and urban areas. Rural residents, migrant workers, and urban residents channel resources such as wage earnings, social grants, agricultural produce, and care to each other through family ties, social networks, and migration (Neves and Du Toit 2013). The preceding chapters showed that the rapid expansion of the Chinese rural economy in the 1980s depended much on the use of land for nonagricultural production, particularly for rural industry. In recent decades, the conversion of rural land for urban use has been the epicenter of land struggles in China. In South Africa, a large number of rural migrant workers and their families live in "unlawful" informal settlements on the edge of the city or periurban areas because these places are close to where they work (Huchzermeyer 2004, 2010; Hunter and Posel 2012). Access to urban land, which provides housing, utilities, employment, and even small business opportunities, should also be the focus of land policy and social movements (Hendricks and Pithouse 2013).

As land plays such a crucial role in both rural and urban livelihoods, the demand for land has been on the rise and land struggles have intensified, forcing the government to take action. According to a land reconciliation survey (*N*=4, 108) in 2004, the majority of African respondents held that the issue of land ownership and redistribution was very important, and more than 70 percent of them also agreed with the statements such as, "When times are tough, one can always survive if one owns some land," and "Land is special: Having land is more important than having money" (Gibson 2009, 35–8). There has been widespread popular discontent about the sluggish process of land reform. The Economic Freedom Fighters (EFF) have emerged as a significant opposition party in the past few election cycles, and is the only entirely new party with significant electoral support in the post-1994 democratic era. The signature issue of the EFF has been a radical critique of the failures of post-apartheid land reform. The party calls for a change in the constitution to allow the government to expropriate land for redistribution without compensation (Alexander 2013, 166–7; Greenberg 2015, 959–61). The action of the EFF was a key factor in the ANC's recent shift in its position on land reform, as noted in the beginning of this section.

Alongside the surging demand for land redistribution have been waves of protest over various livelihood issues such as minimum wages, public service delivery, housing, land grabbing by mining companies, and replacement of local workers by foreign immigrants. By 2007, the number of protests had surpassed the highest mark during apartheid, and this culminated in a new wave of protests before and after the 2012 Marikana Massacre (Alexander 2013; Bond and Mottiar 2013; Schierup 2016). Although not all protests are about land, the land question cannot be ignored because the issues of land, employment, and livelihood security are intimately linked to each other in the neoliberal era of capitalism.

Conclusion: the land question in South Africa and China

The land question in South Africa is very different from that in China due to their divergent histories and distinct geopolitical contexts. In South Africa, the land question centers on how to rectify the historical injustice of 350 years of colonialism and apartheid and how to use land reform to create livelihood opportunities for millions of unemployed or underemployed people. In China, the land question revolves around the choice and contradiction between the two visions of rural development – agrarian capitalism and industrious revolution. The starting point of the land question also differs in the two countries: most of the farmland in South Africa is consolidated into large commercial farms, while in China, smallholder farms still constitute the majority. Nevertheless, the research on the land question in South Africa has offered at least three lessons for China.

First, the pursuit of agricultural modernization, a goal embraced by the Chinese state, should be advanced with extreme caution because of its consequences on employment and livelihood. In the past two decades, the Chinese state has shifted its position from maintaining the use rights of rural households to consolidating land use into large commercial farms. As the history of South Africa shows, the creation of large capitalist farms (with considerable state intervention and support) may lift agricultural production to a higher level, but it would displace millions of peasants and small farmers, who could not secure a job or a livelihood in the city. According to my own calculation, the rural sectors in China have currently provided land-based farm and nonfarm jobs for at least 250 million rural laborers (Zhan and Scully 2018). The unemployment rates in China would rise to match those in South Africa, should land consolidation and expropriation eliminate these jobs. Thus, following Gillian Hart and Giovanni Arrighi, I argue that the consolidation of land through accumulation by dispossession, which created conditions for the success of agrarian capitalism in South Africa, would lead to disastrous results in employment and livelihood, given the enormous population size in China.

Second, the land reform and the demand for land from below in South Africa contrasts with China's ongoing "reverse land reform," which is aimed to consolidate peasants' lands into large farms. The reverse land reform, which compensates land rights with cash, would create intense land struggles in the future if the displaced peasants cannot secure an urban livelihood. As the case of South Africa demonstrates, although the majority of its rural residents have moved to the city, their demand for land has not dissipated and this demand has coalesced with other livelihood problems into various kinds of protests, and this has created a volatile political situation in South Africa. In China, my research found that landless peasants continued to make demand on the government after the land is expropriated. For example, in Wujin of Jiangsu Province, one of my research sites, the demands and protests from older landless peasants have forced the local government to increase their pension standards.

Finally, the fact that the rural households derive their main income from migrant jobs in the city should not be taken as evidence for the declining importance of land. As urban jobs become increasingly precarious, rural land plays a crucial role in the livelihood security of rural residents and migrant workers. In South Africa, the land in the former reserves, though very limited in generating income, has been used to reduce the cost of living and as a safety net, and this to a great extent mitigated extreme poverty and amplified the effects of social grants. Thus the spatially extended livelihood, an important livelihood strategy of low-income families in both rural and urban areas, should be considered a positive measure to offset the precarity in the labor market. This prompts a rethinking of a unidirectional urbanization strategy pursued in China and in other East Asian countries, which I will discuss in detail in the next chapter.

Notes

1 Constant 2010 US dollars.

2 The gross value in 2015 is adjusted based on the accumulated inflation index between 1995 and 2015.

6 Land, welfare, and the East Asian development path revisited

The economic success of Japan and the Asian Tigers has been an inspiration and a target of emulation for China. The Chinese government looked to Singapore as a model when it was deepening market reforms and building an export-oriented economy in the 1990s (Lim and Horesh 2016). The rural crisis and the desire to develop the countryside in the 2000s motivated scholars and officials in China to learn lessons from Japan, South Korea, and Taiwan, which seemed to have achieved a more balanced rural-urban development during the periods of rapid industrialization and urbanization. Chinese scholars are eager to draw lessons from the success of rural cooperatives in Japan and Taiwan, and from the New Village Movement (Saemaul Undong) in South Korea. The latter case has also attracted interest from Chinese officials. After the launch of the program of "building a new socialist countryside" in 2005, tens of thousands of Chinese officials flocked to South Korea to learn about the movement. When I was conducting fieldwork in Tangyuan County in June 2016, I found that the county also sent a delegation of officials to South Korea in 2015. Tangyuan is a remote hinterland county in Heilongjiang Province. Its experience reveals the wide reach of the learning campaign.[1]

It is no surprise that China is keen on learning from its East Asian neighbors. The countries in the region have much in common in terms of culture, demography, and economy. For example, Francesca Bray (1994) argues that the cultivation and consumption of rice has historically shaped technological progress, social, and economic organizations, and the use of land and labor in the region. In recent decades, the appeal of East Asian experiences also comes from the declining shares of the agricultural population to very low levels in Japan, South Korea, and Taiwan, which seem to be a replication of the experiences of the United States and Western Europe and fit well with the ideology of agricultural modernization. Many observers in China thus believe that this will also be the country's future.

This chapter situates China's land question in the East Asian context and reexamines the East Asian development path. As noted in the Introduction, I refer to the East Asian development path as a model of vigorous rural development based on broad access to land before rural labor is absorbed into urban and industrial sectors. Such a model stands in sharp contrast with the displacement of small farmers and the eviction of tenants, as seen in the case of South Africa. Japan, South Korea, and Taiwan all redistributed land from landlords to peasants and promoted small-scale, labor-intensive economic activities prior to and during the periods of rapid industrialization. This is very different from the path of agrarian capitalism in the West or the common perception of agricultural modernization. Thus, contrary to the received wisdom in China that these East Asian economies have followed the "natural" path of agrarian capitalism or agricultural modernization, the East Asian experience has actually been a divergence from it.

The agrarian reforms in East Asia and their positive impacts have been well documented in English literature. This chapter will take a step further and examine recent developments after most rural laborers moved into urban-industrial sectors in Japan, South Korea, and Taiwan. As will be seen, the excessive level of urbanization, a phenomenon often celebrated in China as evidence of modernization, has had negative effects on workers' welfare and well-being due to the restructuring of the global economy and the slowdown of economic growth. The productivist welfare regime in these East Asian economies, which worked fairly well in the era of high economic growth, appears unable to protect workers in the new era, resulting in widespread precarious employment and even urban poverty. In this situation, rural residents and rural-connected urban workers continue to hold the right to small pieces of land for livelihood security, despite the governments' efforts on land consolidation. In recent years, there are signs that an increasing number of urban residents are interested to move back to rural areas, and the governments also recognized the need to revitalize the countryside.

The lessons of the East Asian experience are thus twofold. First, peasants and rural producers were not displaced from the land before they were fully absorbed into urban and industrial sectors, and the East Asian states also provided support to create more employment opportunities in rural areas. Second, access to land still holds importance in the era of precarity even when the majority of the labor force has moved into urban areas. A vibrant rural economy would provide much needed support for the elderly and for at least some precarious urban workers.

The rest of the chapter will be organized as follows: The first section recounts the agrarian reforms in Japan, South Korea, and Taiwan, and the contribution of these reforms to their economic success. The second section discusses economic slowdown and rising precarity in these Asian economies. The third section examines the productivist welfare regime and its inability to provide adequate welfare for urban workers in an era of precarity and population aging. The fourth section describes the current rural conditions and the efforts to revitalize rural areas in the region. The last section examines the implications of East Asian development for China.

Agrarian reform and industrial transformation

In studies of East Asian development, it is often underscored that Japan, South Korea, and Taiwan all implemented land reforms prior to or during the periods of industrialization. In Japan, land reform was started in 1946 under the direction of the American Occupation Force. In the 1930s, the country's rate of tenancy was nearly 50 percent, and only one-third of the farmers held land ownership. The high tenancy rate was associated with the unfavorable terms for tenants, with average rents for rice paddies representing nearly half of the gross value of the annual yield (Dore 1958, 183). Land reform was thus implemented to improve tenant-peasants' conditions and to undercut rural support for communism. This was also a major factor in the land reforms in South Korea and Taiwan in the postwar period. During the land reform, the Japanese government purchased lands from landlords and sold these lands to tenants. It set the maximum holdings of a household at no more than 2.5 hectares for half of the prefectures and 4.5 hectares for everywhere else except for Hokkaidō. As a result of the reform, the share of tenanted land dropped from almost half to 10 percent while the share of owner-farmers increased from one-third to 70 percent, and landless farm households decreased from 27 percent to 0 percent. In total, three million households, 50 percent of the total, gained land in the reform, but most rural households held less than one hectare due to population pressure (McDonald 1997, 58).

Land reform in South Korea consists of two phases. In the first phase (1948–50), the land previously occupied by Japanese colonists was confiscated and distributed to tenant farmers. About 280,000 hectares, or 15 percent of the total arable land was redistributed to 588,000 tenants, which constituted 35 percent of all farm households. The second phase of land reform was targeted at Korean landlords. The government acquired the land owned by absentee landlords or landlords with landholdings that exceeded three hectares. During this phase, a total of 330,000 hectares was acquired and redistributed. The two-phase reform affected 66 percent of farm households and 69 percent of the tenanted area. As a result of the reform, the tenancy rate dropped from 42.1 percent to 7 percent, and the proportion of households that owned their farms increased from 16.5 percent to 71.6 percent (Dorner and Thiesenhusen 1990, 78–80). The reform turned rural South Korea into a smallholder economy: the average farm size was 0.9 hectare in the 1960s, while 79 percent of rural household cultivated less than one hectare (Burmeister 1990a, 713; Francks, Boestel, and Kim 1999, 107–8).

In Taiwan, the Nationalist government had a strong incentive to carry out land reform after it was defeated in the mainland and retreated to the island. In April 1949, the government reduced rent to 37.5 percent of the annual yield, down from previously 50 to 70 percent. Like South Korea, Taiwan was also a Japanese colony, and the government took the land that was occupied by the Japanese after the Second World War. This accounted for 180,000 hectares, about one-fifth of all arable land in the island. Between 1949 and 1953, the government sold or leased 58.9 percent of this land to peasants. The land reform culminated in the implementation of the Land-to-the-Tiller Act in 1953–4, which set a ceiling on landholdings of each household at one to three hectares of paddy lands and two to six hectares of dry land, depending on the grades of the land.

The land above the ceiling must be sold to the government, which in turn transferred these lands to tenants. The policy transferred 154,000 hectares (Dorner and Thiesenhusen 1990, 74–5). The successive measures of the land reform increased the area of farmland cultivated by owner-farmers from 55 percent in 1948 to 84.9 percent in 1956 (Koo 1968, 39).

The redistribution of land rights is an important step to build a prosperous smallholder economy in the countryside, but it is not a sufficient condition. It was even argued that land reform did not significantly boost agricultural productivity in East Asia (Bramall 2004; Kawagoe 1999). As noted in Chapters 1 and 2, a more important condition for the industrious revolution to take place in rural China was that the state provided various supports for smallholders. This was also the case in Japan, South Korea, and Taiwan. In Japan, the government provided price support for staple crops and implemented many schemes of agricultural improvements with generous grants and loans. Efforts were also made to improve rural infrastructure such as roads and irrigation works and to increase the provision of social services by building schools and health clinics (Dore 1958, 186–8, 1984, 220–6). In South Korea, the support for agriculture was very limited in the 1950s, but the government launched various agricultural assistance programs in the 1960s, and areas of support included irrigation expansion, farm improvement, the supply of fertilizers and pesticides, and the strengthening of agricultural research. These efforts culminated in the New Village Movement in the 1970s, during which the government went beyond agriculture to pursue a comprehensive scheme of rural development (Ban, Moon, and Perkins 1982, 163–96; Burmeister 1990a). The Taiwanese government also made great efforts to promote agricultural development during and after the land reform. It promoted agricultural extension, improved irrigation and drainage systems, and provided subsidies and credits for farmers (Kay 2002, 1082; Koo 1966, 155).

An often-raised research question in the literature is whether and how the agrarian reforms were related to the success of industrial transformation in East Asia. By comparing Latin America and East Asia, Christóbal Kay (2002) identifies three positive linkages. First, the agrarian reforms eliminated landlordism, and this removed the interest of powerful landlords and their opposition to the state's industrialization plan. Second, the agrarian reforms and ensuing agricultural growth allowed the state to transfer rural surplus to fund industrialization. Third, the reforms created a more egalitarian social structure and increased purchasing power of rural consumers, thus expanding the domestic market for industrial goods. Other scholars put forward similar arguments (Burmeister 1990b; Koo 1966; Moore 1984). Larry Burmeister (1990b) further suggests that the agrarian reforms contributed to the increase in educational attainment of the rural population in South Korea, which created an educated labor force for industrialization. It should be noted that the effects of agrarian reforms were often intertwined with transnational factors such as easy access to US aid and its markets (Gereffi 1989).

A more important lesson from the agrarian reforms in East Asia, as the analysis in this book suggests, might be that the reforms provided employment opportunities for large numbers of rural laborers before they were able to find jobs in industrial sectors in the city. Like China, Japan, South Korea, and Taiwan all faced strong population pressure and thus confronted the common challenge of securing livelihoods for a large rural population with limited land resources. In this situation, creating small-scale, labor-intensive farm or nonfarm opportunities seemed to be the best way to meet the challenge. Scholars have correctly noted that the agrarian reforms in East Asia resulted from a multiplicity of geopolitical and economic factors in the postwar period, most importantly the intervention of the United States and the need to fight off communism (Bramall 2004; Kay 2002). Nevertheless, the reforms also reflected the East Asian way to deal with population pressure from very early on, that is, the region had long resorted to the industrious revolution for rural development, which prioritizes the absorption of labor in the production process (Sugihara 2003). In view of the rapid population growth in the past century, for many countries in the global South this East Asian development path seemed more relevant than agrarian capitalism. In Latin America, for example,

> a large proportion of the surplus rural population which migrated to urban centres was unable to find industrial employment ... [its] urban surplus population continued to expand preventing any significant trickle-down effect from economic growth and perpetuating, if not exacerbating, income inequalities.
>
> (Kay 2002, 1096)

It should be noted that access to land not only provides the opportunity of farming in East Asia but also a variety of nonfarm job opportunities. It is the combination of farm and nonfarm activities that contributed to the rise in living standards of rural populations despite the small size of landholding in the region. Yujiro Hayami (1998) advocates for the development of rural-based commerce and industry based on East Asian experiences and regards it as an effective way to create sufficient employment for a growing world population:

> In this alternative path, widespread rural industrial activities could be organized in a decentralized manner by exploiting not only the physical labor but also the entrepreneurial ability of rural people.... This rural-based development strategy, if found to be feasible, could alleviate the major difficulty in the tradeoff between growth and equity that confronts developing countries.
>
> (Hayami 1998, 1)

Hayami's proposal was derived from the same historical context as the concept of "industrious revolution," which is examined in this book. He contends that the contributions of small-scale, rural-based enterprises in Japan, which could date back to the Tokugawa period (1603–1868), were no less significant than large, modern corporations in the country's industrialization, because these enterprises made industrial production less capital-intensive than it was in other countries

(Hayami 1998, 2–3). Kaoru Sugihara (2013), who sees Japan as an example of labor-intensive industrialization, has echoed this point. The rapid growth of rural industry was also an integral part of Taiwan's industrialization in the postwar period. By the 1970s, agriculture was rendered the secondary employment in rural Taiwan while rural industry had become the major source of income and employment for the rural population (Ho 1982). The case of South Korea is different, in that its industrial production was highly concentrated in large urban enterprises since it took on the export-oriented industrialization strategy in the 1960s. Nevertheless, the South Korean government had also been promoting rural industry since the 1970s, and by the early 1990s, the workers employed in rural industry reached about three million, accounting for 28.2 percent of the industrial labor force (Lee and Suh 1998, 191; Otsuka 2007). A prerequisite for the development of rural industry and commerce is that peasants and rural entrepreneurs are not displaced from rural communities and have access to rural resources. This has been demonstrated in the case of the Chinese rural industry (Chapter 3), and it also holds true for Japan, South Korea, and Taiwan.

Economic slowdown and the rising precarity

The East Asian manufacturing miracle had drawn rural laborers out of agriculture and rural areas into industry and urban areas, resulting in the shrinking of the agricultural labor force and rural populations (Gereffi and Wyman 1990). This trend was reinforced by large volumes of food imports, which suppressed the prices of agricultural products and placed competitive pressure on the domestic agricultural sector. As Lester R. Brown noted,

> Within 30 years or so, each had gone from being largely self-sufficient in grain to importing most of their supplies. In 1994, Japan imported 72 percent of the grain it consumed, for South Korea the figure was 66 percent, and for Taiwan, 76 percent.
>
> (1995, 14)

The East Asian Food Import Complex, as Philip McMichael (2000) calls it, was previously dependent on the food aid and food exports from the United States, but it has been diversifying its sources of supply in the recent two decades.

The pace of urbanization and proletarianization seemed much faster in East Asia than in many Western countries (Francks, Boestel, and Kim 1999, 4; Koo 1990). In Japan, the share of employment in agriculture had dropped from 30.8 percent in 1960 to 6.2 percent in 1990, and further down to 3.6 percent in 2015. The share of the rural population had decreased from 36.7 percent in 1960 to 22.0 percent in 1990.[2] In South Korea, 79.5 percent of the labor force was engaged in agriculture in 1960, but the figure had decreased dramatically to 18.3 percent in 1990, and further down to 5.2 percent in 2015. In the meantime, many rural residents moved to urban areas, and the rate of urbanization reached 81.6 percent in 2015. A similar process took place in Taiwan, where the shares of agricultural employment and the rural population had fallen from 49.8 percent and 68.6 percent in 1960, to 5.0 percent and 23.1 percent in 2015, respectively (Table 6.1). The fast pace of urbanization and proletarianization had much to do with the rapid expansion of manufacturing sectors, but it should be noted that it also resulted from the urban-biased public investment and service provision.

The East Asian economic miracle came to an end in the 1990s. After the burst of the asset bubble in 1990, Japan entered a long period of economic stagnation from which it has not been able to recover ever since. Although the annual GDP growth rate had already fallen to 4.2 percent between 1974 and 1990, it slumped to a negligible 0.9 percent between 1991 and 2010 (Osawa, Kim, and Kingston 2013, 310). A similar fate fell upon South Korea and Taiwan after the Financial Crisis struck the region in 1997, effectively ending the rapid economic growth in previous decades. The annual GDP growth rate between 1997 and 2015 had decreased to 4.1 percent on average in South Korea and 4.0 percent in Taiwan. And their economic growth has decelerated further in in recent years.[3]

The slowdown of economic growth has forced the East Asian governments to liberalize and deregulate their economies, either as a result of external pressure from the IMF, or as a domestic effort to stimulate the economy and increase firm competitiveness. The various cost-cutting measures adopted by East Asian firms have diluted the previous developmental state policies, exerting adverse impacts on employment and livelihood security of wageworkers. In Japan, the government made a series of revisions to the Temporary Work Agency Law, mostly significantly in 1999 and 2003, to allow employers to extensively use agency temporary workers. Meanwhile, to cut labor costs, large firms have increasingly hired non-regular workers and subcontracted production lines to small and medium enterprises (Song 2012; Watanabe 2012). South Korea was hit badly by the 1997 Financial Crisis, and afterward it implemented neoliberal structural reforms in exchange for a monetary bailout by the IMF. The labor sector was a major target for restructuring, and the goal was to increase labor flexibility for employers. Policies were made to lift the restrictions on the laying-off of regular

Table 6.1 Shares of employment in agriculture and rural population in Japan, South Korea, and Taiwan[4]

	Share of employment in agriculture (%)			*Share of rural population (%)*		
	Japan	*South Korea*	*Taiwan*	*Japan*	*South Korea*	*Taiwan*
1960	30.8	79.5	49.8	36.7	72.3	68.6
1970	16.3	50.5	36.7	28.1	59.3	63.5
1980	–	34	19.5	23.8	43.3	51.3
1990	6.2	18.3	12.9	22	26.2	33.7
2000	5.1	10.6	7.5	21.4	20.4	30.1
2005	4.5	7.9	5.9	14	18.7	27.7
2010	4.1	6.6	5.2	9.1	18.1	25.3
2015	3.6	5.2	5	8.6	18.4	23.1

workers and to legalize the use of "dispatch labor" (Lim and Jang 2006; Song 2012). The 1997 Financial Crisis affected Taiwan less than South Korea. Nevertheless, the heavy dependence on the US market and the desire to join the WTO (World Trade Organization) led the newly elected Democratic Progressive Party to continue and even further the policies of deregulation and privatization, undermining the employment security and labor rights of workers (Kong 2005; Tsai 2001). It should be noted that, as was in the case of Taiwan, some of the deregulation and privatization policies in Japan and South Korea had begun before the economic slowdown and the crisis. In addition, the outsourcing of production lines to overseas, a major cost-cutting measure, was adopted by large firms in all three economies in the 1980s and even earlier, and this had considerably weakened the bargaining power of workers, particularly those in the labor-intensive manufacturing sectors (Ahn, Fukao, and Ito 2008; Harrison 1997; Silver 2003).

A direct result of privatization and deregulation is the swelling of non-regular workers and the precarization of urban employment. In Japan, non-regular workers accounted for 15.3 percent of the labor force in 1984, and this ballooned to 33.7 percent in 2010, in addition to 5.1 percent of the labor force, being unemployed, and 3 percent working as unpaid family workers. In other words, nearly 40 percent of workers in Japan did not have secure employment in 2010 (Osawa, Kim, and Kingston 2013). Non-regular workers in Japan included part-time workers, temporary workers, day laborers, and dispatched laborers. In the 1980s, temporary workers were mainly composed of students and married women, who were not the primary income earners of the household. Since the 1990s, however, an increasing proportion of non-regular workers included younger and middle-aged male workers, and many college graduates in Japan are unable to find a regular job and have to bear with temporary jobs after graduation (Gordon 2017; Osawa, Kim, and Kingston 2013).

The situation in South Korea has been no better. The 1997 Financial Crisis and the ensuing neoliberal structural reforms led to massive layoffs and the extensive use of non-regular workers. By 2004, the proportion of non-regular workers had soared to 37 percent from less than 15 percent in the early 1990s, and it later stabilized but still accounted for over one-third of the labor force in the 2010s (Shin 2013). This statistic was based on the official definition of non-regular employment, which comprises three categories: limited-term workers, part-time workers, and atypical workers (including daily laborers, subcontractors, home workers, and special employment). However, the official definition does not include those who have an open-ended contract (permanent temporary workers) or self-employed workers. The labor advocacy group contended that the share of non-regular workers should be close to 50 percent in the 2010s, much higher than the official figure, about one-third (Lee 2015, 190). For example, many of the self-employed should be classified as non-regular workers as they work longer hours while earning much lower income than regular workers, and many of them are in debt (Shin 2013; Lee 2015).

In Taiwan, non-regular workers, including part-time workers, fixed-term-contract temporary workers, and dispatched workers accounted for 8.8 percent of the labor force in 2010. However, this official statistic excluded the self-employed, which made up 18.3 percent (Hsiao 2013). In addition, the official statistic may have considerably underestimated the scale of non-regular employment. For instance, the category of fixed-term-contract temporary workers only includes those whose contract terms are less than three months. This is an extremely narrow definition of temporary employment, as compared with South Korea's official definition, which sets the threshold at less than two years. The proportion of part-time workers might also have been underestimated. A study using the Luxembourg Income Study Database shows that the proportion of part-time workers was as high as 11.8 percent, much higher than the official figure, 3.7 percent. The study also reveals the low wages of regular workers. The majority of regular workers, 57.8 percent earned less than two-thirds of the medium income, contributing to the problem of "working poor" (Ye and Shi 2017, 43).

In summary, Japan, South Korea, and Taiwan have all witnessed the massive expansion of the non-regular workforce and the precarization of urban employment since the 1990s. This trend is not exceptional to the region, but it has been a worldwide phenomenon resulting from neoliberal globalization. The precarization of employment is particularly notable in many industrialized countries where standard and regular employment was the norm previously (ILO 2016; Standing 2011).

The productivist welfare regime and the crisis of welfare

On New Year's Eve of 2009, a Japanese non-profit organization for the homeless, together with labor unions and volunteers, set up 50 tents at Hibiya Park in the center of downtown Tokyo. The tents were to provide shelter and food for temporary workers who had recently lost jobs and company-provided accommodation. More than 500 people came to the "tent village" (Haken Mura), lining up on the street for blankets, food, health checks, and both legal counseling and employment counseling. The shelter and the plight of the jobless captured national attention over the New Year holiday through extensive media coverage, exposing the harsh reality that millions of workers held non-regular jobs and were often the first to be fired during economic downturns. By the end of 2008, thousands had already lost their jobs in Japan during the Financial Crisis, and at least one million workers met the same fate in 2009, driving the unemployment rate up to 5.1 percent (Chen *et al.* 2012; Kingston 2011, 87–90; Shinoda 2009). The tent village event also exposed the fact that the welfare system in Japan was ill equipped to protect temporary and vulnerable workers in a changing economic situation. Japan was once known for its paternalistic labor system based on lifetime employment and seniority-based wages. As an increasing proportion of the labor force was relegated into non-regular employment, this system seemed unable to provide adequate protection for workers. The same problem is faced with South Korea and Taiwan, which had also prioritized economic growth over welfare provision and social protection for decades. This section will examine the productivist welfare regime in East Asia and reveal its limitations in providing protection and support for workers in the era of slow growth and precarity.

The rapid economic growth in Japan, South Korea and Taiwan before the 1990s was buttressed by a low-spending, growth-oriented welfare regime. Frederic Deyo argues, "East Asian social policy has been driven primarily by the requirements and outcomes of economic development policy" (1992, 289–90). The East Asian governments had managed to keep down expenditures on social welfare and had used the financial resources of social insurance programs to invest in industry and infrastructure (White and Goodman 1998, 14–17). Ian Holliday (2000) conceptualizes this East Asian welfare model as a "productivist welfare regime," which subordinates social policy to "the overriding policy objective of economic growth." The extensions from this general principle include "minimal social rights," "reinforcement of the position of productive elements in society, and state-market-family relationships directed towards growth" (708).

During periods of rapid economic growth, this welfare model seemed to work very well. The expansion of industrial and urban sectors created employment for the majority of workers, particularly the core sections of the labor force. These regular workers were offered secure employment and welfare benefits by their enterprises (large Japanese and Korean firms in particular), even though labor was in general subordinate to capital (Deyo 1989). As for the non-core workers who were not employed or marginally employed, such as the elderly and a proportion of women, they could share the benefits of economic growth through redistributive family and community systems, which are underpinned by Confucian culture in these societies (Jones 1993). As a result, the governments were able to mobilize labor into the production process for economic growth with a low level of social expenditure. While the package of welfare received from the state was small, workers were guaranteed secure employment or could easily find another job in a tight labor market thanks to rapid economic growth. This employment-based growth and welfare model to some extent resembled the rural-based industrious revolution discussed in this book, which is also characteristic of labor being incorporated into rather than excluded from the production process.

The economic slowdown and the neoliberal deregulation of the labor market since the 1990s, however, undermined the key pillars supporting a productivist welfare regime. The economic stagnation in Japan and the impacts of the Financial Crisis on South Korea and Taiwan have considerably increased the proportions of the unemployed and underemployed in the labor force. In addition, the deregulation of the labor market has given rise to a swelling army of non-regular workers. The unemployed, the underemployed, and the non-regular workers, which now account for more than 40 percent of the labor force in Japan, South Korea, and Taiwan, are excluded from employment-based welfare and benefits. This has led to a dualization of the labor market, characterized by the division between regular workers and non-regular or marginal workers (Gordon 2017;

Song 2012). The rising precarity of employment has even threatened regular workers, whose jobs are no longer as secure as previously, as studies on the informalization of the formal economy have suggested (ILO 2016). Worse, population aging and the weakening of the family system have undermined the distributive function of Confucian family and community systems, and as a result, the vulnerable groups such as the elderly, single mothers, the jobless youth and temporary workers have to confront economic risks on their own (Song 2009; Yun 2010).

Ironically, the formulation of and the debate over the East Asian welfare model took place from the late 1990s to the early 2000s, a time when this model had been rapidly collapsing (Aspalter 2006; Gough 2001; Holliday 2000; Kwon and Holliday 2007; White and Goodman 1998). The analysis in this chapter suggests that the key question in the East Asian welfare debate is not whether the East Asian governments have still maintained the productivist welfare regime, but how the authorities cope with the *crisis of welfare* when the previous welfare regime is no longer applicable under the new circumstances. As Kam-wah Chan noted:

> … after the Asian Financial Crisis in the late 1990s, most East Asian metropolises are no longer able to enjoy sustained growth. Many of them began to face similar urban problems encountered by people in the West, such as persistent and rising unemployment, aging population, and family breakdowns…. In many East Asian countries, the declining economy is unable to support even the existing welfare provision, even though this is already considered meagre when compared to many welfare states in the West. There is increasing evidence that welfare development in many East Asian countries is facing crises of a sort not entirely different from the West.
>
> (2007, 245–6)

Paradoxically, Japan, South Korea, and Taiwan have all witnessed welfare expansion since the 1990s, with either the creation of new programs or the expansion of existing programs, such as pension, unemployment benefits, and health care. Up until 1990, Japan had already established a comprehensive welfare system including public pension, health insurance, unemployment insurance, and public assistance. In the 1990s, it started new childcare and long-term-care insurance programs (Aspalter 2006). However, the social expenditure was low as compared with other developed countries. Over the past two decades, the Japanese government has expanded the coverage of social programs by giving more emphasis to previously marginal groups such as the elderly, women and children (Choi 2012; Peng 2015). Its social expenditure has also increased, and the share of social expenditure in GDP is now close to the average level of OECD countries (Hong 2014).

South Korea's social expenditure was very low during the rapid economic growth between the 1960s and 1980s. The government started to reform and extend social welfare in the late 1980s following democratization. Since the 1990s, particularly after the 1997 Financial Crisis, it had revamped the old programs and created new ones. It created a new unemployment insurance program in 1995 and expanded the National Pension Program and the National Health Program in 1999 and 2000, respectively. A Minimum Living Standard Guarantee was introduced in 1999. The welfare system in the country now comprises four major social insurance schemes (industrial accident, health, pension, and unemployment) and a public assistance program (Aspalter 2006; Gough 2001, 183; Kwon and Holliday 2007; Yang 2013). The share of social expenditure in GDP has been rising since the 1990s, but it is still significantly less than that of other OECD countries – less than half of the average of OECD countries (Hong 2014).

Prior to the 1990s, Taiwan's social welfare system was fragmented and catered to the interests of elites and the employees of public sectors, such as civil servants, military personnel, teachers and private school employees. In the 1990s, the reform to the social welfare system became a key issue of political debates in the elections. The most important reform in this period might be the National Health Insurance Law passed in 1994. The 2000s saw a few legislative milestones in the expansion and integration of social welfare programs, especially the Old Age Allowance Act in 2001 and the National Pension Act in 2007 (Aspalter 2006; Hwang 2012). As a result of these reforms, the coverage of health-care provisions, old-age allowance, labor insurance, and pension insurance has been greatly expanded. Nevertheless, the share of social expenditure in GDP has remained stable and is much lower than that of South Korea, attesting to the very limited scope of the social welfare system in Taiwan (Hong 2014).

The expansion of social welfare programs had coincided with the democratization of South Korea and Taiwan. During the change, welfare issues had often become a key theme in political debates between rival parties. This gave rise to the positive diagnosis on how the process of democratization contributed to the expansion of welfare. For example, Huck-ju Kwon (2005) asserts, "The need for economic reform, together with democratization, created institutional space in policy-making for advocacy coalitions, which made successful advances towards greater social (welfare) rights" (477). In retrospect, however, this diagnosis overrated both the importance of democratization and the scale of welfare expansion in East Asia. Soonman Kwon and Ian Holliday (2007) strongly contest the diagnosis and argue that the expansion of the South Korea welfare state was not only limited but also "formed part of wider attempts to boost labour market flexibility," which undermined workers' welfare and rights.

The analysis in this chapter corroborates Kwon and Holliday's argument. The expansion of the welfare systems in the region has been a result of shifting responsibilities from corporations to the state under the guise of neoliberal structural reforms. Although workers may have received more welfare benefits from the state, they lost employment security and the benefits from the employer. Further, welfare provision is often based on personal contributions, regressive taxation (for example, increase in consumption taxes), and the exclusion of non-regular workers.

The outcome is that the majority of workers and their families become worse off after losing crucial social rights and entitlements, resulting in widening inequality, rising poverty, and many other social problems in the region. As compared with South Korea and Taiwan, Japan is reported to have the highest level of social expenditure, close to the average level of OECD countries (Hong 2014). Nevertheless, welfare arrangements in Japan are gravely inadequate to buffer the impacts of structural changes. As social inequality widens, there has been an increase in the size of the poor population. The rate of relative poverty reached 16 percent in 2009. A high percentage (39 percent) of relatively poor households have two or more active workers, suggesting the prevalence of the "working poor" problem. Many non-regular workers are not covered by employment insurance, and they would not receive benefits in the case of unemployment. For those who are covered, unemployment benefits only last for six months, and after that the unemployed can only rely on public assistance. However, only 20 percent of eligible households have actually received such benefits due to the dysfunction of the system (Conrad 2017; Osawa, Kim, and Kingston 2013, 329–32). In short, the Japanese welfare system has not effectively protected the poor, the unemployed and the vulnerable, even if the country already commits the highest level of social expenditure in the region.

Land, welfare, and livelihood security

The insufficiency of the welfare system in East Asia prompts a rethinking of land, welfare, and livelihood security in the era of precarity. Access to land not only opens up land-based employment opportunities, but also provides a measure of social protection. Land and welfare are historically related in East Asia. Broad access to land as a result of the land reforms had partly assumed the function of social welfare when the government-run welfare system was absent or inadequate. Despite large rural-urban population movements, access to land had for a long period continued to provide a source of livelihood security for many households in Japan, South Korea, and Taiwan. However, this role has been gradually eroded, as economic opportunities in rural areas have diminished due to the rapid expansion of urban and industrial sectors on the one hand, and the concentration of public services and investments in the city on the other hand. The excessive reliance on food imports has further undermined the economic role of agriculture and food production for rural households. This section examines the region's agriculture and rural development in recent decades and discusses how the efforts to revitalize rural areas could be a potential way to balance the trend of precarization in the city.

While the size of the agricultural labor force has shrunk rapidly in the region (Table 6.1 above), the pace of decline in the number of farm households has been rather slow. In Japan, agricultural laborers dropped from 12 million to 1.8 million between 1960 and 2015, down 85 percent, whereas the number of farm households had only declined from 6.1 million to 2.2 million. Furthermore, there are at least 1.4 million nonfarm households that possess agricultural land. That is to say, a total of 3.6 million households still hold agricultural land (Francks, Boestel, and Kim 1999, 30; Godo 2013; MAFF 2017). In South Korea, the number of farm units was 1.1 million in 2014, down from 2.4 million in 1960 (KREI 2015, 65). The degree of contraction was much less than that of agricultural labor. This is even more so in the case of Taiwan. The number of farm households stood at 775,000 in 2015, having changed little from 801,000 in 1960 (Taiwanese Government 2017, 103). The change in farm size further demonstrates this point. Despite the massive exodus of agriculture labor, agriculture in Japan, South Korea, and Taiwan remains at a small scale. The average farm size in Japan is about two hectares, and this figure is 1.5 hectares in South Korea and one hectare in Taiwan. Both Japan and South Korea have seen growth in farm size, but the pace of increase has been modest, despite the repeated government efforts to consolidate farms. In Taiwan, the farm size has changed little over the past five decades (Huang 2015; KREI 2015; Jentzsch 2017; McDonald 1997).

This indicates that rural households still hold on to land, even though the income-generating capacity of such land has declined and most of the rural households derive income mainly from jobs in the city. The reason is that access to land offers a source of livelihood security, and this role has increased in the era of precarious employment. According to the longitudinal national surveys conducted by the Cabinet Office of Japan, 83.4 percent of the respondents agreed that rural areas assumes the important function of food production in 2014, up from 63.4 percent in 1990, and 48.7 percent of the respondents agreed that rural areas provide a source of livelihoods in 2014, up from 30 percent in 1990 (Brady 2016, 28). In other words, the importance of land to food and livelihood security has increased despite the declining share of agriculture in employment and household income. The use of rural land is not limited to agriculture. Due to a lack of data, it is difficult to gauge how much land has been used for nonfarm activities, which are now mixed with urban economic activities in general statistics. However, it is reasonable to assume that many households, particularly in Japan and Taiwan, which once had vibrant rural enterprises, still use rural land for nonfarm activities. This increases the income-generating capacity of the land. Even in South Korea, the nonfarm sources of income accounted for more than 40 percent of rural income in 2014, while farm income contributed barely 30 percent (KREI 2015, 90).

Nevertheless, the concentration of resources in urban areas and the excessive reliance on food imports have severely undermined the productive capacity of rural areas, resulting in a range of rural problems including, but not limited to, depopulation, the aging of the farm workforce, the hollowing out of rural communities, the underuse of land, and the decline of agriculture. In recent years, Japan, South Korea, and Taiwan have all undertaken measures to revitalize rural areas and agriculture.

In Japan, the government has offered farming grants to young farmers and launched the Coming Back to Rural Area Movement, which provides skill training, counseling services, and other supportive measures who are interested to move to rural areas. It is shown that an increasing number of young urban residents have moved to rural areas, and many more have expressed interest. In 2016, more than 70,000 people became the newcomers in agriculture, and about one-third of them were under 50 (MAFF 2017). In addition to this, the Japanese government made efforts to diversify rural economic activities by promoting the agricultural processing sector, rural tourism, electricity industry, health care and welfare services, and information and communications industry in rural areas. Other measures include reducing the costs of farm inputs, connecting farmers with consumers, diversifying farm products, and promoting agricultural exports (MAFF 2017). However, it should be noted that Japan's recent agricultural policy reforms are also characterized by neoliberal deregulation, land consolidation, and the corporatization of the farm sector as the government aims to increase the competiveness of Japanese agriculture in the global market (Honma and George Mulgan 2018; Maclachlan and Shimizu, 2016). Some of these measures such as promoting corporate farming would reduce access to land of rural laborers and undermine the efforts for an inclusive revival of rural areas (Jentzsch 2017).

South Korea has also taken an array of measures to revitalize rural areas in the recent decade. It offers loans and skill training services to recruit young farmers and supports farm households specializing in high-value agricultural products such as livestock, fruits, and vegetables. To address the widening rural-urban income gap, it provides crop insurance and direct subsidies, and promotes nonfarm activities such as rural tourism and food processing. There are also programs to promote the linkages between rural and urban areas and to increase the provision of public services such as medical care and children's education in the countryside (Im and Jeong 2014; KREI 2015, 327–32). Taiwan enacted the Rural Rejuvenation Act in 2010, and established a rejuvenation fund of NT$150 billion (approximately 4.8 billion US dollars) for the period between 2010 and 2020. This is to improve rural infrastructure and to conserve rural ecology and culture. In addition, the government also provided start-up funds and training services for young farmers (Huang 2015; Liu 2018). Over the past decade, both the South Korean and Taiwanese governments encouraged land consolidation and farm enlargement under the pressure of international competition and over the concern of the aging of farmers. However, the expansion of scale has been modest, and neither government took coercive measures to seize land from farmers.

The revitalization of rural areas should not be viewed as merely a way to solve rural problems. More importantly, it offers a potential solution to many urban problems in the era of precarity. Access to land and associated benefits such as low living costs, sustainable farming, active lifestyles, and community support in rural areas can, to some extent, alleviate welfare crisis and livelihood risks in the city. In Japan, for instance, the government used rural land to create welfare gardens for people with disabilities, who thus can make a living and be integrated into the community. In South Korea, land has provided a crucial buffer in the era of heightened economic risks and livelihood insecurity. During the Asian Financial Crisis, more than 12,000 urban households had moved back to rural areas after losing jobs in the city. This trend reemerged after the 2008 financial crisis and has accelerated in recent years, reversing the decline of the rural population. In 2014, as many as 44,586 urban households moved back to rural areas. The majority of the returnees are those aged above 40 and with precarious employment, and they have little chance to get a regular job in the city. In the case of Taiwan, moving back to rural areas has also become a viable option for young and middle-aged urban residents (MAFF 2017, 27; KREI 2015, 76–7, 296–7; Sui 2014).

China and East Asian development

The East Asian development path, which is based on broad access to land and vigorous rural development, allowed the region to escape the trap of land concentration and high rates of unemployment seen in South Africa and Latin America. After the majority of rural laborers moved into urban and industrial sectors in the city, the path appeared no longer applicable to the region. Thus, it is commonly perceived that the rural-based development model should be only applied to the early phase of the economic transition toward a modern urban-industrial economy in the region. The analysis in this chapter, however, raises serious questions about this unidirectional linear view of economic development. On the one hand, the excessive urbanization of the population in the region has been contingent on high growth, massive exports, and heavy reliance on food imports. Not all regions in the world (in fact, very few) can replicate this experience as it was derived from the region's unique geopolitical position in the world economy under the hegemony of the United States (Arrighi 1994). On the other hand, economic slowdown, rising precarity and the welfare crisis in the region have exposed the pitfalls of excessive proletarianization and urban-centric development in the neoliberal era. Recently, Japan, South Korea, and Taiwan have all taken measures to revitalize the countryside and rebalance the lopsided rural-urban relations. The East Asian development path, rather than being eclipsed by urbanization and industrialization, seems to gain renewed relevance in the neoliberal era of precarity.

The experiences of Japan, South Korea, and Taiwan offer two lessons for China – one positive and one negative. The positive lesson is that broad access to land in the countryside, as a result of the agrarian reforms, had contributed positively to East Asia's economic success. In this process, the rural population was not displaced from the land before they were fully absorbed into urban and industrial sectors. In China, the land reform also led to the relatively equal distribution of land, and this laid the foundation for economic growth in the 1980s. However, to pursue agricultural modernization, the Chinese government has, in the recent decade, forcefully pushed for the concentration of land and taken away land use rights from peasants, before urban-industrial sectors have the capacity to employ these "surplus" rural laborers. This has swerved the country away from the course of the East Asian development path and moved it toward the version of agrarian capitalism observed in South Africa and Latin America.

The negative lesson is that the excessive levels of urbanization and proletarianization in the region have negatively affected people's livelihood and well-being in a period when economic slowdown and neoliberal reforms rendered urban employment increasingly precarious. In the meantime, the welfare systems in these societies have proven inadequate to protect swelling vulnerable groups. China faces a much more daunting situation than its East Asian neighbors. Not only does it lack key conditions for this extreme level of urbanization, but it also lags behind in the provision of social welfare. China has maintained high economic growth for several decades, but the rate of growth has significantly moderated in recent years when its per capita income is still substantially less than those of Japan, South Korea, and Taiwan. China may pride itself on its large volumes of exports, but it is still far behind its East Asian neighbors in terms of per capita export value: Japan exported 3.6 times as much as China did in 2017; South Korea, 7.5 times; and Taiwan, 7.8 times (World Bank n.d.). While China has increased food imports in the recent decade, it is unimaginable that its huge population can ever rely on the global food market to the same degree as Japan, South Korea, and Taiwan do. The welfare system in China has only covered a smaller urban population, but it is already faced with the severe problem of financial sustainability, not to speak of the insufficient coverage of millions of urban residents. All in all, not only is the excessive level of urbanization undesirable as testified by recent East Asian experiences, but also China does not have sufficient means to provide secure livelihoods for its growing urban population. The land question and the importance of rural development in China should be understood in this context.

Notes

1 The growing interest in the Saemaul Undong may also have to do with the strategy of the South Korean state, which has attempted to promote it as an international aid model (Jeong 2017).

2 To reduce the cost of government, Japan cut the number of towns and villages in the early 2000s by incorporating small towns and villages into large towns and cities. This has greatly reduced the proportion of the rural population in official statistics (Hays 2013).

3 Data on South Korea is derived from The World Bank Open Data and that on Taiwan from the official statistics of the Taiwanese government (https://eng.stat.gov.tw).

4 Data on the shares of employment in agriculture in the period of 1960–90 is derived from Francks, Boestel, and Kim (1999, 37); data on the share of employment in agriculture in the period of 2000–15 is derived from World Bank Open Data (https://data.worldbank.org/); data on the share of rural population is derived from the United Nations' World Urbanization Prospects (https://esa.un.org/Unpd/Wup/).

Conclusion

This book has investigated the land question in China from a historical comparative perspective. It examines how two contrasting development dynamics – agrarian capitalism and industrious revolution – have interacted with China's land institutions and land politics. The book contends that rural land provides a vital source of livelihood and social protection for peasants, small farmers, rural entrepreneurs, and migrant workers and that the importance of this role is heightened rather than diminished in our times against the backdrop of rising urban precarity and population pressure. It also argues that vigorous rural development based on the path of industrious revolution other than agrarian capitalism can better meet the challenge of providing livelihood for a growing population, and mitigate the growing precarity in the city. Thus it questions various arguments that advocate for the forceful displacement of small rural holders from the land in the name of modernization, economic growth, efficiency, profitability, food security, and/or environmental sustainability.

China has been facing population pressure from very early on. Its population reached 150 million at the outset of the eighteenth century, the peak level in the history. Nevertheless, the century continued to see a steady growth of the population, which had more than doubled and reached 350 million in the first decade of the nineteenth century. And yet, the eighteenth century was one of the most prosperous periods in the Chinese history. The economic prosperity not only defies Malthus's theory, but also necessitates a rethinking of the dynamics and potential of a smallholder economy. This book employs the concept of industrious revolution to capture the economic dynamics of eighteenth-century China and contrasts it with agrarian capitalism. The most important differences between the two include access to land and labor absorption. An industrious revolution is based on broad access to land by peasants, small farmers and rural entrepreneurs, whereas agrarian capitalism advances through the displacement of smallholders from the land. The former can support a much larger labor force in the rural economy than the latter. In addition, the surplus generating capacity of land during an industrious revolution is enhanced through state interventions, market exchanges, and community cooperative actions, leading to the improvement in living standards despite the small size of landholdings.

The industrious revolution is not a thing of the past as the literature usually suggests. Rather, it has persisted into contemporary times, particularly in places like East Asia where rural producers have broad access to land, and state interventions created favorable productive and market conditions for rural areas. Modern technologies, which were thought to undermine small rural producers, have actually pushed the industrious revolution to a new height. China is a good example. After the eighteenth-century industrious revolution was unraveled, the country entered a long period of wars and uprisings, culminating in the triumph of the communist revolution in the mid-twentieth century. Besides land reform, another major measure that the communist regime had taken for rural development was to adopt and disseminate modern technologies. In the case of rural industry, community and household enterprises had learnt and acquired manufacturing know-how by collaborating with the state-owned enterprises, participating in state-sponsored skill training, employing urban technicians, and encouraging self-learning and innovation. As a result, the Chinese rural industry in the 1980s had developed into a comprehensive manufacturing system encompassing nearly all of the modern industrial sectors, far surpassing the traditional handicraft industry. In the case of agriculture, the Chinese state had also made efforts to disseminate modern technologies including farm machines, hybrid seeds, best cultivation methods, and inputs such as chemical fertilizers and pesticides. The modern technologies have greatly increased the surplus generating capacity of the land. The second industrious revolution in the 1980s had thus outstripped its eighteenth-century predecessor by a considerable margin in terms of the size of the market and the economic prosperity of rural households and communities.

The communist land reform and the transition to the Household Responsibility System created a rural land tenure system that underpinned the second industrious revolution. However, the rapid urbanization and the rise of agrarian capitalism in recent decades, which are pursued by the Chinese state under the ideology of modernization, have eroded this land system. Land is a vital resource for various economic actors: it provides a source of livelihood for rural residents, it generates profits for capital, and it brings revenue for the government. Thus land has always been a main locus of political and economic struggles in China. In the 1990s, the Chinese state shifted focus from rural to urban areas and provided generous support for cities, particularly large cities in the coastal regions. As the pace of urbanization picked up, the market value of land soared, and local governments have made every effort to turn rural lands into urban lands. The conversion of land has brought local governments an enormous amount of revenue, but land urbanization has taken away peasants' land rights, and the compensations for land loss are often inadequate to guarantee them a secure livelihood. This has led to intense struggles over land rights and compensations. The urban-centric development also drained away rural resources and undercut the surplus-generating capacity of land, leading to a rural crisis in interior provinces in the late 1990s.

Although urbanization encroached upon large tracts of rural land, the land converted into the city still accounts for a smaller proportion of farmland.

However, the rise of agrarian capitalism, which is based on the transfer of farmland from small farm households to large farms and agribusiness companies, would take land rights from most of farmers and turn the Chinese countryside into a place of large capitalist farms. The new land reform, since 2013, as described in the Introduction and Chapter 4, separates use rights and contract rights of farmland, and pushes rural households to relinquish the use rights. The concentration of land in the hands of large farms and agribusiness companies will lead to the eventual demise of the industrious revolution. The "surplus" population released (or evicted) from land due to the spread of agrarian capitalism could move into cities and live a better life, according to the ideologies of agricultural modernization and urbanization. This assumption, however, is seriously contested by the reality, as revealed in the book.

The Chinese land question in world-historical perspective

The Chinese land question, which holds implications for hundreds of millions of people's livelihood and China's economic future, should be understood in a world-historical perspective. The Chinese rural economy diverged from agrarian capitalism in England and embarked on a labor-intensive smallholder development path in the eighteenth century (if not earlier). The importance of this path, called "industrious revolution" in this book, has increased rather than diminished due to the growing population pressure worldwide and the rise of neoliberalism in recent decades, which has led to the informalization and precarization of urban employment. As a result, holding an urban job, which was previously seen as a sign of upward social mobility and increased economic status for rural populations in most countries or regions, no longer guarantees a secure and sufficient livelihood. In this situation, it is imperative to resort to vigorous rural development based on broad access to land, and hence to provide livelihoods for the majority of the humanity and mitigate pervasive precarity under neoliberal capitalism. If China fails to do so, as Giovanni Arrighi reminds us, the country "may well turn into a new epicenter of social and political chaos ..." (2007, 389).

The case of South Africa, discussed in Chapter 5, demonstrates the damaging effects of displacing smallholders and concentrating land in large capitalist farms. The eviction of African peasants and tenants from designated white areas undermined a once-prosperous black peasantry and led to widespread underemployment and poverty in the reserves. The concentration of land did give rise to a strong capitalist agriculture based on large farms and agribusiness companies, a result, which some policymakers and experts in China desire to achieve. However, the surplus population released from land concentration could not be fully absorbed by urban and industrial sectors, even though South Africa has had a larger industrial sector than most of the developing countries. After the removal of the influx control and the end of the apartheid regime, large numbers of rural populations flocked to the city. However, most of them could not find a secure employment, while the unemployment rate has been hovering around 35 percent. The problems such as unemployment, insecure livelihood and glaring social inequality have intensified the struggles for land in recent years, forcing the ruling party to take action on land reform and land redistribution.

The East Asian experiences have been a contrast to the case of South Africa. As Chapter 6 showed, Japan, South Korea, and Taiwan all implemented agrarian reforms after the Second World War and redistributed land from landlords to peasants, creating or strengthening a smallholder economy that provided livelihoods for a large population with limited land. The East Asian countryside was faced with stronger population pressure than South Africa, and the average size of landholdings was also much smaller than the latter. And yet, the region achieved higher standards of living with much less poverty and inequality than South Africa. The rapid growth of urban and industrial sectors in East Asia, buttressed by strong exports, had drawn rural laborers from the countryside into the city, but this had been a gradual process, with most of the rural households retaining land rights even though some of their members moved to the city. In recent decades, the slowdown of economic growth and neoliberal reforms caused growing precarity in the urban labor market, and the welfare system, stressed by population aging and fiscal austerity, is unable to provide sufficient protection for vulnerable groups.

Most of the developing countries would not be able to achieve the East Asian level of exports or rely extensively on food imports to feed the population. Thus it would be more imperative in these countries to promote and strengthen broad access to land among rural smallholders. China is no exception. Although China has been the leading exporter in the world, its exports per capita still lag far behind its East Asian neighbors: Japan outstripped China with 3.6 times exports per capita in 2017; South Korea, 7.5 times; and Taiwan, 7.8 times, as noted in Chapter 6. In addition, China imported a large volume of food from the world, but it can still be classified as self-sufficient according to the United Nations' standard, and the self-sufficiency rate is more than 80 percent, far higher than its East Asian neighbors, whose self-sufficiency rates fall below 40 percent.

The expansion of agrarian capitalism and the intensification of land dispossession have been a worldwide phenomenon in recent decades. Although land is of critical importance to livelihood security, powerful agrarian capital, including large farms, domestic agribusiness companies, and transnational corporations, has intensified land grabbing worldwide, driven by energy and environmental crises and supported by state power (Borras and Franco 2012; Edelman, Oya, and Borras, 2013; Levien 2012; McMichael 2012; Sassen 2010; White *et al.* 2012). This presents a serious threat to people's livelihood and would aggravate urban precarity and poverty by displacing more rural dwellers from the land. The Chinese agrarian capital, with the support of the state, not only seeks to displace small rural producers at home but also moves to take land and resources overseas (Chen *et al.* 2017; Hofman and Ho 2012; Lee 2017). Thus the land question in China is both domestic and international in nature, and the resistance to powerful agrarian capital should transcend the national borders.

Multifunctionality of land and varieties of industrious revolution

The studies of rural land have been heavily focused on agriculture, and this led to some scholars drawing pessimistic conclusions as land for agriculture, grain farming in particular, cannot generate much surplus; and it is concluded that small farmers and peasants are doomed to be overwhelmed by the economies of scale of large farms and the power of agribusiness companies (e.g., Bernstein 2016; Rigg 2006). This book calls attention to the multifunctionality of land. Rural land is not only used for agriculture, but also for a range of nonfarm activities including rural industry and agro-tourism. When the land is used for nonfarm activities, it could generate much more surplus than agriculture. It was the case in China in the eighteenth century, when the land was used for the handicraft industry; it was even more so in recent decades, when land was used to build factories for manufacturing. The land is also used to build houses and other forms of fixed assets, and this blurs the rural-urban boundary. Rural smallholders can benefit greatly from land rights if the process of urbanization does not dispossess them of land but incorporate them into land development. Furthermore, land assumes an important ecological function, and this value should be recognized particularly when peasants and small farmers use land for environment friendly production (Moore 2015). Finally, land constitutes the basis of rural communities, generating social resources such as trust and social support. These resources are crucial for social protection and social reproduction. The importance of this function is elevated due to the precarization of urban employment and the crisis of state-sponsored social welfare.

The multifuctionality of land, as well as other factors, such as state interventions, market conditions, and local resource endowments, have led to the heterogeneous nature of smalholder-based rural development across regions and countries, which I call varieties of industrious revolution. The two county cases in this book are a good example. Wujin County in Jiangsu Province is close to large cities such as Shanghai and Nanjing (the capital of Jiangsu Province), and its geographical location has allowed it to have access to urban technologies and market networks. In contrast, Aohan County in Inner Mongolia is relatively far away from large cities and thus it is difficult for the village to obtain urban resources. In addition, the two cases also vary in conditions of agricultural production, such as infrastructure, soil quality, and precipitation. These differences have led to very different development outcomes in the two counties: Wujin has made great progress in industrial production and the expansion of rural industry reduced agriculture to a secondary role in the local economy. In Aohan, however, rural industry is nearly non-existent and the village relies on agriculture, including animal husbandry, for a major source of income.

Rural revitalization: a new East Asian development path?

In recent years, all East Asian cases (Japan, South Korea, Taiwan, and China) surveyed in this book have formulated strategies or programs of rural revitalization.

This is, on the one hand, to address the problems of rural decline, but on the other hand, it is also aimed to mitigate urban problems and balance rural-urban relations. The previous strategy of urbanization, which is vividly depicted in China as "to enrich peasants by reducing peasants (*jianshao nongmin jiushi fuyu nongmin*)" (e.g., Mao 2003), seems to have reached its limits. Not only do rural laborers who migrated to the city desire to retain land rights, but also there emerges a swelling class of the urban poor and an even large class of urban precariats. In Japan, South Korea, and Taiwan, the excessive urbanization has led to many urban problems in the era of slow growth and the neoliberal reforms to the labor system. The strategy of rural revitalization, which recognizes the importance of land to popular livelihood, attempts to inject new dynamism into rural areas. This may revive a long tradition of rural-based, balanced development in the region and become the new East Asian development path.

This positive diagnosis is accompanied by a caveat. The two contradictory forces identified in this book – agrarian capitalism and industrious revolution – shape the current strategies of rural revitalization in the region. On the one hand, rural revitalization is aimed to strengthen the position of small rural holders with economic incentives, development funds, and increased public services. On the other hand, under the influence of agrarian capitalism, rural revitalization is also used to consolidate farmlands and promote large-scale agriculture. Therefore, the future of the East Asian countryside will depend on the interactions between the two forces. The security of land rights and the resistance to those grabbing land will push a revitalized countryside closer toward the industrious revolution, whereas land concentration and the spread of corporate agriculture will pull it in the opposite direction.

Appendix

List of key land policy documents since the market reform

Rural land policy documents

Table A.1

Year	*Policy document*	*Key points of regulation*
1982	《中国农村会议纪要》(Summary of the Chinese rural conference)	The Household Responsibility System is affirmed. The transfer of land use rights of land is prohibited.
1984	《关于一九八四年农村工作的通知》(Notice on rural work in 1984)	Land contracts should be stable. Redistribution of the contracted land within the village is permitted.
1987	《中华人民共和国土地管理法》(PRC land management law)	The right to convert farmland to nonfarm land is held exclusively by the state.
1993	《关于当前农业和农村经济发展的若干政策措施》(Some policy measures on current agricultural and rural economic development)	The duration of land contracting is extended to another 30 years. The majority of the villagers and upper levels of government must approve it before an adjustment of land distribution in the village can proceed. Transfer of land use rights is allowed, but it should be between the villagers.
1998	《中共中央关于农业和农村工作若干重大问题的决定》(CCP Central Committee's Decision on Major Issues Concerning Agriculture and Rural Areas)	A comprehensive strategy of agricultural modernization is adopted. The role of dragonhead agribusinesses is highlighted.

1998	《中华人民共和国土地管理法》（修订）(PRC land management law, revised)	The compensation standards for land expropriation are specified. The transfer of land use rights is reaffirmed, and the rights can be transferred to parties outside the village.
2001	《中共中央关于做好农户承包地使用权流转工作的通知》(Notice of the CCP Central Committee on properly implementing the work of transferring rural households' contract land)	Farmland should not be transferred to agribusinesses in principle.
2003	《中华人民土地承包法》(PRC land contracting law)	Peasants' land use rights are specified into a law. The land use rights can be transferred to other parties in multiple ways. Redistribution of land within the village must be approved by the township and county governments.
2006	《国民经济和社会发展第十一个五年规划纲要》(The 11th Five Year Plan)	A red line is drawn on the total area of farmland, which must not be less than 120 million hectares.
2008	十七届中全会，《中共中央关于推进农村改革发展若干重大问题的决定》(CCP Central Committee's decision on major issues in furthering rural reform and development)	To establish a market for the transfer of farmland use rights. To scale up agriculture in the form of specialized households, family farms and rural cooperatives.
2013	《中共中央、国务院关于加快发展现代农业，进一步增强农村发展活力的若干意见》(CCPCC and State Council directives on accelerating the development of modern agriculture and enhancing the dynamism of rural development)	To complete land titling for all farmland in five years, i.e., by 2018. Land transfer to agribusinesses and nonfarm enterprises is permitted.
	《中共中央关于全面深化改革若干重大问题的决定》(CCPCC decisions on major issues of deepening the reforms)	The new land reform is initiated. To promote land transfer by classifying land rights into three categories: ownership, contract rights, and operating (use) rights. To establish a unified rural-urban land market for rural construction lands.
2014	《关于全面深化农村改革加快推进农业现代化的若干意见》(Some directives on deepening rural reforms and pushing forward agricultural modernization)	Land use rights can be used as collateral for loans. The separation of three rights of farmland is reaffirmed.

continued

Table A.1 Continued

	《关于引导农村土地经营权有序流转发展农业适度规模的意见》(Directives on leading the orderly transfer of rural use rights and developing the moderate scale of agriculture)	Corporate farms are a key entity of agriculture. To accelerate land transfer and promote long-term land transfers. To establish land transfer markets. To promote large farms. The size of large farms should be 10 to 15 times the average local farm. Financial support including rural subsidies should favor large producers.
2015	《关于农村土地征收、集体经营性建设用地入市、宅基地制度改革试点工作的意见》(Directives on rural land expropriations, the market for collective rural construction land, and the reform on residential land)	To establish the market for rural construction lands. Residential land can be used as collateral. To explore ways for peasants to relinquish residential land once they settle down in the city.
2017	《关于加快构建政策体系培育新型农业经营主体的意见》(Directives on accelerating the building of the policy system to foster new agricultural business entities)	To expand the scale of agriculture. To increase financial support for large farming entities. To build larger dragonhead companies.
2018	《国家乡村振兴战略规划（2018–2022 年）》(National strategic planning for rural revitalization, 2018-2022)	New rural construction lands can be approved if necessary (this is different from previously documents which emphasize restricting the expansion of rural construction land).

Urban land policy documents

Table A.2

1984	《全国城市工作会议纪要》(Summary of the national urban work meeting)	In urban areas, work units and individuals should pay for the use of land.
1988	《中华人民共和国城镇土地使用税暂行条例》(Tentative regulation on urban land use tax in PRC)	To collect land use tax.
1990	《中华人民共和国土地使用权出让和转让暂行条例》(Tentative regulation on the transfer of land use rights in PRC)	The system of transferring land use rights from the state is established.
1998	《国务院关于进一步深化城镇住房制度改革加快住房建设的通知》(State Council notice on further deepening the urban housing reform)	To stop the welfare housing policy. To establish the urban housing market.

2001	《城市房屋拆迁管理条例》(Regulation on the management of urban housing expropriations)	To assess the market price of urban houses and offer cash compensation for house demolition.
2002	《招标拍卖挂牌出让国有土地使用权规定》(Regulation on the auctioning of the use rights of state-owned lands)	Urban lands for businesses such as commerce, tourism, entertainment, and commercial real estate must be transferred through auctioning.
2004	《关于完善征地补偿安置制度的指导意见》(Guidelines on improving the compensation system for land expropriation)	To increase compensation standards for land expropriation. To establish a social security system for land-losing peasants.
	《国务院关于深化改革严格土地管理的决定》(State Council decision on furthering reforms and applying stricter land management regulations)	The increase in urban construction land must be accompanied by the reduction in rural construction land.
2006	《国务院关于加强土地调控有关问题的通知》(State Council notice on strengthening the land regulation)	The living standards of land-losing peasants must not be lower than before the land is expropriated.
2008	《中共中央关于推进农村改革发展若干重大问题的决定》(CCP Central Committee's decision on major issues in furthering rural reform and development)	To control the scale of land expropriations. To increase compensation standards for land expropriations. The policy that the loss of farmland due to urban expansion must be accompanied by the reclamation of new farmland (*zhanbu pingheng*) must be implemented within a prefecture, i.e., the new farmland must be reclaimed within the prefecture.
	《城乡建设用地增减挂钩管理办法》(Methods on the management of the increase-decrease of urban-rural construction lands)	The increase in urban construction land must be accompanied by the reduction in rural construction land.
2010	《国务院办公厅关于进一步严格征地拆迁管理工作切实维护群众合法权益的紧急通知》(State Council emergent notice on applying stricter regulations on land and housing expropriations and protecting the lawful rights of the masses)	To prohibit illegal land and housing expropriations. To increase compensation standards. Long-term livelihoods of land-losing peasants and urban residents must be protected.

continued

Table A.2 Continued

2011	《国有±地上房屋征收与补偿条例》(Regulation on the expropriation and compensation of houses on state-owned lands)	The scope of urban housing expropriations is specified. The compensations for housing expropriations are specified. To prohibit the use of violence in housing expropriations. Compensation must be made before a house is demolished.
2017	《中共中央国务院关于加强耕地保护和改进占补平衡的意见》(CCPCC and State Council directives on enhancing farmland protection and improving the policy of *zhanbu pingheng*)	The new farmland can be reclaimed from another prefecture or another province to make up for the loss of farmland due to urban expansion.

References

Ahlers, Anna. 2014. *Rural Policy Implementation in Contemporary China: New Socialist Countryside*. London, UK: Routledge.

Ahlers, Anna L., and Gunter Schubert. 2009. " 'Building a New Socialist Countryside' – Only a Political Slogan?" *Journal of Current Chinese Affairs* 38 (4): 35–62.

Ahn, Sanghoon, Kyoji Fukao, and Keiko Ito. 2008. "Outsourcing in East Asia and its Impact on the Japanese and Korean Labour Markets." *OECD Trade Policy Papers* (65): 1–89. doi: https://doi.org/10.1787/244366638573.

Ahuja, Vinod, Benu Bidani, Francisco Ferreira, and Michael Walton. 1997. *Everyone's Miracle?: Revisiting Poverty and Inequality in East Asia*. Washington, DC: World Bank Publications.

Alexander, Peter. 2013. "Marikana, Turning Point in South African History." *Review of African Political Economy* 40 (138): 605–19.

Alexander, Peter, and Anita Chan. 2004. "Does China Have an Apartheid Pass System?" *Journal of Ethnic and Migration Studies* 30 (4): 609–29.

Aliber, Michael, and Ben Cousins. 2013. "Livelihoods after Land Reform in South Africa." *Journal of Agrarian Change* 13 (1): 140–65.

Amsden, Alice H. 1989. *Asia's Next Giant: South Korea and Late Industrialization*. New York: Oxford University Press on Demand.

Andreas, Joel. 2010. "A Shanghai Model? On Capitalism with Chinese Characteristics." *New Left Review* (65): 63–85.

Andreas, Joel, and Shaohua Zhan. 2016. "Hukou and Land: Market Reform and Rural Displacement in China." *The Journal of Peasant Studies* 43 (4): 798–827.

Aohan Banner Gazetteer. 1991. *Aohan Banner Gazetteer* [*Aohan qizhi*]. Hohhot, China: Neimenggu renmin chubanshe.

Aohan Banner Irrigation Gazetteer. 1988. *Aohan Banner Irrigation Gazetteer* [*Aohanqi shuili zhi*]. Aohan, Inner Mongolia: Aohan Bureau of Archives.

Aohan Bureau of Archives. 1991. *Aohan Banner Population Gazetteer* [*Aohanqi renkou zhi*]. Aohan, Inner Mongolia: Aohan Bureau of Archives.

Aohan Bureau of Forestry. 1985. *Lüse de lu* [*The green road*]. Aohan, Inner Mongolia: Aohan Bureau of Archives.

Aohan Bureau of Forestry. 1995. "Huihuang de aohan linye [Glorious achievement of Aohan forestry]." *Journal of Inner Mongolia Forestry* [*neimenggu linye*] 18 (7): 1.

Arrighi, Giovanni. 1970. "Labour Supplies in Historical Perspective: A Study of the Proletarianization of the African Peasantry in Rhodesia." *The Journal of Development Studies* 6 (3): 197–234.

Arrighi, Giovanni. 1994. *The Long Twentieth Century: Money, Power, and the Origins of Our Times*. London, UK: Verso Books.

Arrighi, Giovanni. 2007. *Adam Smith in Beijing: Lineages of the Twenty-First Century*. London, UK: Verso Books.

Arrighi, Giovanni, and Beverly Silver. 2001. "Capitalism and World (Dis)order." *Review of International Studies* 27 (5): 257–79.

Arrighi, Giovanni, Nicole Aschoff, and Ben Scully. 2010. "Accumulation by Dispossession and Its Limits: The Southern Africa Paradigm Revisited." *Studies in Comparative International Development* 45 (4): 410–38.

Aspalter, Christian. 2006. "The East Asian Welfare Model." *International Journal of Social Welfare* 15 (4): 290–301.

Atwell, William S. 1982. "International Bullion Flows and the Chinese Economy Circa 1530–1650." *Past & Present* 95 (1): 68–90.

Baek, Seung-Wook. 2005. "Does China Follow 'the East Asian Development Model'?" *Journal of Contemporary Asia* 35 (4): 485–98.

Bai, Jianfeng. 2009. "New Rural Cooperative Medical Care Has Covered 830 Million Peasants." *The People's Daily*, July 14. Accessed April 28, 2018. http://finance.people.com.cn/GB/9646971.html.

Ban, Sung Hwan, Pal Yong Moon, and Dwight H. Perkins. 1982. *Studies in the Modernization of the Republic of Korea: 1945–1975: Rural Development*. Cambridge, MA: Harvard University Press.

Bartlett, Beatrice S. 1991. *Monarchs and Ministers: The Grand Council in Mid-Ch'ing China, 1723–1820*. Berkeley, CA: University of California Press.

Beeson, Mark. 2004. "The rise and fall (?) of the developmental state: The vicissitudes and implications of East Asian interventionism." In *Developmental States: Relevancy, Redundancy or Reconfiguration*, edited by Linda Low, 29–40. New York: Nova Science Publishers, Inc.

Beijing News [Xinjingbao]. 2010. "Sanwei nongcun zhuanjia pou quandi yuanyi [Three rural experts discuss the causes of 'enclosure']." *The Beijing News*, November 5, A01.

Beinart, William. 2001. *Twentieth-Century South Africa*. Oxford, UK: Oxford University Press.

Bernstein, Henry. 2006. "Is There an Agrarian Question in the 21st Century?" *Canadian Journal of Development Studies/Revue canadienne d'études du développement* 27 (4): 449–60.

Bernstein, Henry. 2007. "Agrarian questions of capital and labour: Some theory about land reform (and a periodisation)." In *The Land Question in South Africa: The Challenge of Transformation and Redistribution*, edited by Lungisile Ntsebeza and Ruth Hall, 27–59. Cape Town, South Africa: HSRC Press.

Bernstein, Henry. 2010. *Class Dynamics of Agrarian Change*. Sterling, VA: Kumarian Press.

Bernstein, Henry. 2013. "Commercial Agriculture in South Africa since 1994: 'Natural, Simply Capitalism.'" *Journal of Agrarian Change* 13 (1): 23–46.

Bernstein, Henry. 2016. "Agrarian Political Economy and Modern World Capitalism: the Contributions of Food Regime Analysis." *The Journal of Peasant Studies* 43 (3): 611–47.

Bernstein, Thomas P., and Xiaobo Lü. 2003. *Taxation without Representation in Contemporary Rural China*. Cambridge, UK: Cambridge University Press.

Bo, Yibo. 1991. *Ruogan zhongda juece yu shijian de huigu* [*Retrospect on some significant decisions and events*]. Beijing: Zhonggong zhongyang dangxiao chubanshe.

Bond, Patrick. 2000. *Elite Transition: From Apartheid to Neoliberalism in South Africa*. London, UK: Pluto Press.

Bond, Patrick, and Shauna Mottiar. 2013. "Movements, Protests and a Massacre in South Africa." *Journal of Contemporary African Studies* 31 (2): 283–302.

Borras, Saturnino M., Jr., and Jennifer C. Franco. 2012. "Global Land Grabbing and Trajectories of Agrarian Change: A Preliminary Analysis." *Journal of Agrarian Change* 12 (1): 34–59.

Brady, James. 2016. *Japanese Agriculture: Towards a Sustainable, Trade-Oriented Future*. Osaka: Asia Pacific Institute of Research.

Bramall, Chris. 1993. *In Praise of Maoist Economic Planning: Living Standards and Economic Development in Sichuan since 1931*. Oxford, UK: Clarendon Press.

Bramall, Chris. 2004. "Chinese Land Reform in Long-Run Perspective and in the Wider East Asian Context." *Journal of Agrarian Change* 4 (1–2): 107–41.

Bramall, Chris. 2007. *The Industrialization of Rural China*. Oxford: Oxford University Press.

Bramall, Chris. 2009. *Chinese Economic Development*. London, UK: Routledge.

Brandt, Loren, Debin Ma, and Thomas G. Rawski. 2014. "From Divergence to Convergence: Reevaluating the History behind China's Economic Boom." *Journal of Economic Literature* 52 (1): 45–123.

Braudel, Fernand. 1977. *Afterthoughts on Material Civilization and Capitalism*. Baltimore, MD: Johns Hopkins University Press.

Bray, Francesca. 1994. *The Rice Economies: Technology and Development in Asian Societies*. Berkeley, CA: University of California Press.

Bray, Francesca. 1997. *Technology and Gender: Fabrics of Power in Late Imperial China*. Berkeley, CA: University of California Press.

Brenner, Robert. 1982. "The Agrarian Roots of European Capitalism." *Past & Present* 97 (1): 16–113.

Brenner, Robert, and Christopher Isett. 2002. "England's Divergence from China's Yangzi Delta: Property Relations, Microeconomics, and Patterns of Development." *The Journal of Asian Studies* 61 (2): 609–62.

Brown, Lester R. 1994. "Who Will Feed China?" *World Watch* 7 (5): 10–19.

Brown, Lester R. 1995. *Who Will Feed China? Wake-Up Call for a Small Planet*. New York: W. W. Norton & Company.

Bundy, Colin. 1988. *The Rise and Fall of the South African Peasantry*. 2nd ed. Berkeley, CA: University of California Press.

Buoye, Thomas. 1993. "From Patrimony to Commodity: Changing Concepts of Land and Social Conflict in Guangdong Province during the Qianlong Reign (1736–1795)." *Late Imperial China* 14 (2): 33–59.

Burawoy, Michael. 1976. "The Functions and Reproduction of Migrant Labor: Comparative Material from Southern Africa and the United States." *American Journal of Sociology* 81 (5): 1050–87.

Burmeister, Larry L. 1990a. "South Korea's Rural Development Dilemma: Trade Pressures and Agricultural Sector Adjustment." *Asian Survey* 30 (7): 711–23.

Burmeister, Larry L. 1990b. "State, Industrialization and Agricultural Policy in Korea." *Development and Change* 21 (2): 197–223.

Butler, Anthony. 2017. *Contemporary South Africa*. 3rd ed. London, UK: Palgrave Macmillan.

Byrd, William A., and Qingsong Lin. 1990. *China's Rural Industry: Structure, Development, and Reform*. Oxford, UK: Oxford University Press.

Byrd, William, and Ning Zhu. 1990. "Market interactions and industrial structure." In *China's Rural Industry: Structure, Development, and Reform*, edited by William A. Byrd and Qingsong Lin, 85–111. Oxford, UK: Oxford University Press.

CASS (Chinese Academy of Social Sciences). 1992. *Zhonghua renmin gongheguo jingji dangan ziliao xuanbian (nongcun jingji tizhi juan) 1949–1952*. Beijing: Social Sciences Academic Press.

CCP Archival Research Office. 1993a. *Jianguoyilai zhongyao wenxian xuanbian [Selected important documents since the founding of the state] Vol. 1*. Beijing: Zhongyang wenxian chunbanshe.

CCP Archival Research Office. 1993b. *Jianguoyilai zhongyao wenxian xuanbian [Selected important documents since the founding of the state] Vol. 15*. Beijing: Zhongyang wenxian chunbanshe.

CCTV. 2003. "Liguo Limin: quxiao nongye techan shui [Beneficial to the nation and people: the removal of taxes on special agricultural goods]." Accessed April 16, 2018. www.cctv.com/financial/20030930/101548.shtml.

Chan, Kam Wing, and Li Zhang. 1999. "The Hukou System and Rural-Urban Migration in China: Processes and Changes." *The China Quarterly* 160: 818–55.

Chan, Kam-wah. 2007. "Concluding observations: Is there a crisis of welfare in East Asia?" In *The Crisis of Welfare in East Asia*, edited by James Lee and KaM-Wah Chan, 243–56. Lanham, MD: Lexington Books.

Chang, Ha-Joon. 1993. "The Political Economy of Industrial Policy in Korea." *Cambridge Journal of Economics* 17 (2): 131–57.

Chanye xinxi wang. 2017. "2017 nian zhongguo jiating tudi liuzhuan mianji [The acreage of land transfers from rural families in China in 2017]." Accessed April 30, 2018. www.chyxx.com/industry/201711/579455.html.

Chao, Kang. 1986. *Man and Land in Chinese History: An Economic Analysis*. Stanford, CA: Stanford University Press.

Chayanov, A.V. 1986. *The Theory of Peasant Economy*. Madison, WI: University of Wisconsin Press.

Chayanov, A.V. 1991. *The Theory of Peasant Co-Operatives*. London: I.B. Tauris & Co Ltd.

Chen, Joe, Yun Cheong Choi, Kota Mori, Yasuyuki Sawada, and Saki Sugano. 2012. "Recession, Unemployment, and Suicide in Japan." *Japan Labor Review* 9 (2): 75–92.

Chen, Xinzhou, Jiaxuan Guo, and Changzheng Li. 2002. "Lantian fengbao jingshi nongye chanyehua [The Lantian storm sends a warning to agricultural industrialization]." *Outlook Weekly* [*liaowang xinwen zhoukan*], July 22.

Chen, Xiwen. 2018. "Xiangcun zhenxing kaiqi sannong xiandaihua lujing [Rural revitalization opens the road to rural modernization]." *Liaowang (Outlook Weekly)*, January 24. Accessed May 2, 2018. www.xinhuanet.com/local/2018-01/24/c_1122304398.htm.

Chen, Yangfen, Xiande Li, Lijuan Wang, and Shihai Wang. 2017. "Is China different from Other Investors in Global Land Acquisition? Some Observations from Existing Deals in China's Going Global Strategy." *Land Use Policy* 60: 362–72.

Chen, Yiu Por, Mingxing Liu, and Qi Zhang. 2010. "Development of Financial Intermediation and the Dynamics of Urban–Rural Disparity in China, 1978–1998." *Regional Studies* 44 (9): 1171–87.

Cheng, Tiejun, and Mark Selden. 1994. "The Origins and Social Consequences of China's Hukou System." *The China Quarterly* 139: 644–68.

Chitonge, Horman. 2013. "Land Use and Rural Livelihoods in South Africa: Emerging Evidence from the Eastern Cape." *Agrarian South: Journal of Political Economy* 2 (1): 1–40.

Choi, Young Jun. 2012. "End of the Era of Productivist Welfare Capitalism? Diverging Welfare Regimes in East Asia." *Asian Journal of Social Science* 40 (3): 275–94.

Cline, William R. 1982. "Can the East Asian Model of Development Be Generalized?" *World Development* 10 (2): 81–90.

Cohen, Myron L. 2005. *Kinship, Contract, Community, and State: Anthropological Perspectives on China*. Stanford, CA: Stanford University Press.

Cohen, Paul A. 1984. *Discovering History in China: American Historical Writing on the Recent Chinese Past*. New York: Columbia University Press.

Conrad, Harald. 2017. "Social policy responses to the 'gap society': The structural limitations of the Japanese welfare state and related official discourses since the 1990s." In *Social Inequality in Post-Growth Japan: Transformation during Economic and Demographic Stagnation*, edited by David Chiavacci and Carola Hommerich, 121–33. London, UK: Routledge.

Corbo, Vittorio, Anne Krueger, and Fernando Ossa (eds). 1985. *Export-Oriented Development Strategies: The Success of Five Newly Industrializing Countries*. Boulder, CO: Westview Press.

Cousins, Ben. 2013. "Smallholder Irrigation Schemes, Agrarian Reform and 'Accumulation from Above and from Below' in South Africa." *Journal of Agrarian Change* 13 (1): 116–39.

Cousins, Ben. 2016. "Land Reform in South Africa Is Failing. Can It Be Saved?" *Transformation: Critical Perspectives on Southern Africa* 92 (1): 135–57.

Crossley, Pamela Kyle. 1999. *A Translucent Mirror: History and Identity in Qing Imperial Ideology*. Berkeley, CA: University of California Press.

Crossley, Pamela Kyle, and Evelyn S. Rawski. 1993. "A Profile of the Manchu Language in Ch'ing History." *Harvard Journal of Asiatic Studies* 53 (1): 63–102.

DAFF (Department of Agriculture, Forestry and Fisheries, South Africa). 2016. *Abstract of Agricultural Statistics 2016*. Pretoria, South Africa.

Dai, Yi. 1992. *Qianlongdi jiqi shidai* [*Qianlong emperor and his times*]. Beijing: Zhongguo renmin chubanshe.

Davis, Mike. 2006. *Planet of Slums*. London, UK: Verso Books.

Day, Alexander F. 2013. *The Peasant in Postsocialist China: History, Politics, and Capitalism*. Cambridge, UK: Cambridge University Press.

Day, Alexander F, and Mindi Schneider. 2017. "The End of Alternatives? Capitalist Transformation, Rural Activism and the Politics of Possibility in China." *The Journal of Peasant Studies*: 1–25. doi: 10.1080/03066150.2017.1386179.

De Brauw, Alan, Qiang Li, Chengfang Liu, Scott Rozelle, and Linxiu Zhang. 2008. "Feminization of Agriculture in China? Myths Surrounding Women's Participation in Farming." *The China Quarterly* 194: 327–48.

Deng, Yiming. 1994. "Liangshi tijia nengshi nongmin dedao duoshao haochu [How much peasants can benefit from increasing grain prices]." *Shengchanli zhisheng* [*voices of productive forces*] 2 (8): 27–8.

Deyo, Frederic. 1989. *Beneath the Miracle: Labour Subordination in East Asian Development*. Berkeley, CA: University of California Press.

Deyo, Frederic. 1992. "The political economy of social policy formation: East Asia's newly industrialized countries." In *States and Development in the Asian Pacific Rim*, edited by Richard P. Appelbaum, and Jeffrey W. Henderson, 289–306. Newbury Park, CA: Sage.

Dong, Jun, and Weijie Hong. 2017. "Quanguo nongmin zhuanye hezuoshe shuliang da 193 wan duojia [The number of peasant cooperatives reaches more than 1.93 million]." *Xianhua Net*, September 4. www.xinhuanet.com/2017-09/04/c_129695890.htm.

Dong, Xiao-Yuan. 1996. "Two-tier Land Tenure System and Sustained Economic Growth in Post-1978 Rural China." *World Development* 24 (5): 915–28.

Dore, Ronald P. 1958. "The Japanese Land Reform in Retrospect." *Far Eastern Survey* 27 (12): 183–8.

Dore, Ronald P. 1984. *Land Reform in Japan*. London, UK: The Athlone Press.

Dorner, Peter, and William C. Thiesenhusen. 1990. "Selected Land Reforms in East and Southeast Asia: Their Origins and Impacts." *Asian-Pacific Economic Literature* 4 (1): 65–95.

Du, Lexin, Wenming Zhang, and Zemin Huang. 2006. *Zhongguo yiliao weisheng fazhan baogao* [*Report on the development of health care in China*]. Vol. 2. Beijing: Social Sciences Academic Press.

Du, Ying, and Ruijie Guan. 1996. "Guanyu jiji yindao daxing gongshang qiye jinru nongye lingyu de zhanlue gouxiang [Strategic framework on drawing large industrial and commercial enterprises into agriculture]." *Review of Economic Research [jingji yanjiu cankao]* 18 (d5): 2–16.

Duara, Prasenjit. 1988. *Culture, Power, and the State: Rural North China, 1900–1942*. Stanford, CA: Stanford University Press.

Dunstan, Helen. 1996. *Conflicting Counsels to Confuse the Age: A Documentary Study of Political Economy on Qing China, 1644–1840*. Ann Arbor, MI: Center for Chinese Studies, University of Michigan.

Edelman, Marc, Carlos Oya, and Saturnino M. Borras Jr. 2013. "Global Land Grabs: Historical Processes, Theoretical and Methodological Implications and Current Trajectories." *Third World Quarterly* 34 (9): 1517–31.

Elliott, Mark C. 2001. *The Manchu Way: The Eight Banners and Ethnic Identity in Late Imperial China*. Stanford, CA: Stanford University Press.

Elvin, Mark. 1973. *The Pattern of the Chinese Past: A Social and Economic Interpretation*. Stanford, CA: Stanford University Press.

Evans, Peter B. 1995. *Embedded Autonomy: States and Industrial Transformation*. Princeton, NJ: Princeton University Press.

Evans, Peter B., Dietrich Rueschemeyer, and Theda Skocpol. 1985. *Bringing the State Back in*. Cambridge, UK: Cambridge University Press.

Fan, Shenggen, and Connie Chan-Kang. 2005. "Is Small Beautiful? Farm Size, Productivity, and Poverty in Asian Agriculture." *Agricultural Economics* 32 (s1): 135–46.

Fan, Shenggen, Linxiu Zhang, and Xiaobo Zhang. 2004. "Reforms, Investment, and Poverty in Rural China." *Economic Development and Cultural Change* 52 (2): 395–421.

Fang, Xing. 1997. "Zhengque pingjia qingdai de nongye jingji [Agricultural achievements in the Qing should be correctly evaluated]." *Researches in Chinese Economic History* [*zhongguo jingjishi yanjiu*] 12 (3): 141–50.

Fei, Xiaotong. 1986. *Small Towns in China: Functions, Problems and Prospects*. Beijing: New World Press.

Feng, Erkang. 1985. *Yongzheng zhuan* [*Yongzhen's biography*]. Beijing: Renmin chubanshe.

Feuerwerker, Albert. 1984. "The State and the Economy in Late Imperial China." *Theory and Society* 13 (3): 297–326.

Feuerwerker, Albert. 1992. "Presidential Address: Questions about China's Early Modern Economic History That I Wish I Could Answer." *The Journal of Asian Studies* 51 (4): 757–69.

Francks, Penelope. 2002. "Rural Industry, Growth Linkages, and Economic Development in Nineteenth-Century Japan." *The Journal of Asian Studies* 61 (1): 33–55.

Francks, Penelope, Joanna Boestel, and Choo Hyop Kim. 1999. *Agriculture and Economic Development in East Asia: From Growth to Protectionism in Japan, Korea and Taiwan*. London, UK: Routledge.

Frank, Andre Gunder. 1998. *ReOrient: Global Economy in the Asian Age*. Berkeley, CA: University of California Press.

Friedman, Edward, Paul Pickowicz, and Mark Selden. 1991. *Chinese Village, Socialist State*. New Haven, CT: Yale University Press.

Fu, Yiling. 1957. *Mingdai jiangnan shimin jingji shitan [A preliminary study on civil economy in the Ming dynasty]*. Shanghai: Shanghai renmin chubanshe.

Fu, Yiling. 2007. *Mingqing fengjian tudi suoyouzhi lungang [The outline on feudal land ownership systems in the Ming and Qing Dynasty]*. Beijing: Zhonghua shuju.

Gallagher, Mary, Ching Kwan Lee, and Sarosh Kuruvilla. 2011. "Introduction and argument." In *From Iron Rice Bowl to Informalization: Markets, Workers, and The State in a Changing China*, edited by Sarosh Kuruvilla, Ching Kwan Lee, and Mary Gallagher, 1–16. Ithaca, NY: Cornell University Press.

Gao, Ming, and Yunyun Guo. 2018. "2018 zhongguo xinxing nongye jingying zhuti fazhan fenxi baogao [An analysis report of the development of new agricultural business entities in 2018]." *Farmers' Daily*, February 22, page 04.

Gao, Wangling. 1995. *Shiba shiji zhongguo de jingji fazhan he zhengfu zhengce [Chinese economic development and government policy in the eighteenth century]*. Beijing: China Social Sciences Press.

Gao, Wangling. 1999. *Jingji fazhan yu diqu kaifa: zhongguo chuantong jingji de fazhan xulie [Economic development and reginal development: the developmental stages of Chinese traditional economy]*. Beijing: Haiyang chubanshe.

Gao, Wangling. 2005a. *Zutian guanxi xinlun: dizhu, nongmin he dizu [A new view on the landlord-tenant relationship: landlords, peasants and rents]*. Shanghai: Shanghai shudian chubanshe.

Gao, Wangling. 2005b. "Zutian guanxi xinlun [A new view on the landlord-tenant relationship]." *Researches in Chinese Economic History [Zhongguo jingjishi yanjiu]* 20 (3): 15–24.

Gao, Wangling. 2012. *Qianlong shisannian [Thirteenth year of Qianlong]*. Beijing: Economic Science Press.

Gao, Xiang. 1995. *Kangyongqian sandi tongzhi sixiang yanjiu [A study of the ruling thoughts of Kangxi, Yongzheng and Qianlong emperors]*. Beijing: Zhongguo renmin daxue chubanshe.

Gereffi, Gary. 1989. "Rethinking Development Theory: Insights from East Asia and Latin America." Sociological Forum 4(4): 503-33.

Gereffi, Gary, and Donald L. Wyman. 1990. *Manufacturing Miracles: Paths of Industrialization in Latin America and East Asia*. Princeton, NJ: Princeton University Press.

Gibson, James L. 2009. *Overcoming Historical Injustices: Land Reconciliation in South Africa*. Cambridge, UK: Cambridge University Press.

Giddens, Anthony. 1985. *The Nation-State and Violence*. Berkeley, CA: University of California Press.

Glassman, Jim. 2006. "Primitive Accumulation, Accumulation by Dispossession, Accumulation By 'Extra-Economic' Means." *Progress in Human Geography* 30 (5): 608–25.

Godo, Yoshihisa. 2013. "An Outlook on Japanese Farm Households." http://ap.fftc.agnet.org/ap_db.php?id=66.

Gordon, Andrew. 2017. "New and Enduring Dual Structures of Employment in Japan: The Rise of Non-Regular Labor, 1980s–2010s." *Social Science Japan Journal* 20 (1): 9–36.

Gough, Ian. 2001. "Globalization and Regional Welfare Regimes: The East Asian Case." *Global Social Policy* 1 (2): 163–89.

Guo, Hongdong, Robert W. Jolly, and Jianhua Zhu. 2007. "Contract Farming in China: Perspectives of Farm Households and Agribusiness Firms." *Comparative Economic Studies* 49 (2): 285–312.

Guy, R. Kent. 2010. *Qing Governors and Their Provinces: The Evolution of Territorial Administration in China, 1644–1796*. Seattle, WA: University of Washington Press.

Hall, Ruth. 2007. "Transforming rural South Africa? Taking stock of land reform." In *The Land Question in South Africa: The Challenge of Transformation and Redistribution*, edited by Lungisile Ntsebeza and Ruth Hall, 87–106. Cape Town, South Africa: HSRC Press.

Hall, Ruth. 2009. "Dynamics in the commercial farming sector." In *Another Countryside? Policy Options for Land and Agrarian Reform in South Africa*, edited by Ruth Hall, 120–31. Cape Town, South Africa: University of the Western Cape.

Hall, Ruth, and Thembela Kepe. 2017. "Elite Capture and State Neglect: New Evidence on South Africa's Land Reform." *Review of African Political Economy* 44 (151): 122–30.

Hamilton, Gary G., and Wei-An Chang. 2003. "The importance of commerce in the organization of China's late imperial economy." In *The Resurgence of East Asia: 500, 150 and 50 Year Perspectives*, edited by Giovanni Arrighi, Takeshi Hamashita, and Mark Seldon, 173–213. London, UK: Routledge.

Harrison, Bennett. 1997. *Lean and Mean: The Changing Landscape of Corporate Power in the Age of Flexibility*. New York: Guilford Press.

Hart, Gillian. 1996. "The Agrarian Question and Industrial Dispersal in South Africa: Agro-industrial Linkages through Asian Lenses." *The Journal of Peasant Studies* 23 (2–3): 245–77.

Hart, Gillian Patricia. 2002. *Disabling Globalization: Places of Power in Post-Apartheid South Africa*. Vol. 10. Berkeley, CA: University of California Press.

Harvey, David. 2003. *The New Imperialism*. New York: Oxford University Press.

Hayami, Akira. 1992. "The Industrious Revolution." *Look Japan* 38 (436): 8–10.

Hayami, Yujiro. 1998. "Toward an Alternative Path of Economic Development: An Introduction." In *Toward the Rural-Based Development of Commerce and Industry: Selected Experiences from East Asia*, edited by Yujiro Hayami, 1–20. Washington, DC: The World Bank.

Hays, Jeffrey. 2013. "Urban and Rural Life in Japan." http://factsanddetails.com/japan/cat19/sub122/item646.html#chapter-6.

He, Shenjing, Yuting Liu, Chris Webster, and Fulong Wu. 2009. "Property Rights Redistribution, Entitlement Failure and The Impoverishment of Landless Farmers in China." *Urban Studies* 46 (9): 1925–49.

He, Xuefeng. 2012. *Zuzhi qilai* [*Get organized*]. Jinan: Shandong People's Publishing House.

He, Xuefeng. 2013. *Xiaonong Lichang* [*Small farmers' standpoint*]. Beijing: China University of Political Science and Law Press.

Helliker, Kirk. 2013. "Reproducing white commercial agriculture in South Africa." In *The Promise of Land: Undoing a Century of Dispossession in South Africa*, edited by Fred T. Hendricks, Lungisile Ntsebeza, and Kirk Helliker, 76–102. Sunnyside, South Africa: Jacana Media (pty) Ltd.

Hendricks, Fred T., and Richard Pithouse. 2013. "Reproducing white commercial agriculture in South Africa." In *The Promise of Land: Undoing a Century of Dispossession in South Africa*, edited by Fred T. Hendricks, Lungisile Ntsebeza, and Kirk Helliker, 123–9. Sunnyside, South Africa: Jacana Media (pty) Ltd.

Hinton, William. 1983. *Shenfan: The Continuing Revolution in a Chinese Village*. New York: Random House.

Hinton, William. 1990. *The Great Reversal: The Privatization of China, 1978–1989*. New York: Monthly Review Press.

HLP (the high level panel). 2017. *Report of the High Level Panel on the Assessment of Key Legislation and the Acceleration of Fundamental Change*. Cape Town, South Africa: Parliament of South Africa.

Ho, Peter. 2001. "Who Owns China's Land? Policies, Property Rights and Deliberate Institutional Ambiguity." *The China Quarterly* 166: 394–421.

Ho, Ping-ti. 1959. *Studies on the Population of China, 1368–1953*. Cambridge, MA: Harvard University Press.

Ho, Ping-ti. 1967. "The Significance of the Ch'ing Period in Chinese History." *The Journal of Asian Studies* 26 (2): 189–95.

Ho, Samuel PS. 1982. "Economic Development and Rural Industry in South Korea and Taiwan." *World Development* 10 (11): 973–90.

Hofman, Irna, and Peter Ho. 2012. "China's 'Developmental Outsourcing': A Critical Examination of Chinese Global 'Land Grabs' Discourse." *Journal of Peasant Studies* 39 (1): 1–48.

Holliday, Ian. 2000. "Productivist Welfare Capitalism: Social Policy in East Asia." *Political Studies* 48 (4): 706–23.

Hong, Ijin. 2014. "Trends and Determinants of Social Expenditure in Korea, Japan and Taiwan." *Social Policy & Administration* 48 (6): 647–65.

Honma, Masayoshi, and Aurelia George Mulgan. 2018. "Political Economy Of Agricultural Reform in Japan under Abe's Administration." *Asian Economic Policy Review* 13 (1): 128–44.

Hsiao, Hsin-Huang Michael. 2013. "Precarious Work in Taiwan: A Profile." *American Behavioral Scientist* 57 (3): 373–89.

Hsing, You-tien. 2010. *The Great Urban Transformation: Politics of Land and Property in China*. Oxford, UK: Oxford University Press.

Hu, Angang, and Qungang Wu. 2001. "Nongye qiyehua: zhongguo nongcun xiandaihua de zhongyao tujing [Introducing enterprises into agriculture: an important pathway for rural modernization in China]." *Issues in Agricultural Economy* [*nongye jingji wenti*] 22 (1): 9–21.

Hu, Xuezhi, and Funing Zhong. 2012. "A Study on the Impacts of Rural Population Aging on Grain Production." *Chinese Rural Economy* [*Zhongguo Nongcun Jingji*] 28 (7): 29–39.

Hu, Zhanping, Qian Forrest Zhang, and John A Donaldson. 2017. "Farmers' Cooperatives in China: A Typology of Fraud and Failure." *The China Journal* 78 (1): 1–24.

Huang, Chen-Te. 2015. "The Restructuring Policy of Agro-Manpower and Farmland in Taiwan, R.O.C." FFTC Agricultural Policy Platform. http://ap.fftc.agnet.org/ap_db.php?id=450&print=1.

Huang, Liangui. 1996. "Quanguo nongye chanyehua zuotanhui zai Heilongjiang Zhaodong zhaokai [National forum on agricultural integration held in Zhaodong, Heilongjiang]." *Rural Cooperative Economy and Business Management* [*Nongcun Hezuo Jingji Jingying Guanli*] 14 (4): 3.

Huang, Miantang. 1988. "Qingda gugongren wenti kaoshi [An explanatory investigation of hired laborers in the Qing dynasty]." *Social Science Front* [*shehui kexue zhanxian*] 11 (3): 144–51.

Huang, Pei. 1974. *Autocracy at Work: A Study of the Yung-cheng Period, 1723–1735*. Bloomington, IN: Indiana University Press.

Huang, Philip. 1985. *The Peasant Economy and Social Change in North China*. Stanford, CA: Stanford University Press.

Huang, Philip. 2009. "China's Neglected Informal Economy: Reality and Theory." *Modern China* 35 (4): 405–38.

Huang, Philip. 2011. "China's New-Age Small Farms and Their Vertical Integration: Agribusiness or Co-Ops?" *Modern China* 37 (2): 107–34.

Huang, Philip. 2014. *Chaoyue zuoyou: cong shijian lishi tuanxun zhongguo nongcun fazhan chulu* [*Beyond left and right: exploring China's rural development road based on history and practice*]. Beijing: Falü chubanshe.

Huang, Yasheng. 2008. *Capitalism with Chinese Characteristics: Entrepreneurship and the State*. Cambridge, UK: Cambridge University Press.

Huang, Yuqin. 2012. "From the 'Feminization of Agriculture' to the 'Ageing of Farming Populations': Demographic Transition and Farming in a Central Chinese Village." *Local Economy* 27 (1): 19–32.

Huchzermeyer, Marie. 2004. *Unlawful Occupation: Informal Settlements and Urban Policy in South Africa and Brazil*. Trenton, NJ: Africa World Press.

Huchzermeyer, Marie. 2010. "Pounding at the Tip of the Iceberg: The Dominant Politics of Informal Settlement Eradication in South Africa." *Politikon* 37 (1): 129–48.

Hung, Ho-fung. 2003. "Orientalist Knowledge and Social Theories: China and the European Conceptions of East-West Differences from 1600 to 1900." *Sociological Theory* 21 (3): 254–80.

Hung, Ho-fung. 2011. *Protest with Chinese Characteristics: Demonstrations, Riots, and Petitions in the Mid-Qing Dynasty*. New York: Columbia University Press.

Hunter, Mark, and Dorrit Posel. 2012. "Here to Work: The Socioeconomic Characteristics of Informal Dwellers in Post-Apartheid South Africa." *Environment and Urbanization* 24 (1): 285–304.

Hwang, Gyu-Jin. 2012. "Explaining Welfare State Adaptation in East Asia: The Cases of Japan, Korea and Taiwan." *Asian Journal of Social Science* 40 (2): 174–202.

ILO. 2016. *Non-standard Employment around the World: Understanding Challenges, Shaping Prospects*. Geneva: International Labour Office.

Im, Jeongbin, and Iljeong Jeong. 2014. *The Frame of Agricultural Policy and Recent Major Agricultural Policy in Korea*. FFTC Agricultural Policy Platform.

Jacobs, Ricardo. 2018. "An Urban Proletariat with Peasant Characteristics: Land Occupations and Livestock Raising in South Africa." *The Journal of Peasant Studies* 45 (5–6): 884–903.

Jentzsch, Hanno. 2017. "Abandoned Land, Corporate Farming, and Farmland Banks: A Local Perspective on the Process of Deregulating and Redistributing Farmland in Japan." *Contemporary Japan* 29 (1): 31–46.

Jeong, Hyeseon. 2017. "Globalizing a Rural Past: The Conjunction of International Development Aid and South Korea's Dictatorial Legacy." *Geoforum* 86: 160–8.

Johnson, Chalmers. 1982. *MITI and the Japanese Miracle: The Growth of Industrial Policy: 1925–1975*. Stanford, CA: Stanford University Press.

Jones, Catherine. 1993. "The Pacific Challenge: Confucian Welfare States." In *New Perspectives on the Welfare State in Europe*, edited by Catherine Jones, 198–217. London, UK: Routledge.

Jones, Susan Mann, and Philip A. Kuhn. 1978. "Dynastic decline and the roots of rebellion." In *The Cambridge History of China, Volume 10: The Late Ch'ing, 1800–1911, Part I*, edited by John K. Fairbank, 107–62. Cambridge, UK: Cambridge University Press.

Kalleberg, Arne L. 2009. "Precarious Work, Insecure Workers: Employment Relations in Transition." *American Sociological Review* 74 (1): 1–22.

Kalleberg, Arne L., and Kevin Hewison. 2013. "Precarious Work and the Challenge for Asia." *American Behavioral Scientist* 57 (3): 271–88.

Kawagoe, Toshihiko. 1999. "Agricultural Land Reform in Postwar Japan: Experiences and Issues." *World Bank Policy Research Working Paper* (No. 2111) 1–43. https://doi.org/10.1596/1813-9450-2111.

Kay, Cristóbal. 2002. "Why East Asia Overtook Latin America: Agrarian Reform, Industrialisation and Development." *Third World Quarterly* 23 (6): 1073–1102.

Kingston, Jeff. 2011. *Contemporary Japan: History, Politics, and Social Change Since the 1980s*. 2nd ed. Oxford, UK: John Wiley and Sons.

Kloppenburg, Jack Ralph. 2005. *First the Seed: The Political Economy of Plant Biotechnology*. Madison, WI: University of Wisconsin Press.

Klug, Heinz. 1996. "Historical claims and the right to restitution." In *Agricultural Land Reform in South Africa*, edited by Johan Van Zyl, Johann Kirsten, and Hans P. Binswanger, 390–412. Oxford, UK: Oxford University Press.

Kong, Tat Yan. 2005. "Labour and Neo-Liberal Globalization in South Korea and Taiwan." *Modern Asian Studies* 39 (1): 155–88.

Kong, Xiangzhi, and Zhiqiang Wang. 2004. "Woguo chengzhenhua jinchengzhong shidi nongmin de buchang [Compensation for landless peasants in China's urbanization]." *Economic Theory and Business Management* [*jingji lilun yu jingji guanli*] 23 (5): 60–5.

Koo, Anthony Y. C. 1966. "Economic Consequences of Land Reform in Taiwan." *Asian Survey* 6 (3): 150–7.

Koo, Anthony Y. C. 1968. *The Role of Land Reform in Economic Development: A Case Study of Taiwan*. New York: Frederick A. Praeger Publishers.

Koo, Hagan. 1990. "From Farm to Factory: Proletarianization in Korea." *American Sociological Review* 55 (5): 669–81.

KREI. 2015. *Agriculture in Korea 2015*. Jeollanam-do, Korea: Korea Rural Economic Institute.

Krueger, Anne O. 1978. *Foreign Trade Regimes and Economic Development: Liberalization Attempts and Consequences*. Cambridge, MA: Ballinger for the National Bureau of Economic Research.

Kuhn, Philip A. 1980. *Rebellion and its Enemies in Late Imperial China: Militarization and Social Structure, 1796–1864*. Cambridge, MA: Harvard University Press.

Kwon, Huck-ju. 2005. "Transforming the Developmental Welfare State in East Asia." *Development and Change* 36 (3): 477–97.

Kwon, Soonman, and Ian Holliday. 2007. "The Korean Welfare State: A Paradox of Expansion in an Era of Globalisation and Economic Crisis." *International Journal of Social Welfare* 16 (3): 242–8.

Lall, Sanjaya. 1996. "Paradigms of Development: The East Asian Debate." *Oxford Development Studies* 24 (2): 111–31.

Landesa. 2012. *Landesa 6th 17-Province China Survey: Summary of 2011 Findings*.

Lee, Ching Kwan. 2007. *Against the Law: Labor Protests in China's Rustbelt and Sunbelt*. Berkeley, CA: University of California Press.

Lee, Ching Kwan. 2016. "Precarization or Empowerment? Reflections on Recent Labor Unrest in China." *The Journal of Asian Studies* 75 (2): 317–33.

Lee, Ching Kwan. 2017. *The Specter of Global China: Politics, Labor, and Foreign Investment in Africa*. Chicago, IL: University of Chicago Press.

Lee, Jung-Hwan, and Chong-Hyuk Suh. 1998. "Rural entrepreneurship and industrial development in Korea." In *Toward the Rural-Based Development of Commerce and Industry: Selected Experiences from East Asia*, edited by Yujiro Hayami, 187–210. Washington, DC: The World Bank.

Lee, Yoonkyung. 2015. "Labor after Neoliberalism: The Birth of the Insecure Class in South Korea." *Globalizations* 12 (2): 184–202.

Legassick, Martin. 1974. "South Africa: Capital Accumulation and Violence." *Economy and Society* 3 (3): 253–91.

Levien, Michael. 2012. "The Land Question: Special Economic Zones and the Political Economy of Dispossession in India." *The Journal of Peasant Studies* 39 (3–4): 933–69.

Lewis, William Arthur. 1954. "Economic Development with Unlimited Supplies of Labour." *The Manchester School* 22 (2): 139–91.

Li, Bozhong. 1998. *Agricultural Development in Jiangnan, 1620–1850*. New York: Springer.

Li, Bozhong. 2000. *Jiannan Zaoqi Gongyehua: 1550–1850* [*Early industrialization in South China: 1550–1850*]. Beijing: Social Sciences Academic Press.

Li, Bozhong. 2008. "Zhongsui qunlao: kuazhang haishi xianshi [Work all the year round: reality or exaggeration]?" *Academic Monthly* [*Xueshu Yuekan*] 40 (4): 134–9.

Li, Changping. 2002. *Woxiang zongli shuo shihua* [*I am telling the truth to the prime minister*]. Beijing: Guangming ribao chubanshe.

Li, Changping. 2003. "Shenyan tudi siyouhua [Land privatization should be cautious]." *Reading* [*Dushu*] 25 (6): 93–8.

Li, Changping. 2010. "90 niandai zhongguo nongcun zhengce shi nongmin rijian shiqu zizhuxing [Rural policies in the 1990s gradually deprived peasants of autonomy]." Accessed April 16, 2018. http://book.ifeng.com/yeneizixun/special/90niandai/zhengwen004/detail_2010_09/02/2418767_0.shtml.

Li, Junqing. 2012. "Fanzu daobao liuzhuan moshi kexingxing yanjiu [The case for the land transfer model of reverse contracting]." *Rural Economy* [*nongcun jingji*] 29 (8): 31–4.

Li, Sanmou. 2000. "Qingdai tianqi fanying de tudi guanxi [The land relations in the Qing seen from land sale contracts]." *Agricultural Archaeology* [*nongye kaogu*] 20 (3): 125–32.

Li, Sanmou, and Zhen Li. 1999. "Qingdai yongtianquan xingzhi chongtuan [Rethink permanent tenancy in the Qing dynasty]." *Agricultural History of China* [*zhongguo nongshi*] 19 (3): 19–25.

Liang, Yunyan. 2016. "Guangdongsheng chengzhenhua jinchengzhong shidi nongmin shouru wenti yanjiu [A study on the income of landless peasants in the process of urbanization in Guangdong province]." *Chinese Journal of Agricultural Resources and Regional Planning* [*zhongguo nongye ziyuan yu quhua*] 37 (8): 158–62.

Liao, Hongfeng. 2004. "Nongcun jichu jiaoyu gonggong caizheng zhichu gaige de sikao [Thoughts on the reform of public expenditure on rural basic education]." *Agricultural Research and Economic Management* [*nongye keyan jingji guanli*] 12 (2): 16–9.

Lim, Hyun-Chin, and Jin-Ho Jang. 2006. "Neo-LIBERALISM in Post-Crisis South Korea: Social Conditions and Outcomes." *Journal of Contemporary Asia* 36 (4): 442–63.

Lim, Kean Fan, and Niv Horesh. 2016. "The 'Singapore Fever' in China: Policy Mobility and Mutation." *The China Quarterly* 228: 992–1017.

Lin, Justin Yifu. 1990. "Collectivization and China's Agricultural Crisis in 1959–1961." *Journal of Political Economy* 98 (6): 1228–52.

Lipton, Michael, and Merle Lipton. 1993. "Creating Rural Livelihoods: Some Lessons for South Africa from Experience Elsewhere." *World Development* 21 (9): 1515–48.

Little, Peter D. 1994. *Living Under Contract: Contract Farming and Agrarian Transformation in Sub-Saharan Africa.* Madison, WI: University of Wisconsin Press.

Liu, Hui. 2014. "Zenyang yonghao guojia caizheng zhinong zijin [How to make good use of state funds for rural areas]." *Agricultural Technology and Information* [*nongyekeji yu xinxi*] 31 (4): 8.

Liu, Wan-Yu. 2018. "An Overview of New Agricultural Policies for Taiwan in 2018." FFTC Agricultural Policy Platform. http://ap.fftc.agnet.org/ap_db.php?id=867&print=1.

Liu, Yongcheng. 1980. "Lun qingdai qianqi nongye guyong laodong de xingzhi [On the meaning of agricultural hired labor in the early Qing dynasty]." In *Qingshi Yanjiu Ji* [*Selective studies on the Qing history*], Vol. 1, 91–112. Beijing: Zhongguo renmin daxue chubanshe.

Lufrano, Richard John. 1997. *Honorable Merchants: Commerce and Self-Cultivation in Late Imperial China.* Honolulu, HI: University of Hawaii Press.

Macheng Xianzhi. 1993. *Macheng Xianzhi* [*Macheng County Gazetteer*]. Beijing: Hongqi chubanshe.

Maclachlan, Patricia L., and Kay Shimizu. 2016. "Japanese Farmers in Flux: The Domestic Sources of Agricultural Reform." *Asian Survey* 56 (3): 442–65.

Maddison, Angus. 2007. *Contours of the World Economy 1–2030 AD: Essays in Macroeconomic History.* Oxford, UK: Oxford University Press.

MAFF. 2017. "Summary of the 2016 Annual Report on Food, Agriculture and Rural Areas in Japan." Tokyo, Japan: Ministry of Agriculture, Forestry and Fisheries.

Mann, Susan. 1997. *Precious Records: Women in China's Long Eighteenth Century.* Stanford, CA: Stanford University Press.

Mann, Susan. 2002. "Women, families, and gender relations." In *The Cambridge History of China, Volume 9, Part One: The Ch'ing Empire to 1800*, edited by Willard J. Peterson, 428–72. Cambridge, UK: Cambridge University Press.

Mao, Feng. 2004. "Zhengfu gaiwei shidi nongmin zuoshenmo [What governments should do for landless peasants]." *The World of Survey and Research* [*diaoyan shijie*] 17 (1): 28–29.

Mao, Yushi. 2003. "Sannong wenti de chulu zaiyu jianshao nongmin [The way out of the three rural problems lies in reducing peasants]." *Jiangsu Social Sciences* 2, 4–6.

Marais, Hein. 2011. *South Africa Pushed to the Limit: The Political Economy of Change.* London, UK, Zed Books.

Marks, Robert B., and Chunsheng Chen. 1995. "Price Inflation and its Social, Economic, and Climatic Context in Guangdong Province, 1707–1800." *T'oung Pao* 81 (1–3): 109–52.

McDermott, Joseph P. 1981. "Bondservants in the T'ai-hu Basin during the Late Ming: A Case of Mistaken Identities." *The Journal of Asian Studies* 40 (4): 675–701.

McDonald, Mary G. 1997. "Agricultural Landholding in Japan: Fifty Years after Land Reform." *Geoforum* 28 (1): 55–78.

McMichael, Philip. 2000. "A Global Interpretation of the Rise of the East Asian Food Import Complex." *World Development* 28 (3): 409–24.

McMichael, Philip. 2012. "The Land Grab and Corporate Food Regime Restructuring." *The Journal of Peasant Studies* 39 (3–4): 681–701.

Ministry of Agriculture. 1998. *Summary of the First National Agricultural Census in China (Part I)*. Beijing: China Statistics Press.

Ministry of Agriculture. 2003. *China TVEs Statistical Data: 1978–2002*. Beijing: China Agriculture Press.

Ministry of Agriculture. 2015. "Laoren nongye ye neng you suo wei [Farming by the elderly can also work well]." Accessed May 2, 2018. www.xinhuanet.com/politics/2015-08/24/c_128157372.htm.

Ministry of Agriculture. 2016. "Xinxingshixia nongye chanyehua fazhan liangdian fenchen [The bright spots of agricultural integration in the new situation]." *Xinhuanet*, July 20. Accessed April 29, 2018. www.xinhuanet.com/politics/2016-07/20/c_129163509.htm.

Ministry of Finance. 2007. "Gonggong caizheng fugai nongcun wenti yanjiu baogao [A report on the problems of public rural financing]." www.lunwentianxia.com/product.free.9701172.1/.

Ministry of Finance. 2018. "Caizhengbu 2017 nian caizheng shouzhi qingkuang xinwen fabuhui shilu [Records of the press conference on fiscal revenue and expenditure in 2017]." Accessed April 16, 2018. www.mof.gov.cn/zhengwuxinxi/caizhengxinwen/201801/t20180125_2800163.htm.

Ministry of Water Resources. 1990. *China Water Resources Yearbook 1990*. Beijing: Shuili Shuidian Chubanshe.

Ministry of Water Resources. 1999. *Shuili huihuang 50 nian* [*Glorious 50 years of water conservancy*]. Beijing: Shuili Shuidian Chubanshe.

Moore, Jason W. 2015. *Capitalism in the Web of Life: Ecology and the Accumulation of Capital*. New York: Verso Books.

Moore, Mick. 1984. "Agriculture in Taiwan and South Korea: The Minimalist State? 1." *IDS Bulletin* 15 (2): 57–64.

Murray, Colin. 1987. "Displaced Urbanization: South Africa's Rural Slums." *African Affairs* 86 (344): 311–29.

Myers, Ramon H., and Yeh-chien Wang. 2002. "Economic Developments, 1644–1800." In *The Cambridge History of China Volume 9: Part One: The Ch'ing Empire to 1800*, edited by Willard J. Peterson, 563–646. Cambridge, UK: Cambridge University Press.

Naquin, Susan, and Evelyn Sakakida Rawski. 1987. *Chinese Society in the Eighteenth Century*. New Haven, CT: Yale University Press.

National Development and Reform Commission of China. 2009. *National Agricultural Production Cost and Return Collection 2009*. Beijing: China Statistics Press.

National Development and Reform Commission of China. 2015. *National Agricultural Production Cost and Return Collection 2015*. Beijing: China Statistics Press.

Naughton, Barry. 1994. "Chinese Institutional Innovation and Privatization from Below." *The American Economic Review* 84 (2): 266–70.

NBS (National Bureau of Statistics of China). 1991. *Chinese Rural Yearbook 1991*. Beijing: China Statistics Press.

NBS (National Bureau of Statistics of China). 2001. *China Rural Statistical Yearbook 2001*. Beijing: China Statistics Press.

NBS (National Bureau of Statistics of China). 2009a. *China Rural Statistical Yearbook 2009*. Beijing: China Statistics Press.

NBS (National Bureau of Statistics of China). 2009b. *China Compendium of Statistics: 1949–2008*. Beijing: China Statistics Press.

NBS (National Bureau of Statistics of China). 2015. *2014 Monitoring and Investigation Report on Migrant Workers*. Beijing: China Statistics Press.

NBS (National Bureau of Statistics of China). 2018. "2017 Economic and Social Development Statistical Report of the People's Republic of China." www.stats.gov.cn/tjsj/zxfb/201802/t20180228_1585631.html.

Neves, David, and Andries Du Toit. 2013. "Rural Livelihoods in South Africa: Complexity, Vulnerability and Differentiation." *Journal of Agrarian Change* 13 (1): 93–115.

Neves, David, Michael Samson, Ingrid van Niekerk, Sandile Hlatshwayo, and Andries du Toit. 2009. *The Use and Effectiveness of Social Grants in South Africa*. Johannesburg: Finmark Trust.

Nguyen, Tin, Enjiang Cheng, and Christopher Findlay. 1996. "Land Fragmentation and Farm Productivity in China in the 1990s." *China Economic Review* 7 (2): 169–80.

Nickum, James E. 1978. "Labour Accumulation in Rural China and Its Role since the Cultural Revolution." *Cambridge Journal of Economics* 2 (3): 273–86.

Niu, Jianqiang. 2002. "Mingdai nupu yu shehui [Bondservants and society in the Ming dynasty]." *Journal of Historical Science* [*shixue yuekan*] 36 (4): 98–107.

O'Brien, Kevin J., and Lianjiang Li. 2006. *Rightful Resistance in Rural China*. Cambridge, UK: Cambridge University Press.

Oi, Jean C. 1989. *State and Peasant in Contemporary China: The Political Economy of Village Government*. Vol. 30. Berkeley, CA: University of California Press.

Oi, Jean C. 1999. *Rural China Takes Off: Institutional Foundations of Economic Reform*. Berkeley, CA: University of California Press.

O'Laughlin, Bridget, Henry Bernstein, Ben Cousins, and Pauline E. Peters. 2013. "Introduction: Agrarian Change, Rural Poverty and Land Reform in South Africa since 1994." *Journal of Agrarian Change* 13 (1): 1–15.

Ong, Lynette H. 2014. "State-led Urbanization in China: Skyscrapers, Land Revenue and 'Concentrated Villages.'" *The China Quarterly* 217: 162–79.

Osawa, Machiko, Myoung Jung Kim, and Jeff Kingston. 2013. "Precarious Work in Japan." *American Behavioral Scientist* 57 (3): 309–34.

Ostrom, Elinor. 1990. *Governing the Commons: The Evolution of Institutions for Collective Action*. Cambridge, UK: Cambridge University Press.

Otero, Gerardo. 2012. "The Neoliberal Food Regime in Latin America: State, Agribusiness Transnational Corporations and Biotechnology." *Canadian Journal of Development Studies* 33 (3): 282–94.

Otsuka, Keijiro. 2007. "The rural industrial transition in East Asia: Influences and implications." In *Transforming the Rural Nonfarm Economy: Opportunities and Threats in the Developing World*, edited by Steven Haggblade, Peter Hazell and Thomas Reardon, 216–33. Baltimore, MD: Johns Hopkins University Press.

Palmer, Kim, and John Sender. 2006. "Prospects for On-Farm Self-Employment and Poverty Reduction: An Analysis of the South African Income and Expenditure Survey 2000." *Journal of Contemporary African Studies* 24 (3): 347–76.

Pan, Zhongdong. 1997. "Liangjia tiaozheng de xizhong zhiyou [The worry amid the joy over grain price adjustments]." *Correspondences of Rural Work* [*Nongcun gongzuo tongxun*] 26 (1): 43.

Peng, Ito. 2015. "The 'new' social investment policies in Japan and South Korea." In *Inclusive Growth, Development and Welfare Policy: A Critical Assessment*, edited by Reza Hasmath, 142–60. London, UK: Routledge.

Peng, Kaili, and Hailian Zhu. 2015. "Nongdi chengshi liuzhuan dui butong nianling jieduan shidi nongmin de fuli yingxiang yanjiu [Impacts of land urbanization on the welfare of landless peasants of different ages]." *China Land Sciences* [*Zhongguo tudi kexue*] 29 (1): 71–8.

Perdue, Peter C. 1987. *Exhausting the Earth: State and Peasant in Hunan, 1500–1850*. Boston, MA: Harvard University Asia Center.

Perdue, Peter C. 2005. *China Marches West: The Qing Conquest of Central Eurasia*. Boston, MA: Harvard University Press.

Perkins, Dwight H. 1969. *Agricultural Development in China, 1368–1968*. Chicago: Aldine Publishing Company.

Perkins, Dwight H. 1994. "There are at Least Three Models of East Asian Development." *World Development* 22 (4): 655–61.

Platzky, Laurine, and Cherryl Walker. 1985. *The Surplus People: Forced Removals in South Africa*. Johannesburg, South Africa: Ravan Press.

Pomeranz, Kenneth. 1993. *The Making of a Hinterland: State, Society, and Economy in Inland North China, 1853–1937*. Berkeley, CA: University of California Press.

Pomeranz, Kenneth. 2000. *The Great Divergence: China, Europe, and the Making of the Modern World Economy*. Princeton, NJ: Princeton University Press.

Pomeranz, Kenneth. 2001. "Is There an East Asian Development Path? Long-term Comparisons, Constraints, and Continuities." *Journal of the Economic and Social History of the Orient* 44 (3): 322–62.

Rawski, Evelyn S. 1996. "Presidential Address: Reenvisioning the Qing: The Significance of the Qing Period in Chinese History." *The Journal of Asian Studies* 55 (4): 829–50.

Reed, Bradly W. 1995. "Money and Justice: Clerks, Runners, and the Magistrate's Court in Late Imperial Sichuan." *Modern China* 21 (3): 345–82.

Rigg, Jonathan. 2006. "Land, Farming, Livelihoods, and Poverty: Rethinking the Links in the Rural South." *World Development* 34 (1): 180–202.

Rosenthal, Jean-Laurent, and Roy Bin Wong. 2011. *Before and Beyond Divergence*. Boston, MA: Harvard University Press.

Rowe, William T. 2001. *Saving the World: Chen Hongmou and Elite Consciousness in Eighteenth-Century China*. Stanford, CA: Stanford University Press.

Rowe, William T. 2002. "Social stability and social change." In *The Cambridge History of China Volume 9: Part One: The Ch'ing Empire to 1800*, edited by Willard J. Peterson, 473–562. Cambridge, UK: Cambridge University Press.

Rowe, William T. 2007. *Crimson Rain: Seven Centuries of Violence in a Chinese County*. Stanford, CA: Stanford University Press.

Rowe, William T. 2009. *China's Last Empire: The Great Qing*. Vol. 6. Boston, MA: Harvard University Press.

Sargeson, Sally. 2013. "Violence as Development: Land Expropriation and China's Urbanization." *Journal of Peasant Studies* 40 (6): 1063–85.

Sassen, Saskia. 2010. "A Savage Sorting of Winners and Losers: Contemporary Versions of Primitive Accumulation." *Globalizations* 7 (1–2): 23–50.

Schierup, Carl-Ulrik. 2016. "Under the Rainbow: Migration, Precarity and People Power in Post-Apartheid South Africa." *Critical Sociology* 42 (7–8): 1051–68.

Schmalzer, Sigrid. 2016. *Red Revolution, Green Revolution: Scientific Farming in Socialist China*. Chicago, IL: University of Chicago Press.

Schneider, Mindi. 2014. "Developing the Meat Grab." *Journal of Peasant Studies* 41 (4): 613–33.

Schneider, Mindi. 2017. "Dragon Head Enterprises and the State of Agribusiness in China." *Journal of Agrarian Change* 17 (1): 3–21.

Schurmann, Franz. 1968. *Ideology and Organization in Communist China*. Berkeley, CA: University of California Press.

Scott, James C. 1977. *The Moral Economy of the Peasant: Rebellion and Subsistence in Southeast Asia*. New Haven, CT: Yale University Press.

Scully, Ben, and Edward Webster. 2018. "The Countryside and Capitalism: Rethinking the Cheap Labour Thesis in Post-Apartheid South Africa." In *Race, Class, and the Post-Apartheid Democratic State*, edited by John Reynolds, Ben Fine, and Robert van Niekerk. Scottsville, South Africa: University of KwaZulu-Natal Press.

Seidman, Gay. 1999. "Is South Africa Different? Sociological Comparisons and Theoretical Contributions from the Land of Apartheid." *Annual Review of Sociology* 25 (1): 419–40.

Selden, Mark. 1988. *The Political Economy of Chinese Socialism*. Armond, New York: M.E. Sharpe, Inc.

Sichuan Public Security Bureau. 2004. "Guanyu dangqian sichuansheng zhengdichaiqian yinfa quntixing shijian de diaoyan baogao [A report on recent collective events related to land expropriation in Sichuan province]." *Gongan Yanjiu* [*Public Security Research*] 17 (1): 73–7.

Shi, Qinghua, Hongtao Jin, and Weijian Zhuo. 2011. "Zhengdi yiding jiangdi nongmin shouru ma [Will land expropriation always decrease peasants' income]?" *Management World* [*Guanli Shijie*] 27 (3): 77–82.

Shi, Tao, and Guoying Ma. 2010. "Qingchao qianzhongqi liangshi muchan yanjiu shuping [A survey of research on grain output per *mu* in the Early and Mid Qing Dynasty]." *Historical Research* [*lishi yanjiu*] 50 (2): 143–92.

Shi, Zhihong. 2017. *Agricultural Development in Qing China: A Auantitative Study, 1661–1911*. Beijing: Social Science Academic Press.

Shin, Kwang-Yeong. 2013. "Economic Crisis, Neoliberal Reforms, and the Rise of Precarious Work in South Korea." *American Behavioral Scientist* 57 (3): 335–53.

Shinoda, Toru. 2009. "Which Side Are You On? Hakenmura and the Working Poor as a Tipping Point in Japanese Labor Politics." *The Asia-Pacific Journal* 14 (3): 1–14.

Silver, Beverly J. 2003. *Forces of Labor: Workers' Movements and Globalization Since 1870*. Cambridge, UK: Cambridge University Press.

Skocpol, Theda. 1979. *States and Social Revolutions: A Comparative Analysis of France, Russia, and China*. Cambridge, UK: Cambridge University Press.

Skinner, G. William. 1964. "Marketing and Social Structure in Rural China, Part I." *The Journal of Asian Studies* 24 (1): 3–43.

So, Alvin Y. 2009. "Rethinking the Chinese developmental miracle." In *China and the Transformation of Global Capitalism*, edited by Ho-fung Hung, 50–64. Baltimore, MD: Johns Hopkins University Press.

Solinger, Dorothy J. 1999. *Contesting Citizenship in Urban China: Peasant Migrants, the State, and the Logic of the Market*. Berkeley, CA: University of California Press.

Song, Jesook. 2009. *South Koreans in the Debt Crisis: The Creation of a Neoliberal Welfare Society*. Durham, NC: Duke University Press.

Song, Jiyeoun. 2012. "Economic Distress, Labor Market Reforms, and Dualism in Japan and Korea." *Governance* 25 (3): 415–38.

State Council of China. 1996. "White Paper: The Grain Issue in China." Accessed 22 November 2018. www.iatp.org/files/Grain_Issue_in_China_White_Paper_The.htm.

Standing, Guy. 2011. *The Precariat: The New Dangerous Class*: London, UK: Bloomsbury Publishing.

Stats SA. 2016. *General Household Survey 2015*. Pretoria, South Africa: Statistics South Africa.

Stats SA. 2017. *Agricultural Survey 2016 (Preliminary)*. Pretoria, South Africa: Statistics South Africa.

Stepan, Matthias, and Quan Lu. 2016. "The Establishment of China's New Type Rural Social Insurance Pension: A Process Perspective." *Journal of Current Chinese Affairs* 45 (2): 113–47.

Stockman, Norman. 2000. *Understanding Chinese Society*. Cambridge, UK: Polity.

Stubbs, Richard. 2009. "What Ever Happened to the East Asian Developmental State? The Unfolding Debate." *The Pacific Review* 22 (1): 1–22.

Sugihara, Kaoru. 2003. "The East Asian Path of Economic Development." In *The Resurgence of East Asia: 500, 150 and 50 Year Perspectives*, edited by Giovanni Arrighi, Takeshi Hamashita, and Mark Seldon, 78–123. London: Routledge.

Sugihara, Kaoru. 2004. "The state and the industrious revolution in Tokugawa Japan." In *Working Paper of the Global Economic History Network*: Department of Economic History, LSE.

Sugihara, Kaoru. 2007. "Labour-Intensive Industrialisation in Global History." *Australian Economic History Review* 47 (2): 121–54.

Sugihara, Kaoru. 2013. "Labour-intensive industrialization in global history: an interpretation of East Asian experiences." In *Labour-Intensive Industrialization in Global History*, edited by Gareth Austin and Kaoru Sugihara, 20–64. London, UK: Routledge.

Sui, Cindy. 2014. "Taiwan Transition: From City Life to the Countryside." *BBC News*, 26 November. www.bbc.com/news/business-30204720.

Swider, Sarah. 2015. "Building China: Precarious Employment among Migrant Construction Workers." *Work, Employment and Society* 29 (1): 41–59.

Taiwanese government. 2017. *Statistical Yearbook of the Republic of China 2016*. Taipei: Executive Yuan, Republic of China.

Takeuchi, Hiroki. 2014. *Tax Reform in Rural China: Revenue, Resistance, and Authoritarian Rule*. Cambrdige, UK: Cambridge University Press.

Tang, Jian. 2011. "Review and Discussion on Land Acquisition Reform." *China Land Science* [*Zhongguo Tudi Kexue*] 25 (11): 3–7.

Tawney, Richard Henry. 1932. *Land and Labour in China*. New York: Harcourt, Brace and Company.

Terreblanche, Sampie. 2002. *A History of Inequality in South Africa, 1652–2002*. Scottsville, South Africa: University of Kwazulu Natal Press.

The Economist. 2018. "Dreams of Fields: South Africa Is Getting Land Reform Wrong." *The Economist*, January 25. www.economist.com/printedition/2018-01-27.

Tsai, Ming-Chang. 2001. "Dependency, the State and Class in the Neoliberal Transition of Taiwan." *Third World Quarterly* 22 (3): 359–79.

Unger, Jonathan. 2002. *Transformation of Rural China*. Armond, New York: M.E. Sharpe, Inc.

van der Ploeg, Jan Douwe. 2009. *The New Peasantries: Struggles for Autonomy and Sustainability in an Era of Empire and Globalization*. London, UK: Routledge.

van der Ploeg, Jan Douwe, and Jingzhong Ye. 2016. *China's Peasant Agriculture and Rural Society: Changing Paradigms of Farming*. London, UK: Routledge.

Wade, Robert. 1990. *Governing the Market: Economic Theory and the Role of Government in East Asian Industrialization*. Princeton, NJ: Princeton University Press.

Wakeman Jr., Frederic. 1985. *The Great Enterprise: The Manchu Reconstruction of Imperial Order in Seventeenth-Century China*. Berkeley, CA: University of California Press.

Walker, Kathy Le Mons. 1999. *Chinese Modernity and the Peasant Path: Semicolonialism in the Northern Yangzi Delta*. Stanford, CA: Stanford University Press.

Walker, Kathy Le Mons. 2008. "From Covert to Overt: Everyday Peasant Politics in China and the Implications for Transnational Agrarian Movements." *Journal of Agrarian Change* 8 (2–3): 462–88.

Wallerstein, Immanuel. 1991. "Braudel on Capitalism, or Everything Upside Down." *The Journal of Modern History* 63 (2): 354–61.

Wang, Di. 2001. *Kuachu fengbi de shijie* [*Getting out of a closed world*]. Beijing: Zhonghua shuju.

Wang, Guojiang, and Zhongyou Liu. 2003. "Aohanqi shengtai huanjing jianshe lishi huigu [A historical review of the construction of ecological environment in Aohan Banner]." *Journal of Inner Mongolia Forestry* [*neimenggu linye*] 26 (1) (1): 14–5.

Wang, Shaoguang. 2008. "Learning Mechanism and Adaptability: Lessons from the Change in the Chinese Rural Cooperative Medical System." *China Social Sciences* [*Zhongguo Shehui Kexue*] 29 (6): 111–33.

Wang, Zhizhong. 2010. "Aohanqi de tudi gaige yundong [The land reform movement in Aohan banner]." www.aohan.gov.cn/literaryarticle/detail/282.

Watanabe, Hiroaki Richard. 2012. "Why and How Did Japan Finally Change Its Ways? The Politics of Japanese Labour-Market Deregulation since the 1990s." *Japan Forum* 24 (1): 23–50.

Weideman, Marinda. 2003. *Land Reform, Equity and Growth in South Africa: A Comparative Analysis*. Johannesburg, South Africa: University of the Witwatersrand.

Wen, Tiejun. 2000. *Zhongguo nongcun jiben jingji zhidu yanjiu* [*A study on rural China's basic economic institutions*]. Beijing: Zhongguo jingji chubanshe.

Wen, Tiejun. 2001. "Centenary Reflections on the 'Three Dimensional Problem' of Rural China." *Inter-Asia Cultural Studies* 2 (2): 287–95.

Wen, Tiejun. 2009. "Woguo weishenmo buneng shixing tudi siyouhua [Why our country should not privatize farmland]." *Red Flag Manuscripts* [*hongqi wengao*] 46 (2): 15–7.

Wen, Tiejun. 2011. *Jiedu sunan* [*Explaining sunan*]. Suzhou: Soochow University Press.

Wen, Tiejun. 2016. "A Supplement to Chinese Contemporary Agricultural History." Accessed May 2, 2018. www.rhd361.com/special/news?id=0cedd3f72a314a95866a92532277fcf4.

White, Ben, Saturnino M. Borras Jr., Ruth Hall, Ian Scoones, and Wendy Wolford. 2012. "The New Enclosures: Critical Perspectives on Corporate Land Deals." *The Journal of Peasant Studies* 39 (3–4): 619–47.

White, Gordon, and Roger Goodman. 1998. "Welfare orientalism and the search for an East Asian welfare model." In *The East Asian Welfare Model: Welfare Orientalism and the State*, edited by Roger Goodman, Gordon White, and Huck-ju Kwon, 3–24. London, UK: Routledge.

Whiting, Susan H. 2000. *Power and Wealth in Rural China: The Political Economy of Institutional Change*. Cambridge, UK: Cambridge University Press.

Wiens, Mi Chu. 1980. "Lord and Peasant: The Sixteenth to the Eighteenth Century." *Modern China* 6 (1): 3–39.

Will, Pierre-Etienne. 1990. *Bureaucracy and Famine in Eighteenth-Century China*. Stanford, CA: Stanford University Press.

Will, Pierre-Étienne. 1997. "The 1744 Annual Audits of Magistrate Activity and Their Fate." *Late Imperial China* 18 (2): 1–50.

Will, Pierre-Etienne, and Roy Bin Wong. 1991. *Nourish the People: The State Civilian Granary System in China, 1650–1850*. Ann Arbor, MI: Center for Chinese Studies, University of Michigan.

Wilmsen, Brooke. 2016. "Expanding Capitalism in Rural China through Land Acquisition and Land Reforms." *Journal of Contemporary China* 25 (101): 701–17.
Wittfogel, Karl August. 1957. *Oriental Despotism: a Comparative Study of Total Power*. New Haven, CT: Yale University Press.
Wolpe, Harold. 1972. "Capitalism and Cheap Labour-Power in South Africa: From Segregation to Apartheid." *Economy and Society* 1 (4): 425–56.
Wang, Jinping. 2011. *Chinese Food Security Problems after the Entry of Transnational Capital* (Dissertation). Shenyang, China: Liaoning University.
Wong, Christine PW. 1988. "Interpreting Rural Industrial Growth in the Post-Mao Period." *Modern China* 14 (1): 3–30.
Wong, R. Bin. 1982. "Food Riots in the Qing Dynasty." *The Journal of Asian Studies* 41 (4): 767–88.
Wong, R. Bin. 1997. *China Transformed: Historical Change and the Limits of European Experience*. Ithaca, NY: Cornell University Press.
World Bank. 1993. *The East Asian Miracle: Economic Growth and Public Policy*. Oxford, UK: Oxford University Press.
World Bank. 1994. *South African Agriculture: Structure, Performance and Options for the Future*. Washington, DC: The World Bank.
World Bank. n.d. *World Bank Open Data*.
Wright, Erik Olin. 2000. "Working-Class Power, Capitalist-Class Interests, and Class Compromise." *American Journal of Sociology* 105 (4): 957–1002.
Wu, Chengming. 1983. *Zhongguo zibenzhuyi yu guonei shichang* [*Chinese capitalism and the national market*]. Beijing: China Social Sciences Press.
Wu, Jing. 2017. "The Dilemma of Land-lost Farmers' Employment and the Paths of Improving Their Employment Rate." *Jiangsu Social Sciences* [*Jiangsu Shehui Kexue*] 292: 100–5.
Wujin County Gazetteer. 1988. *Wujin County Gazetteer* [*Wujin xianzhi*]. Shanghai: Shanghai Renmin Chubanshe.
Wujin County Industrial Gazetteer. 1990. *Wujin County Industrial Gazetteer* [*Wujinxian Gongye Zhi*]. Wujin, Jiangsu: Wujin Bureau of Archives.
Wujin government. 1999. *Wujin Yearbook 1999*. Beijing: Fangzhi chubanshe.
Wujin Yearbook Committee. 1990. *Wujin Yearbook 1990* [*Wujin nianjian 1990*]. Shanghai: Shanghai renmin chubanshe.
Wujin Yearbook Committee. 1992. *Wujin Yearbook 1992* [*Wujin nianjian 1992*]. Beijing: Zhongguo shuji chubanshe.
Xiang, Yunzhang. 2012. "Jinnian caizheng zhinong chao 2.5 wanyi [Fiscal support for rural areas exceeds 2.5 trillion yuan this year]." *Jinji Guancha Bao* [*The Economic Observer*], February 6.
Xinhua. 2008. "Chengdu jintudi nongmin zuoshou zujin fanpin dang gongren linggongzi [Chengdu's gold land: peasants collect rent or are hired as workers with wages]." *Sichuan Zaixian*, November 2. Accessed April 30, 2018. http://sichuan.scol.com.cn/cddt/20081102/200811261058.htm.
Xu, Dixin, and Chengming Wu, eds. 1985. *Zhongguo ziben zhuyi fazhan shi* [*The History of Chinese Capitalism*] *(The First Volume)*. Beijing: Renmin Chuban She.
Xu, Wei, ed. 1996. *Yijun tuqi zai sunan* [*The rise of rural enterprises in southern Jiangsu*]. Nanjing: Jiangsu renmin chubanshe.
Xu, Zhun. 2017. "The Development of Capitalist Agriculture in China." *Review of Radical Political Economics* 49 (4): 591–8.

Yan, Hairong. 2003. "Specialization of the Rural: Reinterpreting the Labor Mobility of Rural Young Women in Post-Mao China." *American Ethnologist* 30 (4): 578–96.

Yan, Hairong, and Yiyuan Chen. 2013. "Debating the Rural Cooperative Movement in China, the Past and the Present." *Journal of Peasant Studies* 40 (6): 955–81.

Yan, Hairong, and Yiyuan Chen. 2015. "Agrarian Capitalization Without Capitalism? Capitalist Dynamics From Above and Below in China." *Journal of Agrarian Change* 15 (3): 366–91.

Yan, Hairong, Yiyuan Chen, and Hok Bun Ku. 2016. "China's Soybean Crisis: The Logic of Modernization and Its Discontents." *The Journal of Peasant Studies* 43 (2): 373–95.

Yan, Zhiyao. 2013. "Liuyongdi anzhi yingrufa [Land retaining settlement should become law]." *Caijing Guojia Zhoukan (Economy & Nation Weekly)*, December 22. http://news.hexun.com/2013-12-22/160805486.html.

Yan, Zongdian. 2005. "Shilu qingdai nongye de chengjiu [A preliminary study on agricultural achievements in the Qing]." *Agricultural History of China* [*zhongguo nongshi*] 25(1): 60–6.

Yang, Dennis Tao, and Fang Cai. 2003. "The political economy of China's rural-urban divide." In *How Far Across the River?: Chinese Policy Reform at the Millennium*, edited by Nicholas Hope, Dennis Tao Yang, and Mu Yang Li, 389–416. Stanford, CA: Stanford University Press.

Yang, Guozhen, and Zhiping Chen. 1993. *Mingshi xinbian* [*A new history of the Ming*]. Beijing: Renmin chubanshe.

Yang, Jae-jin. 2013. "Parochial Welfare Politics and the Small Welfare State in South Korea." *Comparative Politics* 45 (4): 457–75.

Ye, Chongyang, and Shijun Shi. 2017. "Working poor mechanism in Taiwan and its policy implication." *Social Policy Research* [*Shehui Zhengce Yanjiu*] 2 (2): 36–54.

Ye, Jingzhong. 2013. "Will a World without Peasants Be Better?" *China Agricultural University Journal of Social Sciences Edition* 30 (3): 12–21.

Ye, Jingzhong. 2015. "Land Transfer and the Pursuit of Agricultural Modernization in China." *Journal of Agrarian Change* 15 (3): 314–37.

Ye, Jingzhong, Chunyu Wang, Huifang Wu, Congzhi He, and Juan Liu. 2013. "Internal Migration and Left-Behind Populations in China." *Journal of Peasant Studies* 40 (6): 1119–46.

Ye, Xian'en. 1983. *Mingqing Huizhou shehui yu tianpuzhi* [*Hui Society in Ming and Qing and the tenant-servant system*]. Hefei, China: Anhui Renmin Chubanshe.

Ying, Fenglin. 2016. "Wanzhou nongye sanxiang butie fafang wanbi [The payment of the three agricultural subsidies was completed in Wanzhou]." *Wanzhou ribao* [*Wanzhou times*], August 5. Accessed April 28, 2018. www.wz.gov.cn/main/xxgk/xxdt/zwyw/64_8496/default.shtml.

Yu, Yao. 2017. "Woguo xinxing nongye zhuti shuliang da 280 wange [The number of new agricultural entities in China reaches 2.8 million]." *Farmers' Daily*, March 8, page 6.

Yun, Ji-Whan. 2010. "The Myth of Confucian Capitalism in South Korea: Overworked Elderly and Underworked Youth." *Pacific Affairs* 83 (2): 237–59.

Zelin, Madeleine. 1984. *The Magistrate's Tael: Rationalizing Fiscal Reform in Eighteenth-century Ch'ing China*. Berkeley, CA: University of California Press.

Zeng, Jinhua. 2016. "Nongye sanxiang butie gaige quanmian tuikai [The reform to the three agricultural subsidies has started nationwide]." *Jingji ribao* [*Economic daily*], April 26. Accessed April 28, 2018. www.ce.cn/xwzx/gnsz/gdxw/201604/26/t20160426_10869135.shtml.

Zhan, Shaohua. 2004. "Preventing the social exclusion of migrant workers: A new perspective on rural development in China." In *Problems of Village and Agriculture during Market Reorientation of the Economy*, edited by Andrzej Rosner, 9–43. Warsaw: IRWiR PAN.

Zhan, Shaohua. 2011. "What Determines Migrant Workers' Life Chances in Contemporary China? Hukou, Social Exclusion, and the Market." *Modern China* 37 (3): 243–85.

Zhan, Shaohua. 2015a. "From Privatization to Deindustrialization: Implications of Chinese Rural Industry and the Ownership Debate Revisited." *World Development* 74: 108–22.

Zhan, Shaohua. 2015b. "From Local State Corporatism to Land Revenue Regime: Urbanization and the Recent Transition of Rural Industry in China." *Journal of Agrarian Change* 15 (3): 413–32.

Zhan, Shaohua. 2017a. "Riding on Self-Sufficiency: Grain Policy and the Rise of Agrarian Capital in China." *Journal of Rural Studies* 54: 151–61.

Zhan, Shaohua. 2017b. "Hukou Reform and Land Politics in China: Rise of a Tripartite Alliance." *The China Journal* 78: 25–49.

Zhan, Shaohua, and Ben Scully. 2018. "From South Africa to China: Land, Migrant Labor and the Semi-Proletarian Thesis Revisited." *The Journal of Peasant Studies* 45 (5–6): 1018–38.

Zhan, Shaohua, and Lingli Huang. 2017. "Internal Spatial Fix: China's Geographical Solution to Food Supply and Its Limits." *Geoforum* 85: 140–52.

Zhan, Shaohua, Hongzhou Zhang, and Dongying He. 2018. "China's Flexible Overseas Food Strategy: Food Trade and Agricultural Investment between Southeast Asia and China in 1990–2015." *Globalizations* 15 (5): 702–21.

Zhang, Hongyu, Qizheng Huang, and Rong Yan. 1996. "Dui midaizi shengzhang fuzezhi de pingshu [Assessing the resposibility system of provincial governors for the rice bag]." *Review of Economic Research* [*Jingji yanjiu cankao*] 18 (88): 2–10.

Zhang, Jinpan, ed. 1998. *Qingchao fazhi shi* [*The legal history of the Qing dynasty*]. Beijing: Zhonghua shuju.

Zhang, Qian Forrest. 2012. "The Political Economy of Contract Farming in China's Agrarian Transition." *Journal of Agrarian Change* 12 (4): 460–83.

Zhang, Qian Forrest. 2015. "Class Differentiation in Rural China: Dynamics of Accumulation, Commodification and State Intervention." *Journal of Agrarian Change* 15 (3): 338–65.

Zhang, Qian Forrest, and John A. Donaldson. 2008. "The Rise of Agrarian Capitalism with Chinese Characteristics: Agricultural Modernization, Agribusiness and Collective Land Rights." *The China Journal* 60: 25–47.

Zhang, Qian Forrest, Carlos Oya, and Jingzhong Ye. 2015. "Bringing Agriculture Back In: The Central Place of Agrarian Change in Rural China Studies." *Journal of Agrarian Change* 15 (3): 299–313.

Zhang, Xiaoshan, and Peng Yuan. 2003. *Zhongguo xiangzhen qiye chanquan gaige beiwanglu* [*Memos on TVEs' ownership reform in China*]. Beijing: Social Sciences Academic Press.

Zhang, Yan. 2006. "Shiba shiji qianhou qingdai nongjia shengji shouru de yanjiu [Research on the farmhouse livelihood in the eighteenth century of Qing dynasty]." *Ancient and Modern Agriculture* [*Gujin nongye*] 20 (1): 67–75.

Zhang, Yi, and Songsong Zhang. 2001. *Zhongguo xiangzhen qiye jianshi* [*A brief history of Chinese TVEs*]. Beijing: China Agriculture Press.

Zhang, Yi, and Yanhong Hao. 2015. "Fazhanzhong de nongmin zhikun [Peasants face difficulties in development]." *The World of Survey and Research* [*Diaoyan shijie*] 28 (11): 27–31.

Zhang, Yulin. 2015. "Great Clearance: China's Enclosure Movement in Comparison with That of England." *Journal of China Agricultural University (Social Sciences)* 32 (1): 19–45.

Zhao, Shukai. 2004. "Xiangzhen gaige: jiantao yu zhanwang [Township reform: criticisms and prospects]." In *2005 nian: zhongguo shehui xingshi fenxin yu yuce [The year of 2005: analyses and predictions on social situation in China*], edited by Xin Ru, Xueyi Lu, and Peilin Li. Beijing: Social Sciences Academic Press.

Zhao, Shukai. 2018. "Baochan daohu zhongde huwan peihe [Hu-Wan alliance in the household contracting reform]." *China Reform* [*Zhongguo gaige*] 33 (2): 100–4.

Zhe, Xiaoye, and Yingying Chen. 2011. "The Mechanism and Governance Logic of the Hierarchical Operation of the Project System: A Sociological Case Study of 'Projects Entering the Village.'" *Social Sciences in China* 32 (4): 126–58.

Zhou, Ying. 2013. "The State of Precarious Work in China." *American Behavioral Scientist* 57 (3): 354–72.

Zhu, Xiaodong. 2012. "Understanding China's Growth: Past, Present, and Future." *Journal of Economic Perspectives* 26 (4): 103–24.

Index

Page numbers in **bold** denote tables, those in *italics* denote figures.

www.ingramcontent.com/pod-product-compliance
Ingram Content Group UK Ltd.
Pitfield, Milton Keynes, MK11 3LW, UK
UKHW011015180926
475701UK00004B/750
9780367662653